THE POSSIBILITY OF DISCUSSION

Answering the question 'How is fruitful discussion possible?', this book addresses the central philosophical issue of how reason shall be understood and how it is limited. This study argues that the understanding of discussion according to which it necessarily starts from putative universal norms and rules for argumentation is problematic, among other reasons since such rules are unfruitful in contexts where there are vast disagreements such as religion.

Inspired by Wittgensteinian ideas, Strandberg develops instead a new way of understanding discussion, truth and rationality which escapes these problems, and shows how this solution can be used to answer the accusation against Wittgensteinian philosophy for being conservative and resulting in fideism.

ASHGATE NEW CRITICAL THINKING IN PHILOSOPHY

The *Ashgate New Critical Thinking in Philosophy* series brings high quality research monograph publishing into focus for authors, the international library market, and student, academic and research readers. Headed by an international editorial advisory board of acclaimed scholars from across the philosophical spectrum, this monograph series presents cutting-edge research from established as well as exciting new authors in the field. Spanning the breadth of philosophy and related disciplinary and interdisciplinary perspectives Ashgate New Critical Thinking in Philosophy takes contemporary philosophical research into new directions and debate.

The Possibility of Discussion
Relativism, Truth and Criticism of Religious Beliefs

HUGO STRANDBERG
Uppsala University, Sweden

ASHGATE

Published by
Ashgate Publishing Limited
Gower House
Croft Road
Aldershot
Hampshire GU11 3HR
England

Ashgate Publishing Company
Suite 420
101 Cherry Street
Burlington, VT 05401-4405
USA

Ashgate website: http://www.ashgate.com

British Library Cataloguing in Publication Data
Strandberg, Hugo
  The Possibility of Discussion: Relativism, Truth and Criticism of Religious Beliefs
  1.Religion – Philosophy. 2.Relativity. I.Title.
  210

Library of Congress Cataloging-in-Publication Data
Strandberg, Hugo, 1975–
  The Possibility of Discussion: Relativism, Truth, and Criticism of Religious Beliefs /
  Hugo Strandberg.
    p.   cm.
  Includes bibliographical references (p.   ) and index.
  1. Faith and reason. 2. Religion – Philosophy. 3. Knowledge, Theory of (Religion)
  4. Wittgenstein, Ludwig, 1889–1951. I. Title.
  BL51.S6737 2006
  210–dc22   2005031882

ISBN 0 7546 5543 1

Printed and bound in Great Britain by Athenaeum Press Ltd., Gateshead, Tyne & Wear.

Contents

Preface   vii

Introduction   1

1   The Unfruitfulness of Rationalistic Discussion of Religious Belief   17

2   Religious Belief and the Diverse Ways We Deal with the World around Us   27

3   Problems of Relativism   43

4   The Demand for Universality   59

5   The Objectivity of Truth   91

6   How Is Fruitful Discussion Possible?   121

7   Wittgenstein, Conservatism and Fideism   149

8   Philosophy of Religion and Enlightenment Thinking   173

Bibliography   181

Index   197

Preface

Aristotle writes about the philosopher: 'Perhaps it is better for him to have colleagues; but still, he is the most self-sufficient of all.'[1] The word 'perhaps' is, to be sure, an understatement, but Aristotle points to two important aspects of what it means to do philosophy. The writing of a philosophical book requires both isolation and discussion with others. It requires isolation not necessarily in a physical sense, but in a moral one, firstly since philosophy is a matter of thinking through a problem for oneself, and secondly since it is only the philosopher him- or herself who is responsible for what has been written. The writing of a philosophical book requires discussion with others, since thoughts are not born in a vacuum. This book could therefore not have been written without influence from many different people. Many have influenced me without my knowing it. Others have influenced me in ways I know of, but which are hard to formulate clearly in a preface such as this. My gratitude to those persons, I will have to express in other ways. My gratitude to some, I believe I am able to formulate, and these I will mention here.

First of all, I want to thank Prof. Eberhard Herrmann, who has read several versions of the chapters of this book. His important questions have forced me to think through many problems again, and to clarify what I have written.

Secondly, I want to thank all the former and present members in the Research Seminar in Philosophy of Religion, for all the stimulating discussions over the years. Those occasions where I have presented preliminary versions of the chapters in this book have, of course, been important, but the opportunity to discuss all kinds of philosophical questions on other occasions or after the seminars I believe has influenced this book at least as much.

Thirdly, I want to thank Dr Erica Appelros and Prof. Ingolf Dalferth, who read and commented on one of the final versions of the whole manuscript. Without their comments, the arguments would be far more unclear than they now are.

Earlier versions of some of the chapters have been read at various conferences. I want to thank everyone who participated in the discussions.

Hugo Strandberg
Uppsala, 29 June 2005

---

1   Aristotle, *The Nicomachean Ethics*, trans. Hippocrates G. Apostle (Dordrecht/Boston, MA, 1975), p. 193 (1177b).

Introduction

In Lars von Trier's mini-series *The Kingdom*, originally created for Danish television, the Professor of Pathology at Rigshospitalet in Copenhagen, Dr Bondo, goes into the ward of a patient.[1] In a previous scene,[2] Bondo has told us that new legislation requires the physician to obtain the relatives' consent for dissection. According to Bondo, this new legislation may make the work of the physicians more difficult, but if consent is asked for openly and without bias, nobody can argue that a dissection is not reasonable, he thinks. In the room, the patient's wife and son sit in front of the bed where the patient lies unconscious. The following conversation takes place between Bondo and the two relatives.

Bondo: Hello, my name is Dr Bondo. I suppose that you are related to Mr Zakariasen?
Mrs Zakariasen: He's my husband. This is our son.
B: I shall say immediately that I am not the doctor who treated your husband, I'm a pathologist. I have requested this interview.
M: Are we to talk in front of him?
B: Mrs. Zakariasen, your husband is deeply unconscious, he cannot hear what we say.
The son: What do you want to say, Mr Bondo?
B: New legislation requires the relatives' consent for dissection.
M: What's a dissection?
S: The physician here would be glad to cut dad into pieces, mother.
B: If we had not had the opportunity to dissect, the medical sciences would still be at a Stone Age stage.
S: Have you observed that dad is still alive? Or is that perhaps just another formality?
B: A prospective dissection will, of course, only take place after death.
S: Would you mind telling us what your personal interests in this case are? Is it not so that you have an interest that goes beyond the more general scientific one?
B: Your father has a hepatoma. I think that I have some great results in my research, but in the last ten years I have not had a single specimen to work on. I need your father's liver badly to be able to conclude my research.
S: So now your beautiful words about the common good are forgotten for the benefit of something that serves your personal career. Can't you understand that we in this situation cannot take your problem quite seriously? In fact, this whole request seems to me rather distasteful.
B: My research may bring about better forms of treatment of hepatomas. It might spare others that suffering you and your father now undergo.
S: With one patient a decade, it is hardly probable that society would establish a treatment on the basis of your research.
B: Nobody can argue that a dissection is not reasonable.
S: We are not arguing, either, we are just saying no. Excuse us, we would like to be alone with dad now.

---

1   This scene takes place about 17 minutes into the second episode, 'Alliancen kallar'.
2   About 31 minutes into the first episode, 'Den hvide flok'.

Here, we are not going to discuss whether dissections are reasonable or not. The focus will be on religion as the field where disagreements are hard to reconcile. The above scene exemplifies several important topics, however, topics which will be discussed, some at length, some more briefly. Here are some examples:

- how hard it can be to reconcile a disagreement by means of argumentation
- how pointless the reference to what is reasonable or rational can be in such situations
- that where the argument takes place and who you, as a partner in the conversation, are influences the outcome of the discussion
- that it is possible to cut off an argumentation by saying that one does not want to argue
- that the objective and impersonal way of discussing a particular subject is not self-evident.

As I have just said, the focus of the philosophical investigations in this book will be on religion as the field where disagreements are hard to reconcile. Religious disagreements can turn up between religious believers and unbelievers, between adherents to different religions, as well as between persons of the same religion or between persons of the same denomination, on some controversial issue. Sometimes such disagreements are serious, sometimes they are not. When they are serious, reconciliation is called for, and it seems desirable that it be attained in a non-violent way, for example by means of discussion.

The focus on *religious* disagreements is not accidental. If you are interested in questions about what have often been called the limitations of reason (questions about what could be shown to others by means of arguments and what you can show yourself the correctness of by means of arguments, and questions about reason's relationship to what lies on the other side of this limit), religion is not only an example, but is in one sense central. The centrality of religion shows itself here in one common picture of the relation between philosophy and religion, a picture according to which philosophy is the very epitome of reason, and religion its very opposite. This picture needs to be questioned, as we will see, but since it is a common picture and influences the ways in which we understand religion and philosophy, investigating what role argumentation, discussion, rationality and the like might play in the context of religion is of central importance. Furthermore, religious disagreements tend to be more hard to reconcile than many other disagreements, and now and then have a violent character. Also for this reason, the focus on *religious* disagreements is not accidental.

Philosophy and Religion

The above picture of the relation between philosophy and religion often finds expression in accounts of the history of philosophy. There, philosophy is often portrayed as having originated through a break with mythological and religious thinking, in the sense that human beings began to reason and formulate arguments when it comes to questions which are of utmost importance.[3] This perhaps says more about the self-understanding of philosophers nowadays than it says about the origin of philosophy, but it is true that beginning at least with Xenophanes, who criticized traditional theology but not religious thinking itself, philosophers have often criticized religious thinking or traditional theology by subjecting it to criteria of rationality not taken from religion itself or theology itself.[4]

This conflict between religion and philosophy later became more severe, when it found expression in the death-sentence against the first martyr of philosophy, Socrates.[5] One of the charges levelled against him was that he did not acknowledge the gods,[6] but when his *Apology*[7] is read more thoroughly, the issue becomes more complicated. Socrates says he acts on divine commission: his questioning is commanded by a god, and if he abstains from such questioning, *that* would be not acknowledging the gods.[8] What this shows is not that some sort of religious belief is unavoidable, but that philosophy too is driven by something which the philosopher has faith in and does not argue for, something which is more important than what philosophy itself can establish, something which gives philosophy itself its importance.[9] To crudely oppose religion and philosophy is, then over-simplified.

Reflections such as the above have led to the breakdown of the philosophical prohibition of religion,[10] a breakdown which will be further touched upon in Chapters 2, 6 and 7. There is, however, a risk involved here: such a permissive attitude may lead to an abstention from criticism. The solution is not, however, to

---

3   See, for example, Francis MacDonald Cornford, *From Religion to Philosophy: A Study in the Origins of Western Speculation* (London, 1912), p. vii; Frederick Copleston, *A History of Philosophy, Volume I: Greece and Rome* (London, 1947), p. 16; Christopher C.W. Taylor, 'Introduction', in C.C.W. Taylor (ed.), *Routledge History of Philosopy, Volume I: From the Beginning to Plato* (London, 1997), p. 2; Richard H. Popkin, 'Origins of Western Philosophic Thinking: Introduction', in Richard H. Popkin (ed.), *The Columbia History of Western Philosophy* (New York, 1999), p. 1.

4   Xenophanes of Colophon, *Fragments: A Text and Translation with a Commentary by J. H. Lester* (Toronto, 1992), p. 25.

5   He was not the first who was sentenced for impiety, however. For example, it is said that Anaxagoras was sentenced for impiety; Diogenes Laertius, *Lives of Eminent Philosophers, In Two Volumes: I*, trans. R.D. Hicks (London, 1925), p. 143 (II.12–14)). Diogenes Laertius has two different versions about the penalty – no matter what, Anaxagoras was reportedly not executed.

6   See, for example, Plato, *The Dialogues of Plato, Volume I: Euthyphro, Apology, Crito, Meno, Gorgias, Menexenus*, trans. R.E. Allen (New Haven, CT/London, 1984), pp. 45, 55–6, 80, 85, 89 (Euthphr. 6ab, 13e–14a, 14e–15a; Ap. 18c, 23d, 26c).

7   Ibid., pp. 79–104.

8   Ibid., pp. 85, 91–2, 96 (Ap. 23abc, 28e–29a, 29d, 33c).

9   Cf. Grace M. Jantzen, 'What's the Difference? Knowledge and Gender in (Post)Modern Philosophy of Religion', *Religious Studies*, 32 (1996): 446.

10 Cf. Gianni Vattimo, 'The Trace of the Trace', trans. David Webb, in Jacques Derrida and Gianni Vattimo (eds), *Religion* (Cambridge, 1998), p. 81.

return to a philosophical fundamentalism, partly for philosophical reasons (reasons we delineated in the above discussion of Socrates' *Apology*), partly since such an attitude is unfruitful in a critical discussion with such religious believers (for example, religious fundamentalists) whom one might like to influence. Such an attitude is unfruitful since such religious believers probably reject that way of discussing the issue from the very beginning. Thus what is called for is to examine how and in what way a fruitful discussion of religious beliefs is possible.

The Question and Some Presuppositions

The question I am going to discuss is thus: 'How is fruitful discussion of religious beliefs possible?' Answering that question also answers the question: 'How is criticism of religious beliefs possible?' Discussion is here exclusively restricted to those cases where there are disagreements. Other cases where one can also hold discussions will not be examined here. The focus will furthermore be on discussions which are about things which make a decisive difference. Beliefs which make a decisive difference are, for example, beliefs whose holding makes one treat other human beings or oneself in a different way from how one would treat them or oneself if one did not hold the belief, or beliefs whose very holding may have certain consequences. One example of the latter kind of beliefs is that in the view of certain religious persons, the beliefs one holds determine whether one will go to heaven or go to hell.

Apart from the reasons for asking this question stated above, there is a reason which is more directly connected to a certain debate in the philosophy of religion. As you will see, my philosophical work is carried out, especially in Chapter 2, in the belief that a Wittgensteinian way of encountering the question could be helpful. When it comes to philosophy of religion, since Kai Nielsen's article 'Wittgensteinian fideism',[11] Wittgensteinian philosophy has been accused of resulting in fideism – that is, the view that an outsider cannot understand or criticize religion. D.Z. Phillips, perhaps the most well-known Wittgensteinian philosopher of religion, has on many occasions tried to show that this accusation is ill-founded.[12] Nevertheless, this accusation has appeared in a great number of textbooks and the like, in philosophy and in philosophy of religion in particular, ever since.[13] The issue therefore needs

---

11   Kai Nielsen, 'Wittgensteinian Fideism', *Philosophy*, 42 (1967).
12   Dewi Zephaniah Phillips, *Belief, Change and Forms of Life* (London, 1986), pp. 4–16, is the most comprehensive example.
13   See, for example, William J. Wainwright, 'Objections to Traditional Theism', in William L. Rowe and William J. Wainwright (eds), *Philosophy of Religion: Selected Readings* (San Diego, CA, 1989), p. 264; Louis P. Pojman, 'Fideism: Faith without/against Reason', in Louis P. Pojman (ed.), *Philosophy of Religion: An Anthology* (Belmont, CA, 1994), pp. 437–8; John Hyman, 'Wittgensteinianism', in Philip L. Quinn and Charles Taliaferro (eds), *A Companion to Philosophy of Religion* (Cambridge, 1997), p. 155; Michael Peterson, William Hasker, Bruce Reichenbach and David Basinger, *Reason and Religious Belief: An Introduction*

to be dealt with more exhaustively, so I am going to show not only *that*, but *how* criticism of religious beliefs is possible, and a Wittgensteinian approach is helpful in *contributing* to such an understanding. To attain such an understanding, many questions must first be dealt with, so the question of fideism will not be directly touched upon until the latter half of Chapter 6 and in Chapter 7. That I devote much space for the discussion of the disagreement between religious believers and non-believers is due to the focus on Wittgensteinian fideism – this disagreement is but one example of a disagreement on a religious issue.

Asking the question of the possibility of fruitful discussion and criticism is not only of relevance for the particular context of the philosophy of religion, however. I will give just a few examples of contexts to which these investigations might have something to contribute – more examples can no doubt be given. Firstly, the question has a general philosophical interest, as we have already seen. The answers to the question of the possibility of fruitful discussion and criticism are obviously important for the understanding of a subject like philosophy whose centre is often said to be critical discussion. Furthermore, the answers have implications for a great number of questions of central philosophical importance, for example questions about universalism and contextualism in epistemology and ethics, and questions about the rationality of science asked in post-Kuhnian philosophy of science. Secondly, the answers to the question of the possibility of fruitful discussion and criticism have implications for questions of central philosophical importance, questions the answers to which at the same time are meant to have extra-philosophical consequences, for example questions asked by feminist philosophers and political philosophers about how it is possible to criticize something without having to succumb to a way of thinking one wants to free oneself from. Thirdly, the answers to the question of the possibility of fruitful discussion and criticism have implications for all such contexts where one wants to influence others, but where how this should be done is not evident, for example in inter-religious dialogue. At the end of Chapter 3, I will give examples of some philosophers who, when discussing some of these issues, do so in a confused way – my investigations here can show other possibilities concerning these issues.

At this point, I would particularly like to stress two of the words in the question 'How is criticism of religious beliefs possible?' The first, 'how', suggests that fruitful discussion of religious beliefs *is* sometimes possible. That it is possible can be seen in concrete cases. The question is therefore (a) what it takes for such discussion to be possible, when it is possible, (b) how we should understand such discussion, and (c) which understandings can account for its occasional possibility and occasional impossibility, and which cannot. These questions hang together, however, and cannot be answered in isolation from each other. The second important word, 'fruitful', is meant to suggest that not every form of discussion is called for. Without this word, the question could be dismissed by somebody saying that discussion is possible

---

to the Philosophy of Religion (New York/Oxford, 1998), p. 177; Paul O'Grady, *Relativism* (Teddington, 2002), pp. 95 and 136.

whenever two persons talk to each other. As seen by the above examples of contexts for which the answer to the question is supposed to have implications, we have stronger demands on discussion than that – we want to understand what it takes to influence somebody else. Thus a fruitful discussion is one in which at least one of the interlocutors is actually influenced by what the other is saying. Through the discussion, this interlocutor comes to realize that some of what she is saying is not quite right, and then she changes her mind on that issue. The focus on 'how' and 'fruitful' means, furthermore, that I am not going to speculate about what is possible or impossible in a situation which is not ours. I will instead try to understand what we are actually doing in the situation we are in: that is, I will try to understand rationality, truth, religious belief and the like *in the role they play in our lives*.

In the following, much focus will be on religious *beliefs*. This could produce the impression that I am committed to a certain view of what is philosophically primary when it comes to religion. This is not so, however. In many cases, a disagreement in a religious context originates because of religious actions: somebody does something that you think should not be done, or does not do what you think should be done. If you, in such a situation, want her to change, you try to show her what you believe is right and wrong, true and false, rational and irrational[14] and the like. In this sense, beliefs are central when it comes to disagreements and discussions of them, without this implying that beliefs are necessarily the essence of religion, that religion is essentially propositional, or that there is a particular essence of religion which can be expressed in a strict definition. In this book, the word 'belief' is used in a minimal sense: if a person would answer 'yes' if she were asked 'Does Jesus live?' (or a question with the same meaning), then she believes that Jesus lives. The word 'belief' is used merely as a tool in this book – I am not claiming that the way the word 'belief' is used in this book is in complete accordance with how the word really is used.

What is presupposed here is that discussions of disagreements are sometimes valuable. In a pluralistic society, this seems to be especially obvious. The reason for discussions of disagreements sometimes being valuable is that not everything is perfect, that change is needed. Letting differences be is then not always good, since it entails that an opportunity for change is missed. That not everything is perfect also means that the possibility that things will get better if *I* change *my* mind is not to be precluded. Therefore, it is as important to retain the possibility of self-criticism as it is to retain the possibility of fruitful discussion with others. Of course, such self-criticism may be occasioned by the other influencing me when we are discussing our disagreement, but for the simplicity of the exposition, in the following, discussion with others and self-criticism is in most cases treated separately.

---

14 That a belief is rational, in my use of the term, implies only that one can legitimately hold it (that a belief is irrational means consequently that holding it is illegitimate). A fruitful discussion of religious beliefs in a situation of disagreement can hence be described as a discussion of what is rational in this minimal sense.

The Problem of Self-reference

The attentive reader has probably discovered a serious problem with this project. What I am going to do is to try to say something about the possibility of discussion, about the limitations of argumentation, and so forth. However, this will be done by means of a discussion, by means of argumentation. This may lead to some problem of self-reference, for example self-referential inconsistency or begging the question by implicitly presupposing what later is claimed to be the conclusion. Such problems, however, can never be avoided completely in discussions about activities such as thinking and discussing. Such discussions are often regarded as the centre of philosophy. This problem therefore highlights something about the status of philosophy.

An obvious consequence of this problem is that the results of the investigations pursued in this book must not have greater pretensions than the investigations themselves say are possible. As I have already suggested and will argue for, there is a limitation to the possibility of argumentation, and there is thus no claim here that my conclusions are reached by means of arguments which will convince everybody. That a philosophical book has no such claim does not, however, mean that it is necessarily worthless and does not deserve to be taken seriously. I will give three examples of kinds of philosophical discussions which have no such claim but nevertheless deserve to be taken seriously.

Firstly, it is possible to assume certain ideas for the sake of argument and show that they are incoherent or the like – such a discussion deserves to be taken seriously by those who hold the ideas shown to be incoherent. Secondly, instead of trying to reach a situation where one can claim to have solved the problem, it is possible to discuss the very formulation of the problem, and show that we are already misled in the formulation of the problem, by preconceived ideas about how things must be,[15] by general, deep-rooted tendencies in our thinking,[16] and by things that are too near us for us to seem them.[17] This can be shown by making overlooked possibilities visible or by pointing out the complexity which tends to be simplified in the formulation of the philosophical problem.[18] Making such possibilities visible can be

---

15   See Ludwig Wittgenstein, *Philosophische Untersuchungen/Philosophical Investigations*, 3rd edn, G.E.M. Anscombe and R. Rhees, trans. G.E.M. Anscombe (Oxford, 2001), pp. 27e, 41e, 43e, 132e (§§ 66, 112, 131, 599); Ludwig Wittgenstein, *The Blue and Brown Books* (Oxford, 1969), pp. 25–7.

16   See ibid., p. 30; Ludwig Wittgenstein, 'Philosophie/Philosophy', trans. C.G. Luckhardt and M.A.E. Aue, in James C. Klagge and Alfred Nordmann (eds), *Philosophical Occasions 1912–1951* (Indianapolis, IN, 1993), pp. 183 and 185.

17   See Wittgenstein, 'Philosophy', p. 179; Wittgenstein, *Philosophical Investigations*, p. 43e (§ 129).

18   See Wittgenstein, *Philosophical Investigations*, pp. 6e, 10e, 27e, 43e (§§ 11, 23, 66, 130–31); Wittgenstein, 'Philosophy', pp. 167 and 171; Wittgenstein, *The Blue and Brown Books*, pp. 12 and 17–18.

done by reminding ourselves of forgotten possibilities.[19] Such a discussion deserves to be taken seriously since it can make us look at the problem in new and perhaps more fruitful ways, and this is done simply by using what we already know. Thirdly, the text which presents the philosophical discussion need not be understood as a scientific text which can be put to use simply as it is. Instead, its *philosophical* value may be retained only when the text is met by a reader who does not simply accept it, but thinks through it and makes it part of her own thinking. The text deserves then to be taken seriously since it can help the reader to think for herself.[20] That calls for some explanation.

Philosophy

In the rest of this introduction, before finally giving an overview of the whole book, I will present some thoughts about philosophy. I will not describe what philosophy is and has always been, nor present the only possible philosophy or some general manifesto. What I will do is rather to present one way of understanding philosophy, a way which is presupposed in the investigations pursued in *this* book. Here, philosophy is not understood simply as a fact-stating discourse. Instead, the focus is on *reflection*. Reading and understanding the rest of the book will therefore be facilitated if the remarks below are borne in mind.

Here, philosophy is primarily the activity of *thinking for oneself* in a thorough way about certain kinds of question. This could be done on one's own, but can also be done together with others. Secondarily, philosophy has a public function. Whether spoken or written, the philosopher then helps others to think for themselves, for example by asking questions, presenting new ways of seeing certain questions, and giving others material to use in their own thinking.

---

19 See Wittgenstein, *Philosophical Investigations*, pp. 36e and 43e (§§ 89 and 127); Wittgenstein, 'Philosophy, pp. 173 and 179; Ludwig Wittgenstein, 'Discussions between Wittgenstein, Waddington, and Thouless: Summer 1941', in James C. Klagge and Alfred Nordmann (eds), *Public and Private Occasions* (Lanham, MD, 2003), p. 382.

20 Cf. Ludwig Wittgenstein, *Vermischte Bemerkungen: Eine Auswahl aus dem Nachlaß/ Culture and Value: A Selection from the Posthumous Remains* (Oxford, 1998), p. 22e; Wittgenstein, 'Philosophy', pp. 161–3. Here, one could also notice the difference between the prefaces to *Tractatus* and *Philosophical Investigations*. In *Tractatus*, Wittgenstein writes: '… the *truth* of the thoughts that are here set forth seems to me unassailable and definitive. I therefore believe myself to have found, on all essential points, the final solution of the problems'; Ludwig Wittgenstein, *Tractatus Logico-Philosophicus/Logisch-Philosohische Abhandlung*, trans. D.F. Pears and B.F. McGuinness (London, 1963), p. 5. In *Philosophical Investigations*, however, he writes: 'I should not like my writing to spare other people the trouble of thinking. But, if possible, to stimulate someone to thoughts of his own'; Wittgenstein, *Philosophical Investigations*, p. xe. Cf. also Eberhard Herrmann, *Religion, Reality, and a Good Life: A Philosophical Approach to Religion* (Tübingen, 2004), p. 32.

In the emphasis on the importance of thinking for oneself, philosophy is more similar to a way of life than a science or a profession.[21] Philosophy *is not* a way of life, however, since it is not itself a doctrine or an answer, but is rather an attempt, for oneself, to deal in a thorough way with questions which are of utmost importance. Especially when it comes to the philosophy of religion, philosophy cannot keep away from questions which affect how one is to live one's life.

This way of understanding philosophy is especially visible in Plato.[22] Here, philosophy is primarily concentrating on ourselves and the lives we are living.[23] Philosophy as a way of producing knowledge is only important secondarily, as a means of attaining a good life, since to live such a life we must know what is good – only when the soul is guided by wisdom and knowledge, is a happy and fortunate life guaranteed.[24] The philosopher is therefore, according to Plato, not a reader of texts, but is engaged in dialogue (which is not the same thing as a debate): only in that way is it possible to think through an issue critically and not merely take over an opinion formulated by somebody else.[25] Since it must be possible to ask questions of one another and answer them in this dialogue, too many people cannot be present at the same time – the philosopher is not a speaker in front of audiences.[26]

Of course, today philosophy has another place and function in society, which means that this understanding cannot be realized in the same way as in the time of Plato, and it is furthermore possible to wonder to what extent Plato idealizes the philosophical reality. However, to consider a way of understanding philosophy which in many respects is antithetic to the present understanding can be valuable, especially in the light of how philosophy has often come to be used for extra-philosophical purposes. If philosophy is about questions one *oneself* is really troubled by, if it is an attempt to come to terms with such questions for *oneself*, philosophy understood as a technique of winning debates or as providing tools for making an opinion one already has more convincing is rather uninteresting.

---

21 Cf. Herrmann, *Religion, Reality, and a Good Life*, pp. 27–8.

22 For a comparison between some of the mentioned aspects of Plato's (and Socrates') way of doing philosophy and Wittgenstein's, see Peter Winch, 'On Wittgenstein', *Philosophical Investigations*, 24 (2001): 183–4.

23 See, for example, Plato, *The Dialogues of Plato, Volume 3: Ion, Hippias Minor, Laches, Protagoras*, trans. R.E. Allen (New Haven, CT/London, 1996), p. 70 (La. 187e–188ab); Plato, *Complete Works*, John M. Cooper (ed.) (Indianapolis, IN, 1997), pp. 510, 1 221–2 (Phdr. 229e–230a; Resp. 618bc, 619de).

24 See, for example, Plato, *The Dialogues of Plato, Volume I*, p. 174 (Men. 88c); Plato, *The Dialogues of Plato, Volume 3*, p. 222 (Prt. 361ab); Plato, *Complete Works*, pp. 719, 1 161, 1 189–91, 1 194 (Euthyd. 281d, 282cd; Resp. 549b, 581c–582d, 583b, 585e–586a).

25 See, for example, Plato, *The Dialogues of Plato, Volume 1*, p. 242 (Grg. 458a); Plato, *The Dialogues of Plato, Volume 3*, p. 188 (Prt. 329a); Plato, *Complete Works*, pp. 551–2, 1 114–5 (Phdr. 275abd; Resp. 492bcd).

26 See, for example, Plato, *The Dialogues of Plato, Volume I*, pp. 240, 243, 259 (Grg. 455a, 459a, 474ab); Plato, *Complete Works*, pp. 544, 727 (Phdr. 268a; Euthyd. 290a). Cf. Oets Kolk Bouwsma, *Wittgenstein: Conversations 1949–1951* (Indianapolis, IN, 1986), p. 57.

That philosophy is about questions one oneself is really troubled by, that it is an activity of thinking for oneself, has been emphasized by Wittgenstein. Once he wrote: 'Work on philosophy ... is really more work on oneself. On one's own conception. On how one sees things. (And what one requires of them.)'[27] In that respect, philosophy has an important personal aspect. In this study, I will discuss a problem which has struck me as important and troublesome. In order to come to terms with the problem, I must, among other things, search for those inclinations in me which lead me astray. Such inclinations can be formulated as philosophical theses and positions, but they are often theses which nobody ever formulates explicitly, although you can often see them as hidden presuppositions in philosophers' argumentations. Some of the positions I show as problematic are thus not positions held by many philosophers explicitly, so the criticisms are not aimed at any specific philosopher, but they could help those, including myself, who are inclined towards a certain position to be free from that inclination. These inclinations are not the only possible ones – you can no doubt be led astray in other ways too. Therefore, I do not aim at exhaustiveness, which would hardly be possible. The inclinations I do discuss are not merely my own, however: I am, of course, a child of my age, thus you can come across these inclinations quite often if you begin to look for them, both in philosophers' argumentations and in other persons' argumentations. That philosophy in one sense is a matter of self-criticism therefore at the same time means that it in one sense is a matter of criticism of culture. Moreover, if you want to find new ways of approaching a philosophical problem, you cannot simply accept the way in which it is usually posed. Instead of discussing with particular philosophers on their own terms, you have to find other ways to describe the problem, which means that you in one sense must discuss with fictive and generalized opponents.

Furthermore, in my work to come to terms with the problem, I use philosophers and ways of doing philosophy which are not accepted by everybody. It would not be wise, however, to try to justify these ways of doing philosophy before the main problem is dealt with. Instead, what shows that these ways of doing philosophy are fruitful is whether they can help us to come to terms with the problem, and as you will see, the conclusions of the investigations pursued in this book justify this procedure.[28] In the end, it is you as a reader who must determine whether what you have read has in any way helped you in your thinking about problems you find troublesome. The belief that there *must* be a way of discussing a particular problem which would make *everybody* come to terms with it is a belief that I show in this book to be problematic.

One consequence of this way of understanding philosophy is that it is not understood as a science. Some respects in which it is not understood as a science

---

27 Wittgenstein writes: 'Die Arbeit an der Philosophie ist ... eigentlich mehr die Arbeit an Einem selbst. An der eignen Auffassung. Daran, wie man die Dinge sieht. (Und was man von ihnen verlangt.)'; Wittgenstein, *Culture and Value*, p. 24. The translator translates as above, but writes 'expects' for 'verlangt'. 'Requires' is a better translation, however.

28 Of course, here the problem of self-reference finds expression again.

have already been mentioned. Another important respect coheres in the specific character of the discussion: in philosophy, there cannot be any presupposed methods of determining the correctness of different solutions to the problem. This does not mean, however, that we cannot speak about philosophical knowledge in another sense than scientific knowledge: that depends on how we define knowledge. A definition according to which only scientific knowledge is real knowledge agrees poorly with the way we usually talk about knowledge, knowing something, or knowing how to do something.

To say, as I did above, that the investigations pursued in this book cannot be guided by any presupposed methods of determining the correctness of different solutions to the problem is *not* to suggest that we should instead try to discover a method for doing that *in* the investigation. The problem is not how and when the method is arrived at. The problem is rather the idea that philosophical work is a matter of finding or constructing a set of different theories or solutions to a problem, and then simply a matter of determining which theory or solution is the right one, in the way a scientist lays down different hypotheses and then, by means of experiments, tries to dismiss some of them. The idea that what we should do is simply evaluate different solutions to a problem overlooks the fact that philosophical theories can seldom be characterized as *mistakes*[29] – that is, as simple errors in thinking or as false hypotheses. A mistake – that is, a simple error in thinking – is rather easy to put right: what is required is only to find the erroneous inference. In philosophy, matters are seldom that easy, however. One reason why matters are seldom that easy is that the formulation of philosophical ideas often points out some important aspect which has previously been neglected, an aspect which our attention is now directed to. Almost all philosophical ideas are therefore correct in some respects, highlighting some important aspect.[30] If a philosophical idea does not satisfy us, we cannot then just construct a new theory or work out an old one, but we must try to do justice to those experiences which made previous philosophers formulate this idea. Balance in the discussion is then what is most important. Ideas formulated by previous philosophers often say something important and correct about some cases or about some aspects, which is not to be forgotten, but the correct observation is then often generalized, by the philosophers in question themselves or by their epigones, to apply in all cases, or emphasized so strongly that other equally important aspects become overlooked. Wittgenstein's discussion of solipsism in *The Blue Book*[31] is a good example of this way of doing philosophy. He shows there a strong sensitivity to what the solipsist is trying to say, and does not disregard her ideas as simple mistakes, but points out at the same time what the solipsist overlooks, how she misrepresents her own ideas, and so on.

---

29 See Wittgenstein, *Philosophical Investigations*, pp. 40e and 93e (§§ 110 and 340).

30 Cf. Ludwig Wittgenstein, *Wittgenstein's Lectures: Cambridge, 1930–1932*, ed. Desmond Lee (Oxford, 1980), p. 21.

31 Wittgenstein, *The Blue and Brown Books*, pp. 48 and 57–73.

Therefore, what we should do is not simply evaluate different philosophical theories in order to see whether we can characterize them as mistakes or not. What we must do instead is to concentrate on the question to which the theories are supposed to be an answer, and ask: What is the problem which the question is supposed to be an expression of? Do the theories do justice to this problem? Is this problem an important problem, and if so, why? In this way, we try to reach the *source* of what we could call the confusion.[32] The word 'confusion', in contrast to 'mistake', is chosen in order to emphasize that a problematic idea is dealt with here not simply by pointing out erroneous inferences, but by revealing the sources of the problematic idea, retaining what is nonetheless of importance in it, and thus showing *the way* from falsity to truth, so to speak. Wittgenstein writes:

> One must start out with error and convert it into truth. That is, one must reveal the source of error, otherwise hearing the truth won't do any good. The truth cannot force its way in when something else is occupying its place. To convince someone of the truth, it is not enough to state it, but rather one must find the *path* from error to truth.[33]

This path is only seldom a straight road. When you are in the brushwood, the best way to take may be a hardly noticeable path which you have to track through its meandering ways. In the same way, my discussion in this book will often not go straight ahead, since freeing oneself from a problematic idea is not easy. By pointing out where we are starting and where we are going, I hope you as a reader will be able to follow me on this path.[34]

For the same reason, the history of the relevant questions, their origin and development, is important in the philosophical discussion in a way in which it is not in the sciences. Comparing different philosophers' treatment of questions similar to the question under discussion can also serve to discover one such way from falsity to truth.

Since almost all philosophical theories here are correct to some extent and we are not trying to settle for any one of them, philosophical problems are not solved by us presenting a final theory. Such a final theory would be unfortunate, since that

---

32   Cf. ibid., p. 59.

33   Ludwig Wittgenstein, 'Bemerkungen über Frazers *Golden Bough*'/'Remarks on Frazer's *Golden Bough*', trans. John Beversluis, in James C. Klagge and Alfred Nordmann (eds), *Philosophical Occasions 1912-1951* (Indianapolis, IN, 1993), p. 119. Translation of Wittgenstein, 'Bemerkungen über Frazers *Golden Bough*'/'Remarks on Frazer's *Golden Bough*', p. 118: 'Man muß beim Irrtum ansetzen und ihn in die Wahrheit überführen. D.h., man muß die Quelle des Irrtums aufdecken, sonst nützt uns das Hören der Wahrheit nichts. Sie kann nicht eindringen, wenn etwas anderes ihren Platz einnimmt. Einen von der Wahrheit zu überzeugen, genügt es nicht, die Wahrheit zu konstatieren, sondern man muß den Weg vom Irrtum zur Wahrheit finden.' In the following, when using a translation in the main text, if the original is in French or German, I will give the original wording in the notes. When there is a citation in a note, and this citation is a translation, the original will not be given.

34   Cf. Ludwig Wittgenstein, 'A Lecture on Ethics', in James C. Klagge and Alfred Nordmann (eds), *Philosophical Occasions 1912-1951* (Indianapolis, IN, 1993), p. 37.

would stop the necessary reflection about what we are doing when we discuss, think, do philosophy, and the like. The problems are instead 'solved' by our making the complexity obvious and visible. As opposed to theories which say how things always are and must be, we point out the range of possibilities, for example by reminding ourselves of forgotten possibilities, and we suggest ways of thinking about and living in this complexity. Philosophy here is not about finding new arguments for the one or the other side in a philosophical debate, not about working out and refining old theories, not about arguing for or against well-defined positions. Instead, philosophy is about working with the question itself, by trying to find a proper way of understanding the question, one which often differs from the way the question has often been understood, and from that understanding, see how the question can be dealt with. In doing that, we are trying to do what philosophers throughout the ages have tried to do, although the pretensions here may be smaller than those of some other philosophers. A discussion of philosophers and philosophical positions can sometimes be of value, but if that were all that was done under the label of philosophy, if philosophy was only a matter of historical knowledge, what I here have called philosophy would no longer be.[35] The possible value of the investigations pursued in this book thus does not originate until they are thought through by a critical reader.

The Structure of the Investigation

To facilitate the reading, I would like to provide an overview of the structure of the investigations which I am going to carry out, before going into the discussion itself.

One way of answering the question 'How is fruitful discussion of religious beliefs possible?' would be to say that there is not much of a problem. When we discuss, we should start from certain putative universal norms and rules for argumentation, and show from these that certain religious beliefs are rational or irrational. In Chapter 1, I give one example of how unfruitful this form of discussion, which I call rationalistic discussion, is when it comes to reconciling religious disagreements. What we then must do is to search for alternatives to rationalistic discussions of religious belief – that is, we must go on asking: How is fruitful discussion of religious beliefs possible?

When I show that rationalistic discussion of religious beliefs is not promising when it comes to many forms of religious disagreements, I question understandings of religious beliefs according to which they are beliefs of a scientific type, based on evidence or on scientific reasoning. In Chapter 2, I discuss this understanding at greater length in order to strengthen my case and explain in more detail why rationalistic discussion of religious beliefs is in many cases not promising. Dealing with this understanding furthermore provides groundwork for another way of

---

35   Cf. Plato, *The Dialogues of Plato, Volume 3*, p. 208 (Prt. 347e–348a).

understanding religious disagreements and fruitful discussion of such disagreements – an understanding I work out in the rest of the book.

In Chapter 2, when I question the understanding of religious beliefs as beliefs of a scientific type, I show that this understanding overlooks how our ways of speaking are conceptually dependent on our ways of acting and living in the world generally. One consequence of this is that disagreements which do not concern whether a mistake has been made within a shared way of making the distinction between true and false, but are about how to reason in a specific area, are possible. The conclusion that different ways of making the distinction between true and false, right and wrong, correct and incorrect are possible, and that there can therefore be no guarantee that a particular disagreement can be reconciled, seems to force us to accept a relativist thesis. Both parties of the disagreement, which the rationalistic discussion was supposed to solve, may be justified relatively in their own way of making the distinction between true and false, and according to the relativist, their different beliefs are then true for the one who holds them. Discussion is then pointless, for there is no disagreement.

In Chapter 3, I discuss how the form of relativism which the remarks in Chapter 2 may give rise to is to be understood. The understanding of relativism this chapter results in is that the relativist suggests that the distinction between true and false should be given up in a situation where it proves impossible to reach an agreement concerning the truth or falsity of the issue in question. Furthermore, I discuss whether and in what way this position is problematic. This discussion shows in the end that relativism is problematic, and what is then needed is to show that from the failure of showing everybody that we are right concerning a certain issue, it does not follow that talking about true and false in this context is senseless.

In Chapter 4, I begin to try to show this, by criticizing the demand for universality, according to which every statement has to be argued for by means of conclusive arguments which show that the statement in question follows from other statements which have already been proven in this way or are self-evident. These arguments must be appreciated by, in principle, everybody. To be rational is then to only hold beliefs which can be shown to be correct in this way. If this conception of rationality is shown to be problematic, the inclination to adopt a relativist position will be far less, since the suggestion that the distinction between true and false should be given up in a situation where it proves not to be possible to reach an agreement concerning the truth or falsity of the issue in question gains strength, in a way which is displayed in Chapter 4, from the demand for universality. The criticism of the demand for universality is formed by showing that being situated in history and society, which makes absolute certainty – which is one aspect of the demand for universality – impossible, is not an obstacle to, but on the contrary a condition for knowledge, true beliefs, rationality and the like in the role they play in our lives. After this discussion, I work out some consequences and implications of this discussion, above all that our inability to give arguments for why we do as we do does not generally delegitimize our ways of doing what we do. Thereafter, I show how rationality could be understood without the demand for universality.

In Chapter 4, my discussion is mainly in terms of rationality. The concept of rationality and the concept of truth are closely linked, however, so in Chapter 5 I analyse the concept of truth in its connection to my problem. This discussion additionally underlines what I have said in Chapter 4: that one can rightly say that one is right and that somebody else is wrong without being able to show this to her. The discussion then aims primarily at showing that it is possible to understand the concept of truth without the demand for universality. This understanding of the concept of truth must not distort what it is supposed to be an understanding of, and for that reason I concentrate on the aspect of the concept of truth which seems to be hard to retain without the demand for universality, namely the objectivity of truth – that is, the fact that the truth of most beliefs is independent of my believing them to be true.

In Chapter 6, I return to the main question: How is fruitful discussion of religious beliefs possible? This question must now be answered, starting with the observation that there is no guarantee that such discussion is always possible. In this chapter, I begin by giving some examples of the failure of rationalistic discussion, examples more concrete than those I have previously given. Thereafter, I begin to discuss the main question. In that discussion, I give an account of how the difference between the case in which fruitful discussion is possible and the case in which it is not, can be understood. Starting from that account, I present some examples of possibly fruitful criticism of particular religious beliefs and forms of belief.

The question 'How is fruitful discussion of religious beliefs possible?' became an urgent one as a result of remarks we made in Chapter 2, relating to Wittgenstein and Wittgensteinian philosophy of religion, and as a result of a common picture of Wittgensteinian philosophy of religion which I have presented here in the introduction. The answer I give in Chapter 6 to the question 'How is fruitful discussion of religious beliefs possible?' could thus also be seen as a way of answering the criticism of Wittgensteinian philosophy of religion for being fideist. In Chapter 7, I show how what I say in Chapter 6 is a way to answer the criticism of Wittgensteinian philosophy of religion for being fideist. Above all, I try to get to the bottom of the problem, by discussing in what sense, if any, Wittgenstein's philosophy could be said to be a critical philosophy.

Lastly, in Chapter 8, I make some observations about what this means for the philosophy of religion as a critical enterprise, since both in Chapter 6 and 7 I have dwelt upon how discussion and criticism of religious beliefs can be understood. Since rationality has no fixed content, my discussion opens up for many different forms of criticism, among others moral, political and existential criticism. Above all, the critical discussion of a specific religious belief may not be cancelled from the philosophical agenda in order to hinder possible improvement and hinder different people from thinking for themselves.

Chapter 1

The Unfruitfulness of Rationalistic Discussion of Religious Beliefs

I hope it is now clear what I mean when I ask 'How is fruitful discussion of religious beliefs possible?', and why I ask this question. It is now time to start answering it.

One simple answer to my question would be to say that there is not much of a problem – now and then it is, of course, difficult to reason in the right way, especially when it comes to religious matters, so it is not so strange that people come to different conclusions. But if everybody is only careful enough in investigations and argumentations, everybody will arrive at the truth, and disagreements will disappear. Hence, what is suggested here is that we should start from certain putative universal norms and rules for argumentation, and show from these that certain religious beliefs are rational (that is, they are legitimately held) or irrational (that is, they are illegitimately held). This form of discussion I will, in the following, call rationalistic discussion. What I am going to do in this chapter is to give one example of how unfruitful this form of discussion is when it comes to reconciling religious disagreements.

The example I will discuss is the disagreements concerning the existence of God. Traditionally, the question about the existence of God has been the central question in the philosophy of religion, and it has mainly been discussed in a rationalistic way. If this way of discussing is unfruitful when it comes to this question, claimed to be crucial, which I will try to show, this indicates that the rationalistic way of discussing is an unfruitful way of reconciling disagreements. If we think that reconciling disagreements is sometimes valuable, in this situation we must search for alternatives to rationalistic discussions of religious belief. The question we then must consider is the one I asked in the introduction: How is fruitful discussion of religious beliefs possible?

Rationalistic Arguments for the Belief that God Exists

When the existence of God has been discussed in a rationalistic way, the discussion has been about arguments for the belief that God exists, for example about the teleological and the cosmological arguments. All these arguments have been criticized in different ways, and I am not going to go into that type of criticism. Let us, on the contrary, assume that they are valid.[1] What does this result in?

Let us assume that the teleological argument is valid. The best way to explain the existence of the world, as it actually is, is then to posit something outside the world which is somehow the cause of the world and which the world is dependent on. However, the teleological argument, rationalistically understood, shows, if it is valid, nothing more than precisely that there exists something outside the world which somehow is the cause of the world and which the world is dependent on – it does not say anything about the properties of this 'something'. On the contrary, many different hypotheses are compatible with the result of this argument, and which of these is correct or more justified, the argument cannot determine. The argument consequently justifies not the belief in a creator (since a creator is a personal being), nor that the cause of the world is an infinite being, nor that this is a being whom we can get in contact with and who is worthy of reverence, or the like.[2] The teleological argument hence does not manage to establish anything of *religious* importance. The argument, even when it is supposed to be valid, does not result in such beliefs which are central to religious believers.[3]

Since what I am focusing on here are disagreements which do make a difference, it is important, when discussing disagreements concerning the existence of God, to understand the belief that God exists, a belief which must be understood in the different ways it shows itself in the lives of religious believers. If the belief that God exists is understood in this way, the attempt to show, in a rationalistic way, that God exists immediately encounters problems, as I have just shown. Even if the arguments were valid, this would not be an argument for the existence of God, if the word 'God' is understood to signify what religious believers believe in, but would only be an argument for the existence of something whose existence is religiously insufficient as well as uninteresting.[4] The traditional arguments for the existence of God are thus dependent on the existence of religious belief in God: if they were presented to a person who had never heard of God or religion, she would not understand the arguments in the sense in which they are intended to be understood – that is, as religiously important arguments. That they have been understood to have religious importance is due to the fact that the word 'God' is not just a few letters,

---

1   Cf. Steven M. Cahn, 'The Irrelevance to Religion of Philosophic Proofs for the Existence of God', *American Philosophical Quarterly*, 6 (1969): 170, who adopts the same strategy and comes to the same conclusion, but argues in a different way.

2   See, for example, David Hume, *Dialogues Concerning Natural Religion* (London, 1991), pp. 129 and 131; Alfred Jules Ayer, *Language, Truth and Logic* (London, 1946), p. 115; Rush Rhees, *Rush Rhees on Religion and Philosophy*, ed. D.Z. Phillips (Cambridge, 1997), p. 5.

3   Cf. Stefan Eriksson, *Ett mönster i livets väv: Tro och religion i ljuset av Wittgensteins filosofi* (Nora, 1998), p. 16.

4   Cf. Ingolf U. Dalferth, *Die Wirklichkeit des Möglichen: Hermeneutische Religionsphilosophie* (Tübingen, 2003), pp. 217–18.

but already has a meaning for us.[5] If the word 'God' did not already have a meaning, the conclusions of the traditional arguments, if they were regarded as valid, would be the existence of something with only vague similarities to God as God is actually understood by believers.

Is there then no way of meeting this problem? One philosopher of religion who has tried to work out an argument for the belief that God exists, where 'God' is given a certain content, is Richard Swinburne.[6] I will therefore turn to Swinburne's project.

Swinburne's Arguments for the Belief that God Exists

What Swinburne is trying to do is to show that the probability of 'the theistic hypothesis' exceeds ½. 'The theistic hypothesis' is here the hypothesis that '… there exists a person without a body (i.e. a spirit) who is eternal, is perfectly free, omnipotent, omniscient, perfectly good, and the creator of all things'[7]. This hypothesis hence has, from the start, a religious content,[8] and Swinburne's project then seems to be more promising than the traditional arguments.

If Swinburne only relied on the traditional arguments, his project would be a failure since, as I have shown, there are many hypotheses which are compatible with those arguments. The theistic hypothesis is one of them, but there are also others, such as the hypothesis that the cause of the world is not a person, is something we cannot get in contact with, or the hypothesis that the cause of the world is a personal being with limited powers. Swinburne must hence be able to give additional arguments for why one of the many hypotheses is to be preferred. By evaluating the probability of the theistic hypothesis and showing that the probability of the hypothesis exceeds ½, Swinburne thinks that he can show why one of the many hypotheses is to be preferred. In the following, I will contrast Swinburne's theistic hypothesis with a hypothesis according to which the cause of the world is a being with limited powers,

---

5   When Thomas Aquinas formulates his five ways (Thomas Aquinas, *Summa Theologica: Complete English Edition in Five Volumes, Volume One* (London, 1981), pp. 13–14), he does not mention God until the end of each of the ways, by formulations such as '… and this we call God'. Hence, what I am assuming is that he is basically right, up until the point when he calls the being whose existence he just has shown 'God'. Calling this being 'God' is not innocent – it is to use a word which has already a meaning for us. Of course, this problem is not so devastating for him, since he does not aim to prove that God exists from a position which neither affirms nor denies the existence of God, as the problem is for Swinburne, who does aim to prove that God exists from such a position.

6   In Richard Swinburne, *The Existence of God* (Oxford, 1991).

7   Ibid., p. 8.

8   That the theistic hypothesis is a genuine expression of the religious belief in God can be questioned, which I do in the next chapter. In this chapter, however, the hypothesis is understood as an expression of the religious belief in God. Even if it is so understood, it must be noticed, however, that a religious believer wants to say a lot more about God than what Swinburne tries to justify, and that his result could thus be said to be rather meagre.

to see whether Swinburne's way of reasoning is a fruitful way to discuss religious beliefs in a context of vast disagreements.

When Swinburne evaluates the probability of the theistic hypothesis, he does so by means of Bayes's theorem. Bayes's theorem can be expressed as a function consisting of three factors that determine the probability of a certain hypothesis.[9] When it comes to a hypothesis like the theistic hypothesis which is meant to explain the existence of everything, these factors can be laid out in the following way. The first factor, which contributes positively to the probability of the hypothesis in question, is a measure of how probable the hypothesis renders the data – that is, of how likely it is that what is the case would be the case if the hypothesis is true. Hence, it is not only a matter of being compatible with the data. When it comes to this factor, it is possible to formulate an internal criticism of Swinburne, by noticing a problem he pays too little attention to. A hypothesis according to which God has limited powers and cannot create any other world than the world which actually has been created would render the data a probability of 1.[10] A hypothesis according to which God has unlimited powers, and therefore can create anything logically possible which there are not overriding reasons not to create,[11] renders the data a very low probability. The problem is simply that if God can create anything, the probability that God would create precisely our world is very low. Swinburne hence needs to show that there are overriding reasons to create precisely our world – that is, that our world is unique in some way – but it is questionable whether this could be done in a rationalistic way.[12]

The second factor, which contributes negatively to the hypothesis in question, is a measure of how probable it is that the data will be found even if we do not assume that the hypothesis in question is true. For Swinburne, this factor plays an important role when he compares the theistic hypothesis with a naturalisitic one, but since we have assumed that arguments like the teleological argument are valid, this comparison is not of interest, and this factor will not make much difference to our comparison.

---

9   For the following account, see Richard Swinburne, *Epistemic Justification* (Oxford, 2001), pp. 103–5. See also Richard Swinburne, *Is There a God?* (Oxford, 1996), pp. 26–7; Richard Swinburne, *An Introduction to Confirmation Theory* (London, 1973), p. 42; Swinburne, *The Existence of God*, pp. 64–5.

10   Some would say that this hypothesis is impermissible, since it is constructed in order to render the data a probability of 1 – that is, it is not constructed independently of the data. According to Swinburne, however, how a hypothesis is constructed does not affect its probability, except for some exceptional cases. See Swinburne, *Epistemic Justification*, pp. 81 and 221–32; Swinburne, *The Existence of God*, pp. 66–7.

11   See Richard Swinburne, *The Coherence of Theism* (Oxford, 1977), p. 160; Swinburne, *The Existence of God*, p. 91.

12   Especially since, according to Swinburne, there is no best of all possible worlds; Swinburne, *The Existence of God*, pp. 113–15. Note that my criticism of Swinburne here does *not* rely on the problem of evil. The issue is hence not why God created a world in which there is evil, but why God created precisely this world when there are so many alternatives.

The last factor, which contributes positively to the hypothesis in question, is the intrinsic probability of the hypothesis. The intrinsic probability of a hypothesis is influenced both by its scope and its simplicity: the greater the scope of the hypothesis, the smaller the intrinsic probability, and the simpler the hypothesis, the greater its intrinsic probability. A hypothesis has greater scope, according to Swinburne's understanding of scope,[13] the more precise it is. It would hence be possible to contrast the theistic hypothesis, which gives precise values to the amount of power, wisdom and so on of God, with a hypothesis which only gives approximate values in these cases, and thus would have smaller scope. However, this is not a suggestion I will make here.

Instead, I will focus on the question of simplicity. Swinburne mentions six facets of simplicity:

> The first facet of simplicity is just a matter of number of things postulated. A hypothesis that postulates one entity (or property of an entity) rather than two … is (other things being equal) simpler. …
>
> Secondly, number of kinds of things. A hypothesis that postulates three kinds of entities (or properties of entities) is (other things being equal) simpler than one that postulates six …
>
> Thirdly, a formulation of a hypothesis that contains a predicate (descriptive of a property) whose sense can be grasped only by someone who understands some other term (when the latter can be understood without understanding the former) will be less simple than an otherwise equally simple formulation of a hypotheses that contains the latter term instead. …
>
> Fourthly, a formulation of a hypothesis in the form of a theory consisting of a few separate laws is (other things being equal) simpler than one consisting of many laws. …
>
> Fifthly, a formulation of a theory in which individual laws relate few variables rather than many is simpler. …
>
> And finally (other things being equal) a mathematical simpler formulation is simpler … Two sub-facets are involved in this facet of mathematical simplicity. One is that fewer terms make an equation or description of some state of affairs simpler … Secondly, other things being equal, an equation or description of some state of affairs is mathematically simpler than another in so far as it uses simpler mathematical entities or relations than that other. A mathematical entity or relation Q is simpler than another one Y if Q can be understood by someone who does not understand Y, but Y cannot be understood by anyone who does not understand Q.[14]

The question is then why a hypothesis according to which God's power, wisdom and so on are infinite is simpler than a hypothesis according to which God's power, wisdom and so on are limited in the respect that God cannot create a different world than the one which is actually created.[15] Swinburne's argumentation for the

---

13 Swinburne, *Epistemic Justification*, p. 82.

14 Ibid., pp. 87–90.

15 Remember that here and in the following, we assume that arguments such as the teleological argument are valid, and that we must therefore compare different hypotheses

simplicity of omnipotence is rather uncomplicated: 'That there is an omnipotent God is a simpler hypothesis than the hypothesis that there is a God who has such-and-such limited power ...'[16]. The reason for this is that there is something special with the value 'infinity': 'There is a neatness about zero and infinity which particular finite numbers lack.'[17]

It is not evident, however, how this is borne out by the six facets of simplicity mentioned above. One could say that an enumeration of everything which God can do (consequently, everything which is not on the list God cannot do) is less simple than the hypothesis according to which God can do anything – this could be motivated by the facet according to which a hypothesis consisting of few separate laws is simpler than one consisting of many laws. On the other hand it is not evident that one can understand what being able to do anything means if one does not understand what being able to do this and that particular thing means. Anyhow, we can construct another hypothesis which is compatible with the data, and in fact renders them more probable than Swinburne's theistic hypothesis does, and which is fairly simple: that God is able to create our world but nothing more. Which of these two hypotheses is simplest is not immediately obvious, and Swinburne can hardly show which of them is simplest without specifying his understanding of simplicity in a controversial way – that is, he can hardly show, in a rationalistic way, which of them is simplest.

It is, moreover, questionable whether the criterion of simplicity can be used in the way Swinburne uses it. Swinburne is right in stressing that when we compare hypotheses, we take their simplicity into account, and right in stressing that we ought to do so. Swinburne is also right in showing that the reasons sometimes given for the role of simplicity, by trying to find something more fundamental, fail since they themselves presuppose the role of simplicity.[18] According to Swinburne, the only reason which can be given for his account of how hypotheses should be evaluated is hence, fundamentally, that it captures and refines our intuitions about how hypotheses should be evaluated.[19] When it comes to the question about the existence of God and the characteristics of God, however, few people evaluate the possible hypotheses in the way Swinburne suggests. Above all, few give the criterion of simplicity such a central role as it has for Swinburne, and that this is so is telling, since what Swinburne is doing is capturing our intuitions, against Swinburne's account. Of course, it is possible for him to say that he also wants to refine our intuitions, but how the refinement should be made is a question which then has to be settled, and Swinburne is then forced to return to our intuitions about refinement.

---

which are compatible with the conclusion of this argument, for example the theistic hypothesis and the hypothesis according to which there is a god with limited powers.

16 Swinburne, *The Existence of God*, p. 94.

17 Ibid., p. 283.

18 Swinburne, *Epistemic Justification*, pp. 99–102.

19 Ibid., pp. 119 and 122–3.

Finally, Swinburne mentions now and then that in different times and places, there have been different understandings of what simplicity involves.[20] It is, of course, true that some of these understandings are not prevalent any more, and it is not hard to see why. However, Swinburne has demonstrated that and how it is possible to show that the theistic hypothesis has a probability which exceeds ½ in a rationalistic way *only* if it is possible to show those who understand simplicity in another way that their understanding is defective, and this Swinburne has not done – he even hints that it cannot be done.[21]

The result of our discussion here is not that Swinburne is necessarily wrong, nor that he is not justified in believing that the theistic hypothesis has a probability which exceeds ½. Such questions we have not discussed. The result of our discussion is, instead, that if we want a fruitful way to discuss religious beliefs, in a context of vast disagreements, Swinburne has not provided us with such a way. His project of comparing the probability of different religions and their hypotheses about God[22] faces the same type of problems we have pointed out above, and we therefore ought to try to find other ways of understanding discussion in these cases.

Arguments for the Belief that God Exists using Revelation

As we have seen, trying to argue in a rationalistic way that God exists by arguing in the same way as one would argue to support a scientific hypothesis is not promising, since such an argument does not end in a belief which is similar to actual religious beliefs. However, there may be a different strategy. One can try to start out from religious experiences, revelations and the like, and in that way show, in a rationalistic way, that God exists. This strategy seems to be more promising, for in a revelation, many characteristics of God may be given.

Of course, if somebody has a religious experience, that could be a sufficient reason for that person to come to believe that there is a God. However, since the question I am discussing is how fruitful discussion of religious beliefs is possible, and discussion is here understood in a rationalistic way, the religious experience, if it is to be counted as evidence, must be judged in an impersonal way – that is, independent of the person who has it.

For this strategy to be possible, there must be rationalistic arguments that show that a certain revelation gives us probable beliefs about the existence and characteristics of God. The revelation must therefore be distinguished by something which makes its coming from God probable – for example, miracles accompanying it. In *Faith and Reason*, Swinburne points to two things that could be evidence for the fact that a revelation is from God: firstly, that the revelation includes true predictions of violations of natural laws, and secondly, that the life of the prophet

---

20 Ibid., pp. 73 and 92; Swinburne, *An Introduction to Confirmation Theory*, pp. 99 and 112–13; Swinburne, *The Existence of God*, p. 56.

21 Swinburne, *Epistemic Justification*, p. 92.

22 Richard Swinburne, *Faith and Reason* (Oxford, 1981), pp. 173–97.

who receives the revelation is accompanied by violations of natural laws.[23] Even if there are philosophers, like David Hume[24] and Antony Flew,[25] who have claimed that such evidence is impossible, I assume here that their arguments for the impossibility of such evidence are not conclusive. Even if this is assumed, however, there are some problems with revelations.

Firstly, there are many different reports, supporting different revelations, and none of them is particularly more credible than the others. Secondly, the question of whether something is a revelation from God or not is never just an empirical question, but also a question about values, be they existential or ethical. Simone Weil says: 'Hitler could die and return to life again fifty times, but I should still not look upon him as the Son of God.'[26] This is something very important, and often neglected. Even if an obvious violation of a natural law should occur, one cannot automatically conclude that God has brought it about, since to say that God has brought something about is to emphasize the *religious* character and significance of the event,[27] and this includes taking an ethical and existential stand. This is the same point Jean-Paul Sartre makes in his discussion of the command to Abraham to slaughter Isaac: '... if I hear voices, who can prove that they proceed from heaven and not from hell ... If a voice speaks to me, it is still I myself who must decide whether the voice is or is not that of an angel.'[28] For these two reasons, it is not possible to show in a rationalistic way that it is probable that there is a God by referring to incredible occurrences.

Rationalistic Arguments for the Belief that God Does Not Exist

My conclusion is hence that the attempt to show in a rationalistic way that God exists is not promising. What has to be discussed now is whether the attempt to show in a rationalistic way that God does not exist – that is, the rationalistic criticism of religion – is promising or not. Often, rationalistic criticism of religion is just a matter of showing that arguments such as Swinburne's are invalid or insufficient, and it is then claimed that if there are no valid rationalistic arguments for the

---

23 Ibid., p. 185.

24 See, for example, David Hume, *An Enquiry Concerning Human Understanding* (Oxford, 1999), pp. 173–4 (§§ 10:12–10:13).

25 See, for example, Antony Flew, *God and Philosophy* (London, 1966), pp. 148–9 (§§ 7.15–7.16).

26 Simone Weil, *Letter to a Priest*, trans. A.F. Willis (London, 2002), p. 34 (§ 25). Translation of Simone Weil, *Lettre à un religieux* (Paris, 1951), p. 58: 'Hitler pourrait mourir et ressusciter cinquante fois que je ne le regarderais pas comme le Fils de Dieu.'

27 See Stefand Eriksson, 'The Resurrection and the Incarnation – Myths, Facts or What?', *Studia Theologica*, 55 (2001): 130–31.

28 Jean-Paul Sartre, *Existentialism and Humanism*, trans. Philip Mairet (Brooklyn, NY, 1948), p. 31. Translation of Jean-Paul Sartre, *L'existentialisme est un humanisme* (Paris, 1946), p. 31: 'Et si j'entends des voix, qu'est-ce qui prouve qu'elles viennent du ciel et non de l'enfer ... Si une voix s'adresse à moi, c'est toujours moi qui déciderai que cette voix est la voix de l'ange ...'.

existence of God, one should not stipulate such a being. This could be motivated by referring to the criterion of simplicity. However, this suggestion seems to rely on the misidentification of the religious belief that there is a God with scientific beliefs where such forms of reasoning are relevant, something I will discuss further in the next chapter. Irrespective of that, however, as a starting point for a fruitful discussion this suggestion is not promising, since religious believers would probably question the criterion of simplicity, since neither it nor how it is to be understood are self-evident.

When it comes to actual arguments for the belief that God does not exist, the problem of evil is a common starting point.[29] Since what I am dealing with here is rationalistic discussion, it is the problem of evil in its logical and evidential forms which are relevant. The evidential form of the argument relies, however, on the misidentification of the religious belief that there is a God with scientific beliefs based on evidence, something I will come back to in the next chapter. The logical form of the argument is different, however. Its conclusion could be said to be that if every possible world were presented to us, none of them would be such that we would say that an omnipotent and all-good God as well as suffering exist.

There are attempts, however, to show that there is no logical contradiction here, for example the so-called free will defence.[30] If one believes that this is a good defence, one can say that it cannot be shown, in a rationalistic way, that God does not exist, along these lines. My point here is different, however. 'Omnipotent' is not a word often used by religious believers. 'Omnipotent' is a word used to give a philosophical and theoretical account of religious expressions. Religious believers say, for example, things like: 'God is much more powerful than we are', 'The world is in God's hands', 'The world is created by and dependent on God', 'My life (our lives) is (are) in God's hands.' The doctrine of God's omnipotence is meant to be a theoretical account of these beliefs, and is only a correct account if it captures what it should capture. If the doctrine of God's omnipotence turns out to be problematic, the reaction of believers could then be that the doctrine fails to capture what it should capture, and they either reject the doctrine of omnipotence on the whole, or redefine it in a less problematic way.[31] This is not, however, to say that the religious beliefs which the doctrine of God's omnipotence should be an account of, for example the belief that the world is in God's hands, are impossibly wrong. If such beliefs are in conflict with central experiences of suffering, scarcity and human responsibility, there is, of course, a problem. Whether such beliefs are in conflict with experiences of, for example, suffering, and if so, what should be done about it, is not a logical

---

29 There are, of course, other arguments which are supposed to show that the concept of God is in some sense incoherent, too. The problems with such arguments are the same as the problems with the argument from the problem of evil, however.

30 See, for example, Alvin Plantinga, *God and Other Minds: A Study in the Rational Justification of Belief in God* (Ithaca, NY, 1967), pp. 131–55.

31 Another possibility is to see God's goodness in another way (and leave the doctrine of omnipotence as it is). Some religious believers talk about natural disasters as a sign of God's wrath, for example, a wrath which also may be executed by seemingly evil human beings.

problem, however, and is hardly something which could be fruitfully discussed in a *rationalistic* way.[32]

Another attempt to show, in a rationalistic way, that God does not exist is by using scientific reductive explanations. However, such attempts are an instance of genetic fallacies: just because something has certain psychological and sociological causes, for example, it need not be wrong or of no value. Reductive explanations would be valid as rationalistic arguments against religious belief if religious belief is understood as a theory which is meant to explain certain phenomena, phenomena which the reductive explanations together with other scientific theories explain in a better way, according to some established way of determining which theory is the better one. As will be shown in the next chapter, however, to understand religious belief as such a scientific theory is to overlook some central features in what we call religious belief.

What I have just said should not be understood as a criticism of criticism of religious beliefs on the whole. Here, I have only shown that *rationalistic* criticism of religious beliefs is not promising. That such criticism is not promising does not mean that there is no good, but non-rationalistic, criticism of religious beliefs – something I will come back to in Chapter 6.

Conclusion

In this chapter, I have shown that rationalistic discussion of religious beliefs is not promising when it comes to many forms of religious disagreements. When doing this, I have questioned such understandings of religious beliefs according to which they are beliefs of a scientific type, based on evidence or on scientific reasoning. In the next chapter, I will discuss this understanding at greater length in order to strengthen my case, and explain in more detail why rationalistic discussion of religious beliefs is not promising in many cases. This is not the main reason for dealing with this understanding, however. The main reason for dealing with this understanding is, rather, that doing so could provide the groundwork for another way of understanding religious disagreements and fruitful discussion of such disagreements, an understanding which I will work out in the rest of this book.

---

32 For more about the relation between religious belief and the doctrine of omnipotence, cf. Dewi Zephaniah Phillips, *The Problem of Evil and the Problem of God* (London, 2004), pp. 6–7, 10–13, 25–6, 178–9.

Chapter 2

Religious Belief and the Diverse Ways We Deal with the World around Us

In this chapter, I will detail the criticism of the understanding of religious beliefs according to which they are beliefs of a scientific type, based on evidence or on scientific reasoning, a criticism which I only hinted at in the last chapter. This understanding of religious beliefs lies behind the understanding of the rationality and irrationality of religious beliefs that I took for granted in that chapter, where a rational belief was understood to be a belief one adopts after having been convinced of its truth by means of an argument starting from certain putative universal norms and rules for argumentation.[1]

Some Characteristics of Religious Belief

I started with the problem of how to reconcile religious disagreements. Reconciling disagreements is obviously more difficult in the context or religion than in the context of science. That this is so shows that disagreements in these two cases must be understood in different ways, and it furthermore indicates that religious beliefs cannot be subordinated to scientific ways of reasoning without being distorted. In the following, I will underline this difference between religious and scientific beliefs additionally by pointing out some examples of such differences, differences which tend to be forgotten. These differences show themselves above all in how religious beliefs are used and how they function.

Firstly, religious belief is characterized by commitment and devotion.[2] If somebody holds a belief, which when linguistically expressed contains the word 'God', but holds it without commitment and devotion, the belief is not called a religious one. Her use of the word 'God' is dependent on the use of this word by religious believers,

---

1   Another possible way to criticize this way of understanding the rationality and irrationality of religious beliefs would be to show that it also misrepresents the scientific practice. I will not pursue this form of criticism here, however.

2   Cf. Martin Heidegger, *Identity and Difference*, trans. Joan Stambaugh (Chicago, IL, 1969), p. 72: '[*Causa sui*] is the right name for the god of philosophy. Man can neither pray nor sacrifice to this god. Before the *causa sui*, man can neither fall to his knees in awe nor can he play music and dance before this god.' Cf. further Rhees, *Rush Rhees on Religion and Philosophy*, pp. 5 and 36. In this sense, criticism of metaphysical thinking is the very opposite to criticism of religious belief.

where it is used with commitment and devotion. This commitment is not a result of a weighing of evidence or the like, and the religious belief is not held tentatively or as highly probable.[3] The commitment is not even a consequence of the belief: if somebody is not committed, her belief is not religious, whereas the commitment can be religious without being connected with articulated beliefs. In that sense, the commitment is conceptually prior to the belief. This does not mean that there is no such thing as religious doubt or uncertainty concerning, for example, the existence of God. However, what makes this doubt and this uncertainty into attitudes towards *religious* beliefs is that they stand in relation to religious commitment, a relation without which they are not understood as religious. The way somebody doubts or is uncertain about a religious belief is therefore very dissimilar from the way somebody doubts or is uncertain about a scientific belief, which again underlines the difference between these forms of beliefs. *Religious* doubt, for example, is not a matter of doubting whether the arguments one thought were valid really are valid. One way of describing religious doubt is instead to describe it as an inability to find meaning in the religious beliefs, in other words that it is a matter of the religious belief being incapable of providing existential satisfaction.

Secondly, the religious belief that there is a God differs considerably from a belief that a certain thing exists. Religious believers say that God is a mystery, that God cannot be completely understood, that God is not of this world. To say that there is a God is thus not to add another being to all those beings one believes there are in the world. To say that there is a God is for example very dissimilar from saying that a particular animal, whose existence has been debated, exists. In the case of the animal, the person who believes in its existence and the person who does not do agree on how the question could be settled, and this is not the case when it comes to God.[4]

Thirdly, science is to a large extent an extension of our everyday dealings with the things around us, of our attempts to understand how they work and to improve our use of them. Religion, on the other hand, is dependent on quite particular experiences of birth, death, joy, sorrow, sexual life, the majesty of and our dependency on nature,

---

3   Cf. Dewi Zephaniah Phillips, *Recovering Religious Concepts: Closing Epistemic Divides* (Basingstoke, 2000), pp. 5–6; Ludwig Wittgenstein, *Lectures and Conversations on Aesthetics, Psychology and Religious Belief*, ed. Cyril Barrett (Oxford, 1966), p. 57. This means that Swinburne's attempt to make the belief that God exists probable, apart from being a failure, also distorts the character of the religious belief in God. Cf. further Cahn, 'The Irrelevance to Religion of Philosophic Proofs for the Existence of God': 170: 'One might expect that religious believers would be vitally interested in discussions of this subject [philosophic proofs for the existence of God]. One might suppose that when a proof of God's existence is presented and eloquently defended, believers would be most enthusiastic, and that when a proof is attacked and persuasively refuted, believers would be seriously disappointed. But this is not at all the case.'

4   Cf. Rhees, *Rush Rhees on Religion and Philosophy*, pp. 20–21; Dewi Zephaniah Phillips, *Faith and Philosophical Enquiry* (London, 1970), pp. 16–17; Dewi Zephaniah Phillips, *Wittgenstein and Religion* (New York, 1993), p. 2.

moral choice, absolute safety and the like – if we did not have these experiences, we would not have religion in the role it plays in human life.[5] Religion responds to these experiences, but it does not try to explain them in a *scientific* manner. Science can affect these experiences, and scientific development can make some of these experiences disappear, but science *itself* is no existential response to them. Religious belief, which develops out of these experiences, therefore has another form of significance than science. This understanding of religious belief, according to which it is an unmediated response to certain experiences, stands in contrast to the metaphysical understanding of religious belief, according to which the concept of God is introduced to serve a theoretical (or practical) purpose, and hence is understood merely instrumentally.

As I have said, religious belief is characterized by commitment and devotion, thus it is not held tentatively or as highly probable. If religious beliefs were the only beliefs which were not based on hypothetical reasoning, they might seem rather peculiar. If that were so, that could be said to indicate either that my description of religious belief must be wrong, or that religious belief must be something defective. To show that these two possible conclusions are confused, I will give some examples of other beliefs, beliefs which are very common, whose character becomes distorted if they are characterized as being based on hypothetical reasoning. This will mainly be done with reference to Wittgenstein, but I am not going to present all his contributions to this topic, since my aim is only to illuminate my main question, and I will not abstain from modifying his points if that could bring about greater clarity.

A Brief Introduction to Wittgenstein's Philosophy

Before going into the discussion of the unhypothetical character of certain beliefs, I will give a brief introduction to Wittgenstein's philosophy. Wittgenstein's main philosophical contribution is not primarily, in my view, individual philosophical investigations, although these too are important, but that he has formulated and given examples of a certain way of doing philosophy. In the introduction to this book, I have already expressed, mainly by reference to Wittgenstein, a certain way of understanding philosophy. To make this way of doing philosophy clearer, I will explain a distinctive feature of Wittgenstein's way of conducting investigations: their conceptual (or grammatical) character.

5　Cf. Richard H. Bell, 'Religion and Wittgenstein's Legacy: Beyond Fideism and Language Games', in Timothy Tessin and Mario von der Ruhr (eds), *Philosophy and the Grammar of Religious Belief* (New York, 1995), pp. 230–31; John Churchill, 'The Squirrel Does Not Infer by Induction: Wittgenstein and the Natural History of Religion', in Timothy Tessin and Mario von der Ruhr (eds), *Philosophy and the Grammar of Religious Belief* (New York, 1995), p. 71; Phillips, *Wittgenstein and Religion*, p. 69; Phillips, *Recovering Religious Concepts*, pp. 204–5; Wittgenstein, 'A Lecture on Ethics', pp. 41–2; Wittgenstein, 'Remarks on Frazer's *Golden Bough*', pp. 127–9.

The word 'conceptual' is to be contrasted with 'empirical' and 'metaphysical'. First, an example of the contrast between 'conceptual' and 'empirical': below, I will say that if yardsticks did not agree, we would not have a system of measuring. If this is understood as an empirical claim, it is an empirical hypothesis about what would happen if our yardsticks ceased to agree with each other. If it is understood as a conceptual claim, however, and this is how this claim should be understood, then it is not a claim about what will happen in the future. The remark says rather that *irrespective* of what will happen in the future, if yardsticks did not agree, we would not have a system of measuring. Furthermore, the claim applies as well to the present: if yardsticks did not agree now, we would not have a system of measuring now. That this is the case is due to the concept of measuring: the relation between measuring and the agreement of yardsticks is not an accidental one, but an *internal* one. This is, of course, due to how we now use words such as 'measuring', what role the activity of measuring plays in our life, and so on.[6] In this context, the phrase 'conceptually prior' can also be explained. The phrase does not refer to some type of empirical priority, for example temporal priority. What it stands for is a certain type of conceptual dependence: for something to be what it conceptually is, something else is needed, whereas the reverse is not true. One example: religious commitment is conceptually prior to religious beliefs, since if somebody is not committed, her belief is not religious, whereas the commitment can be religious without being connected with articulated beliefs.

Second, an example of the contrast between 'conceptual' and 'metaphysical': below, I will say that mistakes are impossible when it comes to 'I have pain', but not when it comes to 'She has pain' (where what is impossible is to have *her* pain). This is not a matter of metaphysical impossibility, but of conceptual impossibility. If it were a matter of metaphysical impossibility, the opposite (that mistakes are possible when it comes to 'I have pain', that it is possible to have another person's pain) should at least be conceivable.[7] To talk about conceptual impossibility can therefore be misleading: to say that something is impossible may make one believe that this 'something' (which is impossible) is a 'thing' which could be conceived. It is therefore, in one sense, better to say that there are nothing like mistakes when it comes to 'I have pain': the phrase 'mistakes when it comes to "I have pain"' does not stand for anything. Those who say that religious beliefs are beliefs of a scientific type and protest against the above analysis of the concept of religious belief by saying that the analysis is an expression of a metaphysical (in the sense of essentialist) understanding of the concept have thus not paid attention to the contrast between 'conceptual' and 'metaphysical': the analysis is supposed to point out the way in

---

6   Cf. Cora Diamond, 'Rules: Looking in the Right Place', in D.Z. Phillips and Peter Winch (eds), *Wittgenstein: Attention to Particulars: Essays in Honour of Rush Rhees (1909–89)* (London, 1989), p. 19.

7   See Severin Schroeder, 'The Demand for Synoptic Representations and the Private Language Discussion: PI 243–315', in Erich Ammereller and Eugen Fischer (eds), *Wittgenstein at Work: Method in the* Philosophical Investigations (London, 2004), pp. 159–60.

which we all use the concept of religious beliefs and to show what understanding we, at least implicitly, have in common, a common understanding without which a disagreement would not be possible, since then we would not be talking about the same thing.

Wittgenstein on Following Rules

I will begin the discussion of the unhypothetical character of certain beliefs by pointing out some important themes in Wittgenstein's discussion of rule following.[8] The problem Wittgenstein is discussing concerning rule following is that a rule considered in isolation can be interpreted in any manner,[9] and hence anything can be said to be in accord with a certain rule. To prevent such an, as we would like to say, erroneous interpretation, we have to give another rule, but this rule can in its turn be interpreted in any manner, so by referring to another rule, we have just pushed the problem to another level.[10] In this situation, it can be tempting to take recourse to an idea of super-rules, rules which cannot possibly be misunderstood, rules which abide in a higher sphere. Such a solution is philosophically unsatisfying, however, since it makes what we tried to understand even more mysterious.[11]

To help us out of this problem of rule following, Wittgenstein points to how we, when somebody says something, in most cases react immediately to what she says, without interpreting what she says, without formulating any hypotheses about what she means.[12] Thus if somebody expresses a rule, the distance between the rule and the application of it is here, in most cases, not bridged by an interpretation – that is, by hypothetically adding another rule – since in most cases, no bridge is needed. That we *always* interpret a specific rule consequently makes no sense: only in some cases is a bridge between rule and application needed. Furthermore, it can be misleading to say that we always *apply* the rule, since that intimates that we first have a rule which we understand independently of *any* application or use of it, a rule which *then* is applied. That we simply react immediately to the rule, without interpreting it, and that we share these reactions, is the background against which we have rules, follow them, and so on. Therefore, what we ought not to do is to isolate rules and the following of rules completely from each other. Doing so gives rise to our problem,

---

8   See Wittgenstein, *Philosophical Investigations*, roughly pp. 63e–75e (roughly §§ 185–242).

9   Ibid., pp. 63e–64e, 68e, 69e (§§ 185, 198, 201).

10 See Ludwig Wittgenstein, *Remarks on the Foundations of Mathematics*, trans. G.E.M. Anscombe (Cambridge, 1978), pp. 79 and 341 (§§ I:113 and VI:38); Wittgenstein, *Philosophical Investigations*, p. 12e (§ 28).

11 See Wittgenstein, *Philosophical Investigations*, pp. 64e and 66e (§§ 188 and 193).

12 See Ludwig Wittgenstein, *Philosophical Grammar*, trans. Anthony Kenny (Berkeley, CA, 1974) p. 47 (§ I:9); Wittgenstein, *Philosophical Investigations*, pp. 69e and 71e (§§ 201–2 and 211).

the problem of how rules can be followed when they can be interpreted in any way, and in this way, what rules are disappears completely from sight.

The tendency to consider the rule and its application in isolation from each other has one of its roots in a simplified way of looking at language. One can be inclined to say that words get their meaning by means of ostensive definitions or rules stating the meaning of a particular word by means of other words. One of the problems with this idea is that an ostensive definition or a rule considered in isolation can be interpreted in any manner,[13] and an ostensive definition or a rule cannot therefore by itself account for the meaning of a word. The connection between meaning and use is then seen only as a one-way connection, from meaning to use: I turn in a specific direction since the signpost tells me to,[14] I fetch somebody a slab when she says 'Fetch me a slab!'[15] since that is what her words mean, and so on. If one only sees the connection between meaning and use as a one-way connection, one can be led to believe that the connection is established by means of magic or accident. However, the connection is not one-way: the signpost would only be a stick of wood if nobody followed it, 'Fetch me a slab!' would only be noises if nobody did fetch the person who utters it a slab. This means that linguistic meaning is not independent of us and our dealings with the world.[16] Wittgenstein's response to this simplified way of understanding the connection between meaning and use is hence to consider words, definitions and rules not in isolation, but in the context in which they are used and in relation to how we deal with the world, relations without which words, definitions and rules are not properly understood.[17] Furthermore, that the connection between meaning and use is not one-way means that there is not anything like rules being constantly applied mistakenly, since the notion of mistake is conceptually connected to what we usually do.

Another way to express the above remark is to say that there is a certain conceptual connection between language, us and the world. Considered in complete isolation, none of these is properly understood. This could be expressed by saying that there is an internal relation between certain facts about the world and about us, and the meaning of particular words. Therefore, if certain things, in the world and in us, were different, certain words, ideas and activities would not be what they now are. This is so not for hypothetical reasons, but for conceptual reasons, since we are not talking about what probably happens or could happen in the future, as I explained above. If things constantly changed their colour, our colour concepts would not retain their

---

13 See Wittgenstein, *Philosophical Investigations*, p. 12e (§ 28).

14 Cf. ibid., p. 68e (§ 198).

15 Cf. ibid., pp. 3e–5e, 7e–8e (§§ 2, 6, 8–10, 17, 19, 20).

16 See Ludwig Wittgenstein, *Wittgenstein's Lectures on the Foundations of Mathematics, Cambridge, 1939*, ed. Cora Diamond (Chicago, IL, 1976), p. 25; Wittgenstein, *Philosophical Investigations*, p. 68e (§ 198).

17 See, for example, Wittgenstein, *Philosophical Investigations*, pp. 2e, 4e, 5e (§§ 1, 6, 9).

meaning;[18] if the result was sometimes 5 and sometimes 7 when we put down three beans (or sticks, fingers, lines) and then another three beans, that would mean the end of what we call sums;[19] if lumps of cheese were to grow or shrink suddenly and for no obvious reason, our procedure of fixing its price by weighing it would lose the point it now has;[20] if things were to disappear and appear again suddenly, substance-concepts such as 'chair' would not have the meaning they now have;[21] if yardsticks did not agree, we would not have a system of measuring;[22] if confusion supervened, we would not have what we now call colour words;[23] if a mathematical proof got ratification from one person but not from another, we would not have what we call calculation.[24] In the same way, if in a community there were no similar reactions to the experiences of birth, death and the like, there would be no religious language in that community.[25]

The connection between language and the world is thus not something whose existence we, when we have a language, are in doubt about and must confirm by means of theoretical, hypothetical reasoning. If there is no such connection, it makes no sense to talk about us having a language at all. The connection between language and the world is already there in our using it. This means that justification, right and wrong linguistic behaviour, making the distinction between true and false and the like do not have their foundation in self-evident theoretical beliefs. Given our shared reactions in a specific context, and given common ways of dealing with the world around us as a precondition, we have a language in which we make the distinction between right and wrong, true and false, and make the distinction between right and wrong applications. There is nothing, however, like taking up a position before or outside every way of making this distinction and trying to justify them, since every such attempt already presupposes language.[26] That we are alike and act in the same

---

18 Cf. Ludwig Wittgenstein, 'Notes for Lectures on "Private Experience" and "Sense Data"', in James C. Klagge and Alfred Nordmann (eds), *Philosophical Occasions 1912–1951* (Indianapolis, IN, 1993), p. 267.

19 See Wittgenstein, *Remarks on the Foundations of Mathematics*, pp. 51–2 (§ I:37).

20 See Wittgenstein, *Philosophical Investigations*, p. 48e (§ 142); Wittgenstein, 'Notes for Lectures on "Private Experience" and "Sense Data"', p. 239.

21 Cf. Wittgenstein, *Philosophical Investigations*, p. 32e (§ 80).

22 See Wittgenstein, *Remarks on the Foundations of Mathematics*, pp. 199–200 (§ III:74).

23 See ibid., p. 200 (§ III:75).

24 See ibid., p. 365 (§ VII:9).

25 Nothing is dependent on precisely *these* examples. If you do not find them convincing, it is possible to find other examples which are perhaps more convincing. Cf. Ludwig Wittgenstein, *Wittgenstein's Lectures: Cambridge, 1932–1935*, ed. Alice Ambrose (New York, 1979) p. 97; Wittgenstein, *Lectures on the Foundations of Mathematics*, p. 103.

26 See Ludwig Wittgenstein, 'The Language of Sense Data and Private Experience', in James C. Klagge and Alfred Nordmann (eds), *Philosophical Occasions 1912–1951* (Indianapolis, IN, 1993), p. 352; Wittgenstein, *Lectures on the Foundations of Mathematics*, p. 95; Wittgenstein, *Philosophical Grammar*, p. 184 (§ I:133).

way is hence a *precondition* for us having a communicative language at all, it is not a *reason* which makes our language correct judged from some sort of way of making the distinction between true and false which is there before that language. If the reasons turn out to be false, what they support stands in need of other reasons, whereas if the preconditions are not there, there is no language either.

One possible objection to what has so far been said is that this implies that what is true is what is normal, that human agreement decides what is true, or that the majority decides what is true. This is not so. What is true is that our ways of talking are dependent on facts about the world and about us, but this dependence has to be understood in the right way. In language, there are established ways of making the distinction between true and false in specific areas. That we act in the same way is only a precondition for a certain activity, not a part of the content of what we say when we say something.[27] If there were no certain shared reactions, we would not have the mathematical language we have, for example, but a mathematical statement is not *about* these preconditions. Agreement does not decide what is correct in an already existing language, but is just a precondition for language.[28] This means that if we had no common ways of talking, there would not be anything to be right and wrong about. When we have a way of making the distinction between true and false, we determine what is true and false. If there were no such agreement, clock readings would not be false or incorrect, but there would not be anything like measurements of time at all.[29] In the same way, if the same calculation did not give the same answer at different times and when carried out by different persons, the 'calculations' would not be false or incorrect, but there would not be anything like calculations at all.[30]

In the following, I will go on to present some examples of ways of speaking which one could be inclined to regard as based on theoretical, hypothetical reasoning, ways of speaking which, however, turn out to be philosophically problematic if seen in that way.

---

27 See Wittgenstein, *Remarks on the Foundations of Mathematics*, pp. 323 and 365 (§§ VI:21 and VII:9).

28 See Wittgenstein, *Remarks on the Foundations of Mathematics*, pp. 353 and 355 (§§ VI:49 and VII:1); Wittgenstein, *Lectures on the Foundations of Mathematics*, pp. 107 and 183–4; Wittgenstein, *Philosophical Investigations*, p. 75e (§ 241). For more about this and related topics, see Martin Gustafsson, 'The rule-follower and his community: remarks on an apparent tension in Wittgenstein's discussions of rule-following', *Language Sciences*, 26 (2004): 135–6, 139, 144–5.

29 Cf. Gordon P. Baker and Peter M.S. Hacker, *An Analytical Commentary on the Philosophical Investigations, Volume 2: Wittgenstein: Rules, Grammar and Necessity* (Oxford, 1985), p. 229.

30 See Wittgenstein, *Remarks on the Foundations of Mathematics*, pp. 198 and 356 (§§ III:73 and VII:2); Wittgenstein, *Lectures on the Foundations of Mathematics*, p. 102.

Pain

One example of ways of speaking which one could be inclined to regard as based on theoretical, hypothetical reasoning, is how we talk about pain. When it comes to pain, one can be inclined to say that one knows one's own pain with certainty, but in the case of others, only infers that they are in pain by means of analogy between their behaviour and one's own when one is in pain. Conversely, one can be inclined to say that nobody can know how I feel, that nobody can feel my pain. Our feelings are hidden from others, and at best I can only know your feelings indirectly, and you can only know my feelings indirectly. Not until a person learns to speak does it become possible for her to describe her feelings to others, but even then, this is only a faint and defective description compared to the knowledge one has of one's own feelings.

Such sayings as, for example, 'One can never know whether another person is in pain'[31] are often an expression of a metaphysical thesis about how things *must* be. The path away from such sayings can be pointed out by reminding the one who utters them of certain facts she overlooks. One of them is that the use of the sentences 'I have pain' and 'She has pain' are dissimilar. It is therefore not true that they are on the same level, the only difference being that the first is used with much more certainty than the second. 'I have pain' is, in one sense, not a statement *about* a specific person, as 'She has pain', or 'I have broken my arm' for that matter, is. In the latter two cases, there is a possibility of error[32] – that is, the wrong person has been picked out – whereas in the first case, a mistake – that is, I have mistaken somebody else for me – is as impossible as it is to moan with pain by mistake, having mistaken somebody else for me.[33]

This means that it is misleading to say that 'I have pain' is used only as a description. The sentence can instead be seen as a new form of pain-behaviour which we learn as children to replace the primitive[34] and inarticulate pain-behaviour with which we react without reasoning when being hurt.[35] Hence, 'I have pain' does not refer to pain-behaviour, but is a pain-behaviour, one could say.[36] The use of 'I have

---

31 Cf. Wittgenstein, *Philosophical Investigations*, p. 86e (§ 303).

32 That it is possible to say 'I have broken my arm' but pick out the wrong person could sound a little mysterious. However, Wittgenstein gives an example: 'It is possible that, say in an accident, I should feel a pain in my arm, see a broken arm at my side, and think it is mine, when really it is my neighbour's'; Wittgenstein, *The Blue and Brown Books*, p. 67. The point is that this is not possible when saying 'I have pain.'

33 See Wittgenstein, *The Blue and Brown Books*, p. 67.

34 'Primitive' is not used pejoratively in this context. When I talk about 'primitive behaviour' here and in the following, I am only saying that our ways of talking about pain, for example, are dependent on such behaviour, and that this behaviour is hence conceptually prior to such ways of talking.

35 See Wittgenstein, *Philosophical Investigations*, pp. 75e–76e (§ 244).

36 See Ludwig Wittgenstein, 'Notes for the "Philosophical Lecture"', in James C. Klagge and Alfred Nordmann (eds), *Philosophical Occasions 1912–1951* (Indianapolis, IN, 1993), p.

pain' and 'She has pain' is dissimilar: the difference between them could be seen as the difference between moaning, and saying that somebody moans. In opposition to a far too intellectualized picture of our use of the sentence 'I have pain', Wittgenstein stresses its connections to primitive pain-behaviour.

By pointing out these differences, Wittgenstein makes us less inclined to consider the difference between 'I have pain' and 'She has pain' as a matter of different degrees of certainty, an idea which can make us believe that saying 'She has pain' must always be a matter of formulating a hypothesis. This belief is confused. Also, the sentence 'She has pain' has a connection to primitive behaviour, but a different one to 'I have pain.' It is a far too intellectualized picture to think that we only see the behaviour of others, and from this conjecture what lies behind by means of hypothetical reasoning.[37] Only in some cases do we do this, whereas we usually just react immediately to the cries of others by a reaction of sympathy or the like.[38] One might therefore say that the primitive form of 'She has pain' is a moaning too – namely, what Wittgenstein calls a moan of compassion.[39]

Induction, Cause and Effect

Although drawing a general conclusion from a number of cases by means of induction and establishing that something is the cause of a certain effect are important ways of reasoning in human life, we can be inclined to say that the evidence is always insufficient for a conclusion to be drawn in these cases. When it comes to induction, one then says that one can never conclude from one case to another, that all we can know is isolated occurrences in the past. When it comes to cause and effect, one then says that we cannot know what is the cause of a certain effect, or even that talk about the cause of something is always illegitimate, since when we talk about causes, we add something which cannot be seen to what can be seen. Wittgenstein's remarks concerning these issues are meant to point out how inductive reasoning and searching for a cause are rooted in ways of acting which are conceptually prior to reasoning, and that these ways of reasoning are therefore not founded on theoretical, hypothetical thinking.

449.

37 See Ludwig Wittgenstein, *Zettel*, trans. G.E.M. Anscombe (Berkeley, CA/Los Angeles, CA, 1967), p. 95e (§§ 537 and 540–41); Ludwig Wittgenstein, *Bemerkungen über die Philosophie der Psychologie, Band II/Remarks on the Philosophy of Psychology, Volume II*, trans. C.G. Luckhardt and M.A.E. Aue (Chicago, IL, 1980) p. 33e (§ 170).

38 See Wittgenstein, *Philosophical Investigations*, p. 86e (§ 303); Wittgenstein, 'Notes for Lectures on "Private Experience" and "Sense Data"', p. 287; Ludwig Wittgenstein, 'Ursache und Wirkung: Intuitives Erfassen'/'Cause and Effect: Intuitive Awareness', trans. Peter Winch, in James C. Klagge and Alfred Nordmann (eds), *Philosophical Occasions 1912–1951* (Indianapolis, IN, 1993), p. 381.

39 See Wittgenstein, 'Notes for Lectures on "Private Experience" and "Sense Data"', p. 261.

Wittgenstein points to the fact that acting in an inductive way is part of our ways of acting even before hypothetical reasoning comes in – acting confidently in an inductive way is simply what we do.[40] This and the other examples discussed in this chapter are not supposed to be a proof against scepticism – for example, scepticism about inductive reasoning – but makes us less inclined to be attracted by such scepticism. When we reason hypothetically about the future, this is done against the background of all those cases where we do not reason hypothetically about the future, but just act confidently. If one, for example, tries to be a little cautious, and therefore says that what we have seen in the past only gives us reason to *believe* that this will also happen in the future or that what we have seen in the past only makes sayings about the future *probable*, one is still doing this against the background of confident acting in an inductive way. Without such acting, it would even be illegitimate to talk about 'reason to believe' and 'making probable'. Hence, this means that without confident acting in an inductive way, we have no hypothetical reasoning about the future either. This is not to deny that now and then we are wrong in particular cases, but if we try to show that inductive reasoning is wrong *generally* by referring to *particular* failures of this way of reasoning, we already presuppose this way of reasoning, since we then reason inductively from the particular to the general. This is not to deny that this form of reasoning could be given up. This would lead to a very different form of life than the present. What could happen is, for example, that this way of reasoning led to different results at different times or for different persons, and it would then undermine itself.

The same goes for searching for a cause. Wittgenstein gives several examples of how we immediately react to the cause without first determining that this is the cause by means of hypothetical reasoning.[41] In these cases, it is not a matter of formulating hypotheses, investigating or carrying out experiments. That we in these cases just act, without doubt, is a precondition for the possibility of doubting our ways of finding causes in particular cases – without such confident acting, the doubt we have in particular cases would not stand in contrast to anything. It is thus possible that we, in certain cases, point out the wrong cause when we react instinctively, but nevertheless we in fact react in this way, and therefore we talk about cause and effect as we do.[42]

There is, however, a *specific* problem with our talk about cause and effect. One can be inclined to say that talk about the cause of something is always illegitimate, since when we talk about causes, we add something which cannot be seen to what can be seen. One of the problems with saying so is that it is presupposed that the causal relation, to be something legitimate, has to be some sort of thing. Is it really

---

40 See Ludwig Wittgenstein, *Über Gewissheit/On Certainty*, trans. Denis Paul and G.E.M. Anscombe (Oxford, 1974), p. 37e (§ 287); Wittgenstein, *Philosophical Grammar*, p. 109 (§ I:67); Wittgenstein, *Philosophical Investigations*, pp. 113e–114e (§§ 466 and 472–4).

41 See Wittgenstein, 'Cause and Effect', pp. 373, 387, 410. See also Norman Malcolm, *Nothing Is Hidden: Wittgenstein's Criticism of His Early Thought* (Oxford, 1986), p. 150.

42 See Wittgenstein, 'Cause and Effect', pp. 373 and 377.

true that everything which can be seen is some sort of thing? Is it not possible to see that somebody is happy without this having to be regarded as a hypothetical conclusion from seeing particular things? To say that what we *really* see is only shapes, colours and movements and that everything else is hypothetical conclusions drawn from these is to misrepresent our ways of seeing.[43] If that were so, we would not see chairs and tables either, but would have to understand them as hypothetical conclusions drawn from our seeing shapes, colours and movements. That we see colours, shapes and movements as well as causal relations does not mean that we see them in exactly the same way, however. One can imagine a person who sees a particular incident and can make an accurate animated cartoon of it, but does not recognize causes and effects in it, without being inclined to say that it is her sight that is defective.[44]

Colour Words

Another example of ways of speaking which one could be inclined to regard as based on theoretical, hypothetical reasoning is our use of colour words. One can be inclined to think that colour words name private, inner sensations. Thus one can be tempted to say things like 'Only I know what I really mean by "green"',[45] or believe that only by means of hypothetical reasoning can one can be justified in saying 'I know what she sees when she says that she sees something blue.'

   However, to say that colour words stand for something necessarily private eliminates the distinction between right and wrong applications of the words, between believing that you use them rightly and actually doing it. If we assume that colour words stand for something necessarily private, it makes no sense for somebody to say to me that I am wrong when I say 'That patch is red.' It makes no sense either for me to say that I was wrong when I said 'That patch is red.' If I begin to suspect that I was wrong, the problem is not only that I cannot find out whether I was wrong or not, but even that it makes no sense to talk about 'finding out' here – to look at the patch once more is of no help. Since we talk about right and wrong use of colour words, this shows that such words do not get their meaning by means of being attached to private sensations, and hence that we do not infer by means of hypothetical reasoning what somebody sees when she says that she sees something blue.

   Our problem thus depends on leaving the public character of language out of consideration. This means that the answer to the question 'How do I know that when I do what I call seeing green I do what you call seeing green' could simply be said

---

   43 Cf. Ludwig Wittgenstein, *Bemerkungen über die Philosophie der Psychologie, Band I/Remarks on the Philosophy of Psychology, Volume I*, trans. G.E.M. Anscombe (Chicago, IL, 1980), pp. 192e–193e (§§ 1 101–2).

   44 Cf. ibid., p. 193e (§ 1 103).

   45 See Wittgenstein, 'Notes for Lectures on "Private Experience" and "Sense Data"', p. 208.

to be that words like 'green' belong to and are used in a common language, and are used to apply to objects in the common world.[46] If inner sensations need to be involved here at all, we could simply say that our inner sensations when we see red are the same, but this is not because of a discovery we have made as a result of some queer sort of investigation, but is simply how we use terms like 'the same'.

Our linguistic usage depends on certain facts about the world and about us. These facts are preconditions for the language to exist, but are not part of the content of what we say when we use colour words. That we use colour words as we do is conceptually dependent on the agreement of reactions, in this case that people describe the same things as green:

> … the phenomenon of language is based on regularity, on agreement in action. Here it is of the greatest importance that all or the enormous majority of us agree in certain things. I can, e.g., be quite sure that the colour of this object will be called 'green' by far the most of the human beings who see it.[47]

Differences between Religious Belief and the above Examples

The examples which have been discussed show that there are many beliefs, beliefs which are very common, whose character becomes distorted if they are characterized as based on hypothetical reasoning. This shows that religious beliefs are not the only beliefs which are not based on hypothetical reasoning, and are hence not peculiar for that reason. The similarities between religious beliefs and the above examples must not be exaggerated, however. The example of pain may, for example, lead one to fail to notice important differences between pain language and religious language. The way moaning and shouting is primitive in pain language is dissimilar from the way the experience of, for example, the majesty of nature and the religious reactions and ways of expressing oneself which can come up immediately there – that is, not as a result of hypothetical reasoning – are primitive in religious language.[48] (One similarity is, of course, that if we did not have such experiences and reactions, we

---

46 See Wittgenstein, *Philosophical Investigations*, p. 81e (§ 275); Wittgenstein, 'Notes for Lectures on "Private Experience" and "Sense Data"', pp. 216–17.

47 Wittgenstein, *Remarks on the Foundations of Mathematics*, p. 342 (§ VI:39). Translation of Ludwig Wittgenstein, *Bemerkungen über die Grundlagen der Mathematik* (Frankfurt am Main, 1974), p. 342: '… das Phänomen der Sprache beruht auf der Regelmäßigkeit, auf der Übereinstimmung im Handeln. Hier ist es von der größten Wichtigkeit, daß wir alle, oder die ungeheure Mehrzahl in gewissen Dingen übereinstimmen. Ich kann, z. B., ganz sicher sein, daß die Farbe dieses Gegenstandes von den allermeisten Menschen die ihn sehen "grün" genannt wird.' See also Wittgenstein, 'Notes for Lectures on "Private Experience" and "Sense Data"', p. 234.

48 Many who have talked about primitive reactions in connection to religious belief have not pointed this out clearly enough, and their accounts have in this respect not been exhaustive. See, for example, Peter Winch, *Trying to Make Sense* (Oxford, 1987), pp. 110–11;

would not have pain language and religious language in the role they play in our lives.) Concerning pain, we never move particularly far from moaning and shouting. We learn to discriminate by developing a sensitivity for different kinds and locations of pain, and we learn to talk instead of moaning, but that is about it. Concerning religion, a certain sensitivity and discriminatory capacity is also developed, but talk about God, for example, is found far beyond the situations where there are existential experiences, and this talk about God is not comparable with talk about pain when we are not in pain. Furthermore, religion seems not only to be a way of acting in response to such experiences or talking about them, but also a way of evoking them, by means of singing, meditation and so on.

That religious belief is not based on hypothetical reasoning might perhaps seem to be most correct in the case where a person, even as a child, learns to speak and act religiously, and therefore has a religious language to use when she has particular experiences of birth, death and the like. That religious belief in this case is initially not based on hypothetical reasoning is obvious. This is not to say that the religious belief in this case cannot be felt to be inadequate later on, but it is misleading to say that religious belief in this case actually is, and always ought to be, based on hypothetical reasoning. Religious actions one has learnt as a child one simply does, without any reasoning behind it, just as we use the language we learn as children and act in general in the way we have learnt. This is not, however, to say that there could never be reasons for taking a critical attitude to religious beliefs, and this I will come back to.[49]

However, the philosophical discussion of religion often starts from a picture according to which a person is initially not a religious believer, but later chooses to be one. I have just pointed to the fact that this picture leaves out other possibilities.[50] The picture according to which a person is initially not a religious believer but later becomes one due to hypothetical reasoning is, however, not even a correct picture of one particular case. Firstly, what it means to become a religious believer later in life is misunderstood if that process is considered in complete isolation. The person

---

Brian R. Clack, *Wittgenstein, Frazer and Religion* (New York, 1999), p. 85. However, Winch and Clack do not claim that their accounts are exhaustive.

49 See Chapter 6.

50 One reason why these possibilities are often excluded is perhaps that *in* religion, it is sometimes said that it does not suffice to only act and speak religiously, but that one must also be convinced. Such sayings could, for example, be a way of emphasizing the importance of not having false intentions, the importance of acting with the focus on God and not on social status. The conviction which is emphasized here in religion is not, however, based on hypothetical reasoning and is not something isolated from the way religious persons speak and act, a conviction which is then later added to their speech and acting, but on the contrary shows itself in *how* they speak and act. That it is possible to fake conviction and devotion does not refute this; on the contrary: to fake devotion is dependent on what you fake when you fake devotion. The person who fakes devotion must thus act in the way a devoted person acts, otherwise nobody would believe her. In this sense, devotion is conceptually prior to fake devotion.

who later in life becomes a religious believer becomes this in a world where the words 'religious believer' already have a meaning. This meaning includes, among other things, the devotion characteristic of the persons who already speak and act religiously. Secondly, to analyse the process of becoming a religious believer as a matter of applying already established criteria is to disregard the important notion of conversion. One other way of describing the process of becoming a believer is instead to describe it as a matter of feeling a need for, in relation to experiences of birth, death and the like, a way of acting and speaking, and feeling that a certain way of speaking and acting is adequate, in a very general sense, in relation to these experiences.

Conclusion

If our diverse ways of speaking were based on theoretical, hypothetical thinking, this could guarantee there being only one way to make the distinction between true and false, rational and irrational and the like. If that were the case and we thought we had discovered two different ways of making this distinction, this would mean that we had not reached the base yet, that there was still theoretical work to be done. What then had to be done would be to show that one (or both) of these ways of making the distinction between true and false is wrong according to a more basic way of making the distinction between true and false. We have come to see, however, that this idea overlooks how our ways of speaking are conceptually dependent on our ways of acting and living in the world generally. Therefore, disagreements could be possible which are not a matter of disagreements concerning whether a mistake has been made within a shared way of making the distinction between true and false, but are a matter of disagreements about how to reason in a specific area.[51] Such disagreements are the linguistic expression of different ways of acting. That such disagreements are possible is not so strange: if one wants to convince somebody, by means of arguing, that she is wrong, one must argue in the way she finds correct in this area, no matter how crazy one might think this way of reasoning is. If in such a situation one tries to argue against the way the other argues, one finds oneself presupposing what should be argued. Nonetheless, one could feel that such a situation must be impossible, and try to find philosophical reasons for this being impossible, but when it comes to concrete cases, one must find concrete ways to overcome the disagreements anyhow.

In this chapter, I have shown that the picture of religious beliefs according to which they are beliefs of a scientific type, based on evidence or on scientific reasoning, overlooks certain characteristics of religious belief. I have further given some examples of how the belief that the distinction between true and false, between rational and irrational, is made in the same way in all areas of human life overlooks certain things. It overlooks that these ways of talking are not based on hypothetical

---

51 Cf. Rhees, *Rush Rhees on Religion and Philosophy*, pp. 20–21; Wittgenstein, *Lectures and Conversations on Aesthetics, Psychology and Religious Belief*, p. 53.

reasoning, but that these distinctions are rooted in the diverse ways we deal with the world around us. Yet one could feel that in a disputed area like religion, the distinction *must* be made in ways which are universal, and this feeling may be prompted by a feeling of uneasiness concerning the possible relativist implications of the following remarks by Wittgenstein:

> Supposing we met people who did not regard that as a telling reason. Now, how do we imagine this? Instead of the physicist, they consult an oracle. (And for that we consider them primitive.) Is it wrong for them to consult an oracle and be guided by it? – If we call this 'wrong' aren't we using our language-game as a base from which to *combat* theirs?
>
> And are we right or wrong to combat it? Of course there are all sorts of slogans which will be used to support our proceedings.
>
> Where two principles really do meet which cannot be reconciled with one another, then each man declares the other a fool or heretic.
>
> I said I would 'combat' the other man, – but wouldn't I give him *reasons*? Certainly; but how far do they go? At the end of reasons comes *persuasion*. (Think what happens when missionaries convert natives.)[52]

Reading this, one can begin to wonder (no matter how what Wittgenstein writes here should be understood):[53] if there are many ways of making the distinction between true and false, does this not mean that there are many 'truths'? Does this not mean that what is true is relative to a certain way of making this distinction, and therefore that there is nothing like true *simpliciter*? Does this not mean that one ought to abstain from saying that the way one makes the distinction between true and false is the right one or that it is better than some other way of making this distinction, since it is always possible that one is unable to show to certain people that it is the right one or that it is better than some other way? Does this not mean that one cannot criticize the religious beliefs of others, which means that fruitful discussion is not possible although one can wish that it were? Do not all these questions show that I must be mistaken, since relativism is obviously wrong? In the next chapter, I will discuss what form, if any, of relativism what I have said here entails, and whether relativism is obviously wrong.

---

52 Wittgenstein, *On Certainty*, pp. 80e–81e (§§ 609–12): 'Angenommen, wir träfen Leute, die das nicht als triftigen Grund betrachteten. Nun, wie stellen wir uns das vor? Sie befragen statt des Physikers etwa ein Orakel. (Und wir halten sie darum für primitiv.) Ist es falsch, daß sie ein Orakel befragen und sich nach ihm richten? – Wenn wir dies "falsch" nennen, gehen wir nicht schon von unserm Sprachspiel aus und *bekämpfen* das ihre? / Und haben wir recht oder unrecht darin, daß wir's bekämpfen? Man wird freilich unser Vorgehen mit allerlei Schlagworten (slogans) aufstützen. / Wo sich wirklich zwei Prinzipe treffen, die sich nicht mit einander aussöhnen, da erklärt jeder den Andern für einen Narren und Ketzer. / Ich sagte, ich würde den Andern "bekämpfen", – aber würde ich ihm denn nicht *Gründe* geben? Doch; aber wie weit reichen sie? Am Ende der Gründe steht die *Überredung*. (Denke daran, was geschieht, wenn Missionäre die Eingeborenen bekehren.)'

53 For an interpretation of Wittgensein's remarks, see Hillary Putnam, *Renewing Philosophy* (Cambridge, MA, 1992), pp. 172–6.

Chapter 3

Problems of Relativism

The conclusion that different ways of making the distinction between true and false, right and wrong, correct and incorrect are possible, and that there can therefore be no guarantee that a particular disagreement can be reconciled, may make us accept a relativist thesis. Both parties of the disagreement, which the rationalistic discussion was supposed to solve, may be justified relatively in their own way of making the distinction between true and false, and according to the relativist, their different beliefs are then true for the one who holds them. Discussion is then pointless, for there is no disagreement.

Relativism can be specified in many ways, into different relativist theses. These are often classified in different ways, firstly according to what it is that is relative (truth, justification and the like), secondly according to what the relative thing is relative to (conceptual schemes, cultures and the like), and thirdly if the relativist thesis in question is supposed to apply in general or only in some particular contexts (ethics, religion and the like).[1] The relativist thesis which cropped up at the end of the last chapter cannot yet be put into these boxes, however – it is still rather unclear. Furthermore, the philosophical discussions of relativism have often been defective, since they have only concerned well-defined and specified relativist theses. This way of discussing relativism is defective since it agrees poorly with the character of this position: relativists are in most cases not primarily advocates of elaborated theses, but have been struck by a problem, which they then try to express in different ways. What is philosophically interesting is primarily this problem, and only secondarily different ways of expressing it in theses.

---

1   For some different ways of defining what relativism is and classifying different varieties of relativism, see, for example, Maria Baghramian, *Relativism* (London, 2004), pp. 2–9; Richard J. Bernstein, *Beyond Objectivism and Relativism: Science, Hermeneutics, and Praxis* (Oxford, 1983), p. 8; Steve Edwards, 'Formulating a Plausible Relativism', *Philosophia*, 22 (1993); Susan Haack, *Manifesto of a Passionate Moderate: Unfashionable Essays* (Chicago, IL, 1998), pp. 149–52; Martin Hollis and Steven Lukes, 'Introduction', in Martin Hollis and Steven Lukes (eds), *Rationality and Relativism* (Oxford, 1982), pp. 5–12; William Max Knorpp, 'What Relativism Isn't', *Philosophy*, 73 (1998); Max Kölbel, 'Indexical Relativism versus Genuine Relativism', *International Journal of Philosophical Studies*, 12 (2004): 298–300; Paul O'Grady, 'Wittgenstein and Relativism', *International Journal of Philosophical Studies*, 12 (2004): 323–5; John Preston, 'On Some Objections to Relativism', *Ratio*, 5 (1992): 57–8; Steven Rappaport, 'Must a Metaphysical Relativist Be a Truth Relativist?, *Philosophia*, 22 (1993): 75.

I will therefore do two things in this chapter. Firstly, I am going to confront the problem we came across at the end of the last chapter with two standard arguments against relativism, to see whether there are any relativist theses which are possible at all. This discussion will hence serve as a way of specifying a relativist position. Relativism is often supposed to be obviously wrong,[2] but as we will see, this is not so for all forms of relativism. That a position is not obviously wrong does not, however, imply that it is not problematic. What I will do secondly, therefore, is to discuss some suggestions as to why relativism is problematic. This discussion shows in the end that relativism *is* problematic, and thus gives us problems and questions which must be discussed in subsequent chapters.

The two standard arguments against relativism which I will discuss go back at least to Plato. The first argument is that relativism is in some sense self-refuting, and I will begin by presenting Plato's version of the argument.

The First Standard Argument against Relativism

The relativist idea Plato is discussing is '… that as each thing appears to me, so it is for me, and as it appears to you, so it is for you …'[3] or '… that a thing is for any individual what it seems to him to be …'[4]. If something appears to me to be sour, for example, then that thing is sour to me – that is, there is nothing like sour *simpliciter*.[5] The relativist idea is a general expression of this point about something tasting sour. However, if this is so generally, what is the status of relativism itself? If everything is as it appears to each one of us, then the person who proposes this idea is no wiser than anyone else, and we do not have to take it seriously. According to relativism, if it appears to someone to be false, then it is false to that person![6]

Plato's argument is not as good as it may appear, however. Of course, if somebody only asserts the relativist idea without arguments, Plato's argument is correct. The idea can be preceded by extensive argumentation, however, which may make it appear to us to be true. These arguments must, of course, start out from the non-relativist way of talking about truth and falsity they object to, but if they are

---

2   See, for example, Hilary Putnam, *Reason, Truth and History* (Cambridge, 1981), p. 119; Baghramian, *Relativism*, pp. 136 and 327.

3   Plato, *The Theaetetus of Plato*, trans. M.J. Levett and Myles Burnyeat (Indianapolis, IN, 1990), p. 272 (Tht. 152a).

4   Ibid., p. 285 (Tht. 161c).

5   Ibid., p. 283 (Tht. 160bc).

6   See ibid., pp. 285 and 297–8 (Tht. 161de and 170e–171b). See also Plato, *Complete Works*, pp. 104, 723–5 (Cra. 386cd; Euthyd. 286c–288a). For other variants of the same argument, see, for example, Nancy K. Frankenberry and Hans H. Penner, 'From Functionalism to Relativism: Introduction', in Nancy K. Frankenberry and Hans H. Penner (eds), *Language, Truth, and Religous Belief: Studies in Twentieth-century Theory and Method in Religion* (Atlanta, GA, 1999), p. 277; Robert Kirk, *Relativism and Reality: A Contemporary Introduction* (London, 1999), p. 40; Baghramian, *Relativism*, pp. 132–6 and 141.

successful, they will make us reject this way of talking (for example, by means of reductio-argumentation – that is, by means of showing that this way of talking is self-contradictory or leads to absurd consequences).[7] The relativist does not have to argue positively for relativism, but can argue negatively against any other position, and when there seems to be no other tenable alternative, then relativism may be adopted. Then the arguments themselves must also be rejected, but since relativism then appears to us to be true, this does not matter.[8]

Plato's argument, although unsuccessful, makes the point of this relativist idea more visible, however. Relativism is better expressed as a matter of giving up a certain way of talking and acting. The point of the example with the thing that tastes sour is that it makes no sense to ask: 'This thing tastes sour to me, but is it *really* sour?' The point is, furthermore, that if one person says that something tastes sour and another person says that it does not, it makes no sense for them to discuss which of them is right, for it makes no sense to say that they disagree. Therefore, the point of the example is that we should give up making the distinction between true and false in this context.

One may react differently to this particular example of the thing that tastes sour, but the crux of the matter is that a relativist idea makes a more general point: we should give up making the distinction between true and false in many, most or every context. The question is not whether that is possible or not, for it definitely is possible,[9] but whether there could be good arguments for such a suggestion.

Relativism and Pyrrhonism

Relativism, understood in this way, is nearly related to Pyrrhonism, one form of ancient scepticism. By taking account of Pyrrhonism, the relativist can strengthen her case and find arguments for her suggestion.[10]

---

7   The arguments for relativism could thus be used 'under erasure' (cf. Jacques Derrida, *Of Grammatology*, corr. edn, trans. Gayatri Chakravorty Spivak (Baltimore, MD, 1997), p. 60) or function as a ladder which is thrown away after one has climbed up on it; cf. Wittgenstein, *Tractatus*, p. 151 (§ 6.54).

8   Cf. Theodor W. Adorno, *Negative Dialectics*, trans. E.B. Ashton (New York, 1973), pp. 35–6.

9   That this is logically possible is denied by many anti-relativists. Of course, giving up making the distinction between true and false in every context is not possible without extensive changes in the way we live, but one way for humankind to give up making this distinction would be to stop communicating. It is highly improbable that we will do this, but it is not logically impossible.

10   For an example of an account of the relations between relativism and Pyrrhonism, see Baghramian, *Relativism*, pp. 41–8. Baghramian fails to notice the distinctive non-doctrinal character of Sextus's scepticism, however, and consequently also fails to see how the relativist can escape certain criticisms by learning from Pyrrhonism.

Sextus Empiricus,[11] when describing Pyrrhonism, describes it as a way of life,[12] as a way of acquiring tranquility when being troubled by questions where there is disagreement. When investigating such questions, the Pyrrhonist acquires the ability to formulate a counter-argument against every argument for a specific belief. This ability thus results in a situation where there is as much to be said for a specific claim as against it, and the Pyrrhonist then suspends judgement on the subject in question. The tranquility she has searched for then arrives, completely unexpected.[13]

Hence, what the Pyrrhonist shuns is only to hold something as true which is not evident – that is, to have an opinion on a question where there are different opinions.[14] The Pyrrhonist can thus say that something seems to her to be in a certain way if by saying that she does not mean that this also *is* in that way.[15] Pyrrhonism is hence, in similarity to relativism, a way of reacting to the fact that there are vast disagreements on many questions. The difference between them, that the Pyrrhonist abstains from having an opinion and that the relativist says that the opinions are true for the persons who have them, is then smaller than one might believe. Pyrrhonism and relativism are at one in their practical result: everyone says only how things appear to them, without making claims for everyone.

Relativism is often, as we have seen, accused of being a contradictory position. It is therefore interesting to see how Sextus Empiricus tries to avoid the same charge against Pyrrhonism. Firstly, this is done by describing Pyrrhonism as an ability (to formulate counter-arguments to every arguments for a specific position),[16] or as a way of life, a way of acquiring tranquility, and not as a theory. Secondly, the Pyrrhonist can, as we have seen, say that something seems to her to be in a certain way, which allows her to say that her ability appears to her to bring about tranquility, and so on.[17] Thirdly, the counter-arguments she is able to formulate, she need not believe in. It suffices that they neutralize the arguments for a specific position by attacking them from inside, so to speak.[18] Since arguments for specific theoretical positions will no doubt continue to appear, suspending judgement is not something one does once and for all. The Pyrrhonist must probably start to argue again now and then to retain her tranquility.[19]

---

11 For good expositions of Sextus Empiricus's account of Pyrrhonism, see Michael Williams, 'Scepticism without Theory', *Review of Metaphysics*, 41 (1988); and David R. Hiley, *Philosophy in Question: Essays on a Pyrrhonian Theme* (Chicago, IL, 1988), pp. 10–18.

12 Sextus Empiricus, *Outlines of Scepticism*, trans. Julia Annas and Jonathan Barnes (Cambridge, 1994), p. 7 (§ I:17).

13 Ibid., pp. 20–21 (§§ I:28–I:29). See further ibid., pp. 4–6 and 49 (§§ I:8–I:10, I:14, I:196).

14 Ibid., pp. 6 and 9. (§§ I:13 and I:22).

15 Ibid., pp. 6–7 (§§ I:13–I:15).

16 Ibid., p. 4 (§ I:8).

17 Ibid., pp. 49–51 and 61–2 (§§ I:198–I:199, I:202–I:203, I:233).

18 Ibid., pp. 52 and 216 (§§ I:206, III:280–III:281).

19 Ibid., p. 3 (§ I:1–I:3).

Relativism can be defended in the same way. Relativism need not be understood as a doctrine or theory, but could be understood as a way of acquiring tranquility or the like when being troubled by questions where there is disagreement, and it is precisely the existence of vast disagreements which is under focus in this study. The relativist can furthermore avoid the charge of inconsistency by saying only that things seem to be in a certain way to her, and by abstaining from positive arguments for relativism. The relativist argues instead only *against* the positions of others, by, for the sake of argument, accepting their ways of arguing and revealing problems in them. In our attempt to specify relativism, we have thus now specified it to mean the suggestion that we, in a Pyrrhonian spirit, should give up making the distinction between true and false in all contexts where there are disagreements.

The Second Standard Argument against Relativism

The second standard argument against relativism is only hinted at by Plato, when he writes that in matters of health and disease, it is obvious, also to the relativist, that some persons excel the rest of us in knowledge.[20] Hilary Putnam says that his view is not a relativism which says that anything goes or that every conceptual system is as good as any other, and he then goes on to give an argument similar to Plato's:

> If anyone really believed that, and if they were foolish enough to pick a conceptual system that told them they could fly and to act upon it by jumping out of the window, they would, if they were lucky enough to survive, see the weakness of the latter view at once.[21]

Another way of expressing the same argument is to point at the success of science, the results of which we have all around us and cannot live without. Therefore science cannot be taken to be merely true for us, but must be taken as simply true.

The point of the argument is hence that as we are actually living, there are beliefs which are so self-evident to us that we cannot say that they are merely true for us, but must say that they are true *simpliciter*. However, the problem with the argument is that since it points to beliefs which appear to (almost) all of us as true, these beliefs are not beliefs which trouble the Pyrrhonian relativist.[22] If somebody really did claim that she could fly or that science were wrong, the relativist can simply say that this appears to her to be false, without feeling a need to make any absolute or universal claims. To the relativist, as well as to anyone else, it seems as if one cannot jump out of the window without hurting oneself. The relativist can also say that science appears to her to be true, and she can thus live a life benefiting from it.

The anti-relativist can make another move, however. She can say that the point is primarily not whether the results of science are accepted or not. The point is rather

20 Plato, *The Theaetetus of Plato*, p. 299 (Tht. 171e).

21 Putnam, *Reason, Truth and History*, p. 54.

22 Cf. Michael P. Lynch, *Truth in Context: An Essay on Pluralism and Objectivity* (Cambridge, 1998), p. 142.

that the scientific attitude which lies behind these results is characterized by an outlook free from any particular perspective. The scientific attitude is characterized by treating all ideas (one's own as well as others') in the same way, not adopting any position before having examined it thoroughly, being attentive to one's own mistakes, and immediately correcting mistakes when they are discovered, and so on. The scientific attitude is hence in opposition to relativism.

However, if this is supposed to be an argument against relativism, the scientific attitude itself must not be a particular perspective or attitude and must thus have no real alternatives, but must be superior to all other attitudes one can take to reality, and should be adopted in all areas of human life. In this context, Thomas Kuhn has pointed out that the scientific attitude is not as prevalent in science as one might believe, and that furthermore, science would not have made the progress it has if scientists were not somewhat dogmatic.[23] My point is different, however. For the anti-relativist to make her point, the scientific attitude must be superior to all other attitudes one can take to reality, and have no real alternatives. If it is superior in that sense, it must be taken always and everywhere. Therefore, the scientific attitude must be taken to this attitude itself – that is, the scientific attitude must be examined thoroughly before it is adopted. However, this is seldom done, and most importantly, an examination cannot be started if we always have to examine the means of examination first. When the scientific attitude turns against itself, it turns out that it is not superior to all other attitudes, in the sense that it has no real alternatives, since it is itself not based on examination, but on what we could call trust.[24] Of course, the relativist accepts the results of science, in the sense that they appear to her to be true, but when it comes to the scientific attitude, it cannot be taken in all areas of human life, and it is not evident in which areas it should be taken, or how it is to find more concrete expression in diverse areas of human life.

Referring to the scientific attitude is hence not a tenable counter-argument against relativism. Relativism can, on the contrary, be seen as a consequence of the scientific attitude itself. If all ideas (one's own as well as the ideas of others) are treated in the same way, and no position is adopted before having examined it thoroughly, one may be reluctant to adopt a specific position before being able to show everybody that it is true. Instead, one may say that the different possible positions are true for those who have adopted them. That relativism may be a consequence of a scientific attitude pursued *in absurdum* is a theme I will continue discussing in the next chapter.

However, Plato's and Putnam's arguments, as well as the insistence on the inescapable results of science, although unsuccessful in themselves, point to the important fact that there are situations where expressions like 'I was wrong' or 'I made a mistake' no doubt have application. The situation where the ice first seems

---

23 Thomas S. Kuhn, *The Structure of Scientific Revolutions* (Chicago, IL, 1970), for example pp. 77–82, 146, 151–2, 157.

24 Cf. Dewi Zephaniah Phillips, *Religion and Friendly Fire: Examining Assumptions in Contemporary Philosophy of Religion* (Aldershot/Burlington, VT, 2004), pp. 117 and 120–21.

to a person to bear her weight, but breaks when she is walking on it and she gets wet and cold, is an example of a situation where a saying like 'The ice seemed to me to bear me, but it didn't' comes naturally.

Although there might be philosophical arguments for giving up the distinction between true and false, such arguments appear futile compared to the certainty with which we speak about true and false in situations like the above. However, this means only that the most general relativist idea, the idea according to which the distinction between true and false should be given up in all contexts, is opposed to how we sometimes, without reflection, talk about true and false. Whether it makes sense to distinguish between true and false, for example when it comes to taste – that is, whether there is something like sour *simpliciter* – or when it comes to works of art – that is, whether there is something like beautiful *simpliciter* – is not shown by the above remark. There could thus be reasons for giving up the distinction between true and false in such contexts where the Pyrrhonian relativist thinks that the distinction should be given up, where there are disagreements.

The problem which appeared at the end of the last chapter was that different ways of making the distinction between true and false, right and wrong, correct and incorrect are possible. The relativism which this can give rise to is thus not a general one, since if two persons make the distinction between true and false in the same way, they can talk about beliefs being true and false and themselves being right or mistaken. However, does it make sense to speak about these ways of making the distinction between true and false themselves being true or false, right or wrong, correct or incorrect? It seems possible for the relativist to deny this.

The problem is that there can be no arguments that, without begging the question, show that a certain way of making the distinction between true and false itself is true or correct, since in order to show this, a way of making the distinction between true and false must already be there.[25] Of course, it is sometimes possible to give arguments that show that a certain way of making the distinction between true and false is false or incorrect, by showing that it is self-contradictory or the like. There are no reasons, however, to think that there is only one non-contradictory way of making the distinction between true and false in all areas of life, which means that the absence of self-contradiction is not enough to show that a specific way of making this distinction is the right one. Since there can be no arguments that, without begging the question, show that a certain way of making the distinction between true and false itself is true or correct, the relativist denies that it makes sense to say that a specific way of making the distinction between true and false is the right one.

The relativist's denial gains strength from the anti-relativist's attempt to argue that her way of making the distinction between true and false is the right one, since the relativist exposes how these arguments beg the question. In the same way, the relativist's answer gains strength from the anti-relativist's dismissal of the question, since the relativist shows that the anti-relativist's way of making the distinction

---

25 Cf. Paul K. Moser, *Philosophy after Objectivity: Making Sense in Perspective* (New York, 1993), p. 64.

between true and false is not the only one. In both cases, the relativist shows that if the anti-relativist's attitude, only giving arguments which beg the question or giving no arguments at all for her way of making the distinction between true and false, is allowed, we can support any position we prefer, which is a relativism as good as any.

Subjective and Arbitrary

We have now seen that it is possible to formulate a relativism which is not self-contradictory or *obviously* wrong. However, this does not mean that this relativism is not problematic. In the following, we will examine some suggestions as to why relativism is problematic.

The first way of expressing the problem with relativism is to say that according to relativism, the choice between different ways of making the distinction between true and false must be subjective and arbitrary.[26] This is a misunderstanding of relativism, however. It is of course possible to create different artificial sets of standards of evaluation, in a similar way to it being possible to create different logics by construing the semantics differently. If in such a situation we had to choose one of them, the choice would perhaps be subjective and arbitrary. When we talk about different ways of making the distinction between true and false, however, we are not talking about some kind of axioms, but about shared ways of acting. This means that the objection that the choice is subjective and arbitrary misses the point, since it depends on the idea that it is necessary to choose here. Ways of making the distinction between true and false are, on the contrary, in most cases adopted by means of upbringing or by means of a process which is better not described as a matter of choice.[27]

Of course, arbitrariness and subjectivity in the sense of contingency is involved here. It is not, however, a matter of arbitrary or subjective *choice*, nor is it a matter of arbitrariness and subjectivity in the sense of insignificance to the individual.[28] If it were a matter of choice, the situation in which a way of making the distinction between true and false is adopted would be a situation in which you stand outside every such way and try to pick one of them. The only way to do this would then be to decide by lot or the like, but picturing human beings as deliberatively choosing how they should make the distinction between true and false is an over-intellectualized representation of how ways of making the distinction between true and false are adopted.

---

26 Harvey Siegel, for example, thinks that this is the problem. See Harvey Siegel, *Relativism Refuted: A Critique of Contemporary Epistemological Relativism* (Dordrecht, 1987), pp. 10 and 52.

27 Cf. the way the relation between religious belief and choice was discussed in the last chapter.

28 Cf. Martin O'Neill, 'Explaining "The Hardness of the Logical Must": Wittgenstein on Grammar, Arbitrariness and Logical Necessity', *Philosophical Investigations*, 24 (2001): 15.

However, the most important reason why it is not a matter of subjectivity and arbitrariness here is that for something to be a way of making the distinction between true and false, there must be some sort of consistency in how this distinction is made, a consistency which is not hidden to other people.[29] Hence, the degree to which a way of making the distinction between true and false can be different from other such ways is limited. Furthermore, unless there is some sort of agreement about how the distinction between true and false is made in a certain context, discussion would not be possible in that context, and the distinction would not have the kind of significance it has for us. Hence, in most cases our ways of making the distinction between true and false are shared with others, and thus not subjective. If people were using their own subjective evaluative standards, and chose standards totally by chance, there would be a complete breakdown of discussion, in contrast to occasional and local breakdowns of discussion which no doubt occur. Hence it is an important part of what we call making the distinction between true and false that there is some sort of agreement here.[30]

Davidson's Argument against Relativism

What I have just said bears some similarities to Donald Davidson's argument in, above all, 'On the Very Idea of a Conceptual Scheme'.[31] Davidson argues that no matter how vast the disagreement between two persons may be, there must be an agreement in basic[32] beliefs for it to make sense to talk about there being a disagreement. Davidson's argument is that to be a language user, the interpretee must, in the basic cases, mostly be in agreement with the interpreter. On the one hand, this has to do with understanding. Davidson argues that if we had evidence for something being impossible to interpret in our language, this would at the same time be evidence for this not being speech behaviour.[33] On the other hand, this has to do with the amount of possible disagreements. If we want to interpret what somebody says, without prior knowledge of the meanings of her words, we must take for granted that she uses her words in the right way in most cases, taking explicable errors into account, of course. Not until we have come to understand her words, her language, is it possible to detect vast disagreements between us.[34]

---

29 This is so for conceptual reasons, not metaphysical one. Thus if somebody were extremely inconsistent, she would not be doing what we call making the distinction between true and false.

30 Cf. Wittgenstein, *Remarks on the Foundations of Mathematics*, p. 80 (§ I:116); Michael P. Hodges, 'The Status of Ethical Judgements in the *Philosophical Investigations*', *Philosophical Investigations*, 18 (1995), esp. 103.

31 Donald Davidson, *Inquiries into Truth and Interpretation* (Oxford, 2001), pp. 183–98.

32 See the section 'The Principle of Charity as a Condition for Interpretation' in Chapter 5 for an explanation of what 'basic' means here.

33 Ibid., pp. 185–6. See also Wittgenstein, *Philosophical Investigations*, p. 70e (§ 207).

34 See, for example, Davidson, *Inquiries into Truth and Interpretation*, pp. 196–7.

This argument is often understood not as an argument against a general relativism, but against one relativistic idea, the idea of incommensurability, as put forward by Kuhn and Feyerabend.[35] The kind of relativism we are discussing here is affected by Davidson's argument, however. If Davidson is right, a situation where I meet and try to discuss with someone with a radically different way of making the distinction between true and false is not possible, because if I believe that her way of making this distinction is radically different, I have in fact not understood her.

There are some problems with Davidson's argumentation, however. These will not be discussed until Chapter 5, since his argumentation, as I have presented it here, is basically correct, which can be seen from simple examples. Among other examples, Davidson gives the following:

> Let someone say … 'There's a hippopotamus in the refrigerator'; am I necessarily right in reporting him as having said that there is a hippopotamus in the refrigerator? Perhaps; but under questioning he goes on, 'It's roundish, has a wrinkled skin, does not mind being touched. It has a pleasant taste, at least the juice, and it costs a dime. I squeeze two or three for breakfast.' After some finite amount of such talk we slip over the line where it is plausible or even possible to say correctly that he said there was a hippopotamus in the refrigerator, for it becomes clear he means something else by at least some of his words than I do. The simplest hypothesis so far is that my word 'hippopotamus' no longer translates his word 'hippopotamus'; my word 'orange' might do better.[36]

What this example shows, and this is one of the things we can learn from Davidson, is that an interpretation according to which the beliefs of the one whose speech we interpret are very different from ours, is not actually an interpretation. For attribution of disagreement to be possible, there must be a background of shared beliefs against which talk of agreement and disagreement makes sense.

This means that if we let somebody taste many different things which we say taste sweet and she says that they taste sour, this indicates that she does not use the words 'sweet' and 'sour' as we do. Furthermore, if somebody likes to watch works of art she calls ugly and has such works of art on the walls at home, but looks with disgust at works of art she calls beautiful, this indicates that she does not use the words 'ugly' and 'beautiful' as we do. Hence, although it is possible to give up the distinction between true and false when it comes to, for example, taste or works of art, if the differences between two persons' judgements are too great or the differences between the contexts of use are too great, this indicates that they are not talking about the same thing.

That the different ways of making the distinction between true and false are not too different is, however, a conceptual point. This means that Davidson's observation cannot be used to argue against a specific way of making the distinction between true and false, but can merely be used to understand it. Davidson's observation therefore does not help us in reconciling real disagreements, for example by revealing

---

35   Cf. Siegel, *Relativism Refuted*, pp. 38–42.

36   Davidson, *Inquiries into Truth and Interpretation*, pp. 100–101.

problems in the positions of the conflicting parties. What the observation helps us with is preventing us from believing that the problem is bigger than it is.

Criterial and Non-criterial Notions of Reasoning

If the problem with relativism is not properly understood when it is expressed as a problem of arbitrariness and subjectivity, is relativism then a problem since it presupposes a problematic conception of reasoning? One possible objection to the Pyrrhonian relativist's way of arguing is this: the Pyrrhonian relativist draws the conclusion that it is impossible to show everybody which set of evaluative standards is the best from the fact that there is no set of evaluative standards which is self-evident to everybody. However, this is a valid inference only if you presuppose that all forms of reasoning are a matter of applying evaluative standards, and why should this be presupposed? The point of the objection is thus that the focus has been only on a criterial notion of reasoning, whereas there is also a non-criterial notion, a notion which makes us capable of evaluating the evaluative standards themselves, a notion which has been overlooked.[37]

What I have written in Chapter 2 concerning following rules suggests that this objection is partly correct. There, it was shown that what is needed in order to bridge the distance between rule and application is not an interpretation, that is, another rule. What we have to see is that in most cases, no bridge is needed. We follow the rule without interpreting it, and what makes rules – that is, something which can be followed rightly or wrongly – what they are is that we actually follow a specific rule in the same way – that is, that there is an agreement in action. The same goes for reasoning. A criterial notion of reasoning suffers from the same problem as an understanding of rule following which only focuses on the formulable rules. The non-criterial aspect of reasoning is then what is conceptually prior. Words like 'criteria' and 'evaluative standards' should therefore not be understood in isolation from the shared ways of acting which are a presupposition for reasoning. Not paying attention to the shared ways of acting results in a simplistic understanding of the relations between criteria and the practice of reasoning. Hence, the above objection is right in two basic respects. Firstly, the very learning of how to make the distinction between true and false is not primarily a matter of learning formulations, but a matter of learning to do something. Secondly, what a certain way of making the distinction between true and false involves shows itself not primarily in formulations, but in the way the distinction is made. Agreement and disagreement is hence primarily a matter of agreement and disagreement in action.

The insufficiency of a criterial notion of reasoning, especially the fact that criteria cannot themselves stipulate how they are to be applied and therefore can be interpreted differently, can make us think that we have resources for reconciling vast disagreements. The insufficiency of a criterial notion of reasoning can make us think

---

37 Cf. Nikolas Kompridis, 'So We Need Something Else for Reason to Mean', *International Journal of Philosophical Studies*, 8 (2000), esp. 279.

that there is another kind of reasoning which helps us to apply the formal criteria in the right way. Since this kind of reasoning is not bound to criteria, the thought that this kind of reasoning is presuppositionless and universal can arise. What must be noticed, however, is that non-criterial reasoning is not another kind of reasoning, but an ineliminable aspect of reasoning on the whole, as we have seen above in connection to Chapter 2. When we have argued that different ways of reasoning are possible, this has thus been made primarily with reference to the non-criterial aspect. That the objection in some respects is right, in the respects I gave an account of in the last paragraph, does not mean that it shows a solution to the relativist problem. The objection suggests that argumentation is not a matter of applying criteria formulated in advance. Such an understanding of argumentation does not preclude the possibility of conflicts which cannot be reconciled argumentatively, however.

This is not the only way of understanding the objection that I have only considered a criterial notion of reasoning, and disregarded the non-criterial notion, however. The objection can also be understood as an insistence that the process of questioning and changing our criteria of rationality is a rational process, and this process obviously cannot be a matter of applying criteria.[38] Hilary Putnam formulates a variant of this argument when he says that in philosophy, we must be able to examine critically the criteria themselves, and that the notion of argumentation which is required in philosophy cannot then be identified with the criteria:

> I don't at all think that rational argumentation and rational justification are impossible in philosophy, but rather I have been driven to recognize something which is probably evident to laymen if not to philosophers, namely that we cannot appeal to *public* norms to decide what is and is not rationally argued in philosophy.[39]

Of course, to be rational, rational argumentation must agree with our conception of what it is for argumentation to be rational. This conception is not a matter of formulated rules, but shows itself in what forms of argumentation we actually treat as rational. This means, however, that to be rational, rational justification must be in accord with this conception of rationality, and rational justification of this conception is then a matter of begging the question. This does not mean that it is impossible to detect defects in our conception of rationality and change it for the better, or that it is impossible to help persons with other conceptions to change them for the better. What it means is that in situations of vast disagreements concerning conceptions of rationality, you may not be able to show those you disagree with that your conception is more rational. A non-criterial understanding of reasoning does not make such disagreement impossible. The problem with relativism is thus not a matter of whether we understand reasoning criterially or non-criterially, for the practical problem can appear nonetheless.

---

38 See ibid., esp. 275.

39 Putnam, *Reason, Truth and History*, p. 111. See also Kompridis, 'So We Need Something Else for Reason to Mean': 275.

The Actual Problem with Relativism

As we have seen, the problem with relativism, as relativism has been formulated in this chapter, is not properly understood if it is expressed as a problem of arbitrariness and subjectivity, or as a problem about different conceptions of reasoning. Furthermore, the first standard argument against relativism fails. It is only the second standard argument which is successful, but only partly. The second standard argument pointed out how futile philosophical arguments which aim to convince us that the distinction between true and false should be given up are when compared to the certainty with which we speak about true and false in certain situations.

The question I asked in the introduction – How is fruitful discussion of religious beliefs possible? – was asked since discussion of religious beliefs should be upheld in a pluralistic society. In such a society, there are no doubt religious disagreements, and some of these disagreements ought to be discussed, since some beliefs have disastrous consequences for those who believe them and for others.[40] Relativism clashes with this, since if everybody is right concerning some types of questions, it is pointless even to *try* to discuss in that context.

This is not an argument which proves that relativism concerning religious questions is wrong. What it does is to give a reason for searching for a way of retaining the distinction between true and false in this context.[41] What must therefore be shown in subsequent chapters is that one can rightly say that one is right and that somebody else is wrong without necessarily being able to show this to her – that is, that what I have said in Chapters 1 and 2 does not make relativism inevitable.

In a situation of vast disagreement, we can hope that discussion is possible and try to achieve it, but there is no assurance that it is possible. Anti-relativists, however, often believe that it must be the case that it is possible to discuss. Karl Popper, when criticizing Thomas Kuhn's suggestion that, as Popper formulates it, '… the rationality of science presupposes the acceptance of a common framework.'[42], says that '… a critical discussion … of the various frameworks is always possible.'[43] and that '… in science … a critical discussion of the competing theories, of the competing frameworks, is always possible'.[44] Kai Nielsen, when criticizing what he calls Wittgensteinian fideism, presupposes that there are no limits to the possibility

---

40 One disputed question is, of course, which beliefs have that character.

41 Richard Bernstein says that relativism leads '… to cynicism and a growing sense of impotence'; Bernstein, *Beyond Objectivism and Relativism*, p. 4. This is not presented as an argument against relativism, but as a reason for discussing the issue, in the way I have argued above. See also Putnam, *Reason, Truth and History*, p. 153. Harvey Siegel, on the other hand, presents the impotence of relativism as a strong *argument against* relativism; Siegel, *Relativism Refuted*, pp. 20–21 and 30–31.

42 Karl Popper, 'Normal Science and Its Dangers', in Imre Lakatos and Alan Musgrave (eds), *Criticism and the Growth of Knowledge: Proceedings of the International Colloquium in the Philosophy of Science, London, 1965, Volume 4* (Cambridge, 1970), p. 56.

43 Ibid., p. 56.

44 Ibid., p. 57.

of the intelligible criticism of the practices, forms of life or modes of social life of others.[45] Of course, such limits may not be drawn beforehand, but Nielsen presumes that cases where discussion turns out to be impossible cannot even be detected. Hilary Putnam, after having said that 'We can only hope to produce a more rational *conception* of rationality or a better *conception* of morality if we operate from *within* our tradition ...',[46] goes on to ask: 'Does this dialogue have an ideal terminus? Is there a *true* conception of rationality, a *true* morality, even if all *we* ever have are our *conceptions* of these?'[47] Richard Rorty would answer no, says Putnam, since for him '... there is only the dialogue; no ideal end can be posited or should be needed'.[48] Putnam then asks the rhetorical question, how Rorty's view differs from self-refuting relativism,[49] intimating that for us to escape relativism, we must posit a position towards which everybody is in some sense heading. Finally, Harvey Siegel says that there are only two alternatives: either claims to knowledge can be fairly, non-question-beggingly assessed, or we must embrace relativism. However, according to Siegel, relativism is self-refuting, so he draws the conclusion that it must be possible to assess claims to knowledge without begging the question, and that further, it must be possible to justify rationality rationally without begging the question.[50]

My discussion in the following chapters will show that these are not the only alternatives.[51] The only alternative to relativism is not an assurance that discussion is always possible. The relativist supposes that if in a particular case we cannot show everybody that we are right, it does not make sense to talk about true and false in this context. This conclusion is not necessary, however, as I will show.

Conclusion

In this chapter, I have shown that a relativism developed in a Pyrrhonist way is not untenable in the way often assumed. However, this form of relativism, a position which gives up the distinction between true and false in certain contexts, stands in

---

45 Nielsen, 'Wittgensteinian Fideism', esp. 206–7.

46 Putnam, *Reason, Truth and History*, p. 216.

47 Ibid., p. 216.

48 Ibid., p. 216.

49 Ibid., p. 216.

50 Siegel, *Relativism Refuted*, pp. 10, 30–31, 162, 168–9.

51 My discussion of relativism is in that respect similar to many discussions in feminist philosophy, where the discussion of relativism is more balanced than perhaps anywhere else. See, for example, Nancy Fraser and Linda J. Nicholson, 'Social Criticism without Philosophy: An Encounter between Feminism and Postmodernism', in Linda J. Nicholson (ed.), *Feminism/Postmodernism* (New York, 1990), pp. 26–7; Jane Flax, 'Postmodernism and Gender Relations in Feminist Theory', in Linda J. Nicholson (ed.), *Feminism/Postmodernism* (New York, 1990), pp. 42–3; Sandra Harding, 'Feminism, Science, and the Anti-Enlightenment Critiques', in Linda J. Nicholson (ed.), *Feminism/Postmodernism* (New York, 1990), pp. 85–7; Anna Yeatman, 'A Feminist Theory of Social Differentiation', in Linda J. Nicholson (ed.), *Feminism/Postmodernism* (New York, 1990), pp. 293–4.

opposition to how we in many contexts sometimes, without reflection, use words and phrases such as 'true', 'false', 'having made a mistake' and the like. In a situation where we cannot show those we disagree with that they are wrong and we are right, the matter is different. Here, it is possible for the relativist to deny the sense of making the distinction between true and false. However, the question I asked in the introduction – How is fruitful discussion of religious beliefs possible? – was asked since discussion of religious beliefs should be upheld in a pluralistic society. Relativism clashes with this, since if everybody is right concerning some type of questions, it is pointless even to *try* to discuss in that context. What is needed is hence to show that from the failure to show everybody that we are right, it does not follow that talking about true and false in this context is senseless.

In the next chapter, I will begin that discussion by criticizing the demand for universality and the conception of rationality which is connected to it. If this conception is shown to be problematic, the inclination to adopt a relativist position will be far less. This criticism will be conducted by showing that being situated in history and society, which makes absolute certainty – one aspect of the demand for universality – impossible is not an obstacle to, but on the contrary, a condition for knowledge, true beliefs, rationality and the like in the role they play in our lives.

Chapter 4

The Demand for Universality

Relativism, as I formulated it in the last chapter, suggests that the distinction between true and false should be given up in a situation where it proves not to be possible to reach an agreement concerning the truth or falsity of the issue in question. This suggestion gains strength, in a way which will be displayed below, from the demand for universality,[1] according to which every statement has to be argued for by means of conclusive arguments which show that the statement in question follows from other statements which have already been proven in this way or are self-evident. These arguments must be appreciated by, in principle, everybody. To be rational is then to hold only beliefs which can be shown to be correct in this way. When we are incapable of living up to this demand for universality, this failure can find an expression in a relativist way of talking about truth and rationality.

This demand for universality can be connected to the following two sources. Firstly, it comes from the legitimately felt need to overcome disagreements. The demand for universality is an exaggerated expression of this *wish* for universality, as an attempt to force what we sometimes wish. This felt need to overcome disagreements is also one of the sources of *relativism*. In contexts where overcoming disagreements is fairly easy, there is no problem. In contexts where it seems to be impossible to overcome disagreements, the matter is different, however. Since every disagreement, according to the demand for universality, *must* be possible to reconcile, one can be inclined to react to this situation as the Pyrrhonian relativist does: she says that, as a matter of fact, there are no disagreements here, just different points of view or the like. The failure to live up to the demand for universality thus, for the relativist, leads to a reinterpretation of the context in question, to a reinterpretation according

---

1 Such a demand for universality can be understood in different ways. It can be understood in a more Kantian sense, according to which I must be able to universalize my holding of a specific belief – that is, my holding a specific belief is legitimate if anybody who was in the same situation as me would hold the same belief. This suggestion is problematic. The problem is that it is not at all clear what 'same' means. One way to make the distinction between same and different in this context is to say that every situation in one sense is the same – that is to say that in principle, everybody must agree with me. This is problematic for reasons delineated below. Another way to make the distinction between same and different in this context is to say that every situation is unique. However, this means that the demand for universality, understood in this way, becomes totally uninteresting. In this chapter, I will not discuss the demand for universality understood in this more Kantian sense, but only in the sense delineated below.

to which what might appear to be disagreements are no disagreements, and thereby the feeling that there are disagreements which must be overcome is suppressed.

Secondly, if something is seen from only one point of view, it is possible for it to become distorted or the knowledge of it to become defective. Therefore, it is often good to try to see things from different points of view. So far, this is right. The demand to see things from different points of view can be pushed to extremes, however, as it often has been in the epistemological tradition, by raising the demand for absolute certainty. Then a point of view is needed which is everyone's and nobody's, and one has to free oneself from every form of commitment, from one's body, from society and history, and from one's upbringing. This picture of human beings in the epistemological tradition can, according to Charles Taylor, be summed up in three anthropological beliefs:[2] (i) the picture of the subject as ideally disengaged, that is free and rational to the extent it has distinguished itself from the world, in its natural and social aspects, around it; (ii) a punctual view of the self, ready to treat these worlds instrumentally, and (iii) an atomistic construal of society as constituted by individual purposes. When we come to see that absolute certainty seldom is attainable, the only possible reaction, if we continue to hold on to the demand for universality, is to say that we seldom have real knowledge. Instead, the Pyrrhonian relativist suggests that in such situations, we should give up the distinction between true and false, and hence stop talking about knowledge.

These two main sources of the demand for universality are both connected to the scientific attitude I mentioned in the last chapter. However, what I will suggest in this chapter is that the demand for universality is not a proper extension of this attitude, by, among other things, pointing out that commitment, embodiment, upbringing and being situated in society and history is not an obstacle to, but on the contrary a condition for knowledge, true beliefs, rationality and the like, in the role they play in our lives. By paying attention to this fact, one becomes less inclined to believe that every disagreement *must* be possible to reconcile, and hence also less inclined to adopt a relativist position – that is, less inclined to give up making the distinction between true and false in a certain context. Pointing out this fact will be done in a way which, in a broad sense, could be called phenomenological. I will begin by discussing Heidegger rather extensively. Apart from being a part in the discussion of situatedness, embodiment and the like in the first half of this chapter, the discussion of Heidegger will also serve as an introduction to this discussion.

After the discussion of situatedness, embodiment and the like, I will work out some consequences and implications of this discussion, above all that our inability to give arguments for why we do as we do does not generally delegitimize our ways of doing what we do. Thereafter, I show how rationality could be understood without the demand for universality. This understanding of rationality contains, among other things, an emphasis on the aspect of development in our notion of rationality.

---

2   Charles Taylor, *Philosophical Arguments* (Cambridge/London, 1995), p. 7.

Heidegger and the Situatedness of Dasein

The demand for universality and its insistence on absolute certainty, achieved by taking up a point of view which is everyone's and nobody's, and by freeing oneself from every form of commitment, from one's body, from society and history, and from one's upbringing, is criticized by Martin Heidegger. In *Being and Time*,[3] Heidegger begins by writing that we must again ask the question of Being (of the meaning of Being).[4] What it means to ask this question is not obvious, however, so Heidegger goes on to write that we first have to ask how this question should be formulated.[5] The entity[6] which asks the question of Being is the entity which Heidegger calls 'Dasein' – that is, the entity which each of us is. To be able to formulate the question of Being adequately, we must hence first elucidate and explicate the Being of this entity.[7] Moreover, Dasein is the only kind of entity for which its Being is an issue – that is, which always comports itself towards its Being in some way or another.[8] If the Being of Dasein thus is explicated, what it means for an entity to comport itself actively towards the Being of every entity, including itself, will be elucidated. Heidegger's analysis of the Being of Dasein in the rest of *Being and Time* is hence in some respect part of the answer to the question of Being, but above all it is a way to become able to formulate the question adequately.

The method of Heidegger's investigation is phenomenological,[9] which, according to Heidegger, means letting that which shows itself be seen from itself in the very way in which it shows itself from itself.[10] This means that Heidegger wants to describe that which shows itself in the way it shows itself before any theoretical accounts of it have been given. In relation to Dasein, Heidegger therefore wants to describe it as it is proximally and for the most part – that is, in its average everydayness.[11] Heidegger thus describes how something is what it is, not how it must be. His descriptions should therefore not be understood as counter-arguments against somebody who really believes, for example, that there is no external reality. What Heidegger's

---

3   Martin Heidegger, *Being and Time*, trans. John Macquarrie and Edward Robinson (Oxford, 1962).

4   Heidegger, *Being and Time*, p. 21 (2). Here and in the following, I give the reference to Martin Heidegger, *Sein und Zeit* (Tübingen, 2001) in parentheses. The reason for this is that in most translations, the pagination of the German original is given in the margins, which means that if the original is referred to, it is possible to find the right page in most versions of the text.

5   Heidegger, *Being and Time*, p. 24 (4).

6   John Macquarrie and Edward Robinson choose 'entity' as the translation of *Seiendes*. See ibid., p. 22 for their discussion of their choice. The term 'entity' may bring about misleading associations, but I will use it here nonetheless.

7   Ibid., pp. 26–7 (7).

8   Ibid., p. 32 (12).

9   Ibid., pp. 49–50 (27).

10   Ibid., p. 58 (34).

11   Ibid., pp. 37–8 (16). See also ibid., p. 69 (43).

descriptions show in relation to this example is rather that someone who does not believe that there is no external reality does not have to give arguments for that. This does not mean, however, that they 'believe' in the existence of the external world – this is merely another way to endorse the same inappropriate way of approaching the problem. The 'scandal of philosophy' is therefore not, as Kant supposed,[12] that no proof of the existence of an external world has been given, but that such proofs are expected and attempted again and again. What Heidegger tries to show is that what the proofs try to prove is always already presupposed in such proofs, since the entity which expects and attempts such proofs, Dasein, is an entity which essentially is-in-the-world.[13]

Heidegger starts his description of the Being of Dasein by stating that to Dasein, Being-in-a-world is something that belongs essentially.[14] Being-in-the-world is not a question of Being-in in the sense in which the water is in the glass or the garment is in the cupboard – that is, it is not a matter of two entities extended in space with regard to their location in that space. Instead, the Being-in of Dasein should be understood as a matter of residing or dwelling at the world as that which is familiar to Dasein.[15] Two points are especially important here. Firstly, Dasein cannot be isolated from the world. It is not the case that Dasein is, to begin with, and then has a certain relation to the world which it now and then adopts.[16] Secondly, the world is not just there, disengaged from human activities and purposes – present-at-hand, as Heidegger calls it.[17]

The relation Dasein has to the world is described by Heidegger using words such as 'concern' (*Besorgen*), in order to emphasize the active, engaged and practical nature of that relation.[18] In the same way, our everyday Being-in-the-world is labelled by Heidegger as our dealings in the world and with entities within-the-world.[19] Consequently, the kind of dealing which is closest to us is that kind of concern which puts things to use, not a purely theoretical cognition.[20] These things, which we encounter in concern, Heidegger calls 'equipment' (*Zeug*). They are characterized by their relation to practical activities, by being something in-order-to. Because of that relation, an equipment is proximally and for the most part in relation to other equipment.[21] Dasein is therefore primarily related to a totality of equipment, not to individual items.[22]

---

12 Immanuel Kant, *Critique of Pure Reason*, trans. Paul Guyer and Allen W. Wood (Cambridge, 1998), p. 121 (B xxxix).

13 Heidegger, *Being and Time*, p. 249 (205).

14 Ibid., p. 33 (13).

15 Ibid., pp. 79–80 (54).

16 Ibid., p. 84 (57).

17 Ibid., p. 81 (55).

18 Ibid., pp. 83–4 (57).

19 Ibid., p. 95 (66–7).

20 Ibid., p. 95 (67).

21 Ibid., p. 97 (68).

22 Ibid., p. 98 (69).

The kind of Being of equipment Heidegger calls readiness-to-hand, in contrast to presence-at-hand. When an entity is ready-at-hand, it is situated between Dasein and what Dasein is focused on. What the everyday dealings dwell with is namely not primarily the equipment, but the work, that which is to be produced.[23] An individual tool does not become conspicuous, obtrusive or obstinate until it cannot be used, is missing or stands in the way.[24]

Also Nature, which is not equipment, is not simply present-at-hand. When used by Dasein in its dealings with the world, as timber or water power, it is ready-to-hand. However, also when it is not so used, it is primarily not simply there, neutral as on object of examination, but enthralls us and is familiar to us: 'The botanist's plants are not the flowers of the hedgerow; the "source" which the geographer establishes for a river is not the "springhead in the dale".'[25]

The work which is to be produced is not isolated, but points to, for example, the material of which it is made, which in its turn points to that out of which it has been made, and so on. In that way, the world is not just a collection of unrelated things, but is a totality of relations.[26] To that which the work points to, belongs other entities with Dasein's kind of Being, for example in the capacities as users or wearers of the work.[27] This means that, in the same way as Dasein always is in a world, an isolated 'I' without Others is not proximally given.[28] The world is always a world I share with Others. Being-in-the-world is hence a matter of Being-with Others.[29]

That the Others are encountered from out of the world in which Dasein essentially dwells concernfully, means that theoretical 'explanations' of the existence of those which are not me starts out from a defective understanding of the Being of Dasein. Such 'explanations' start out from an isolated 'I', which first encounters itself, and then encounters other entities which are like itself. Heidegger points out, in contrast to this, that Dasein finds 'itself' proximally in what it does, uses, expects, avoids and the like – that is, in what it is proximally concerned with, not in some inner punctual centre of actions.[30] What Dasein is proximally concerned with, it encounters in its environment, where other entities with Dasein's kind of Being are also encountered. Dasein finds there 'itself' not only in relation to what is present-at-hand, but also in relation to those entities with the same kind of Being as Dasein, entities towards

---

23 Ibid., pp. 98–9 (69).

24 Ibid., pp. 102–4 (73–4). See also Martin Heidegger, *Poetry, Language, Thought*, trans. Albert Hofstadter (New York, 1971), pp. 33–4.

25 Heidegger, *Being and Time*, p. 100. Translation of Heidegger, *Sein und Zeit*, p. 70: 'Die Pflanzen des Botanikers sind nicht Blumen am Rain, das geographisch fixierte "Entspringen" eines Flusses ist nicht die "Quelle im Grund".'

26 Heidegger, *Being and Time*, p. 100 (70).

27 Ibid., p. 100 (70–71).

28 Ibid., p. 152 (116).

29 Ibid., p. 155 (118).

30 Ibid., p. 155 (119).

which Dasein as Being-with comports itself, a relation which is characterized by Heidegger as 'solicitude' (*Fürsorge*).[31]

Since Dasein's relation to the world primarily is one of concern, it is 'fascinated' (*benommen*) by the world with which it is concerned, and is in the first place not simply staring at a world of entities being present-at-hand. Not until Dasein explicitly refrains from dealing actively with particular entities – from, for example, using them – is it possible for it to look purely at what it encounters.[32] This means that when Dasein directs itself towards something and tries to get knowledge of it, it does not first get out of some inner sphere, but is always already outside at the entities it encounters in the always already discovered world. It is hence not the process of attaining theoretical knowledge which creates the subject's first contact with the world.[33]

When Dasein refrains from dealing actively with particular entities, and simply looks at them, what it sees is primarily not something absolutely neutral, isolated from any relation to Dasein's activities and purposes. To achieve a purely theoretical grasp of the object requires a good deal of effort:

> It requires a very artificial and complicated frame of mind to 'hear' a 'pure noise'. The fact that motor-cycles and waggons are what we proximally hear is the phenomenal evidence that in every case Dasein, as Being-in-the-world, already dwells *alongside* what is ready-to-hand within-the-world; it certainly does not dwell proximally alongside 'sensations'; nor would it first have to give shape to the swirl of sensations to provide the springboard from which the subject leaps off and finally arrives at a 'world'. Dasein, as essentially understanding, is proximally alongside what is understood. Likewise, when we are explicitly hearing the discourse of another, we proximally understand what is said, or – to put it more exactly – we are already with him, in advance, alongside the entity which the discourse is about.[34]

Thus it is not the case that when seeing or hearing we, so to speak, throw a meaning over some naked thing which is present-at-hand. When something is encountered within-the-world, it rather always already has an involvement in Dasein's activities.[35]

---

31 Ibid., p. 157 (121).

32 Ibid., pp. 88–9 (61).

33 Ibid., pp. 89–90 (62).

34 Ibid., p. 207. Translation of Heidegger, *Sein und Zeit*, p. 164: 'Es bedarf schon einer sehr künstlichen und komplizierten Einstellung, um ein "reines Geräusch" zu "hören". Daß wir aber zunächst Motorräder und Wagen hören, ist der phänomenale Beleg dafür, daß das Dasein als In-der-Welt-sein je schon *beim* innerweltlich Zuhandenen sich aufhält und zunächst gar nicht bei "Empfindungen", deren Gewühl zuerst geformt werden müßte, um das Sprungbrett abzugeben, von dem das Subjekt abspringt, um schließlich zu einer "Welt" zu gelangen. Das Dasein ist als wesenhaft verstehendes zunächst beim Verstandenen. Auch im ausdrücklichen Hören der Rede des Anderen verstehen wir zunächst das Gesagte, genauer, wir sind im Vorhinein schon mit dem Anderen bei dem Seienden, worüber die Rede ist.' See also Heidegger, *Poetry, Language, Thought*, p. 26.

35 Heidegger, *Being and Time*, pp. 190–91 (149–50).

Heidegger therefore points out that the demand for universality results in a defective way of understanding knowledge, true beliefs, rationality and the like. Heidegger shows that the knower is not an isolated subject, but an active entity situated in a particular time and place, related to other human beings and to what she encounters in the world, and with interests and purposes. To see the subject's relation to the world as passive, neutral or instrumental, as the epistemological tradition does, is hence to emphasize what is only possible secondarily. Knowing is furthermore not the first attitude we take up to the things in the world. Commitment, embodiment, upbringing, and being situated in society and history are hence not, as such, obstacles to knowledge, true beliefs, rationality and the like, but on the contrary, conditions for them in the role they play in our lives.

This does *not* mean that distancing oneself from the world which is encountered as closest to us and in which we are concernfully absorbed is always wrong. As we have seen, Dasein is proximally and for the most part at the world of its concern,[36] and it finds 'itself' proximally in what it is proximally concerned with, and not in some inner punctual centre of actions. Since Dasein finds 'itself' proximally in what it is proximally concerned with, the difference between Dasein's kind of Being and the kind of Being of those entities Dasein is concerned with tends to be neglected, and Dasein then understands its own Being in terms of that entity towards which it comports itself proximally: the world.[37] Dasein's Being-in-the-world is thereby concealed, and the belief that the existence of the external world must be proved arises easily.[38] Philosophical thinking thus requires a certain distance to our everyday dealings in order to see them properly,[39] but this is always done on the basis of our everyday dealings, without which philosophical thinking in the role it plays in our lives would not be possible.

Heidegger sums up the characteristics of the Being of Dasein in the word 'care' (*Sorge*), which he explicates as 'ahead-of-itself-Being-already-in-(the-world) as Being-alongside (entities encountered within-the-world)'.[40] Care has an obvious temporal structure: 'The primordial unity of the structure of care lies in temporality. The "ahead-of-itself" is grounded in the future. In the "Being-already-in ...", the character of "having been" is made known. "Being-alongside ..." becomes possible in making present.'[41] This temporality Heidegger does not explicate in terms of history, although such an explication lies quite near to what he is actually saying, and

---

36 Ibid., pp. 167 and 220 (129 and 175).

37 Ibid., p. 36 (15).

38 Ibid., p. 250 (206).

39 Ibid., pp. 264–5 (222).

40 See ibid., for example p. 237. For the German equivalent, see Heidegger, *Sein und Zeit*, for example p. 192: 'Sich-vorweg-schon-sein-in-(der-Welt-) als Sein-bei (innerweltlich begegnendem Seienden)'.

41 Heidegger, *Being and Time*, p. 375; italics removed. Translation of Heidegger, *Sein und Zeit*, p. 327: '*Die ursprüngliche Einheit der Sorgestruktur liegt in der Zeitlichkeit. Das Sich-vorweg gründet in der Zukunft. Das Schon-sein-in ... bekundet in sich die Gewesenheit. Das Sein-bei ... wird ermöglicht im Gegenwärtigen.*'

is compatible with it. Since what we are interested in here is to show, among other things, that being situated in history is not an obstacle to, but on the contrary one condition for, knowledge, true beliefs, rationality and the like in the role they play in our lives, in the following we will turn to Hans-Georg Gadamer, who has gone into more detail about the senses in which Dasein is situated in history.

Gadamer and History

Throughout *Truth and Method*,[42] Gadamer mentions the fact of human finitude now and then. This finitude finds different expressions. It is a matter of being situated in history as a link in a chain,[43] of being constantly dependent on the given circumstances,[44] of being situated within traditions,[45] of being always already affected by history,[46] of always finding oneself within a situation.[47] Gadamer therefore stresses mostly how we are conditioned by the past. This makes him say things like '... history does not belong to us; we belong to it'.[48] This is something more general than only a matter of history in the strict sense, however: 'Long before we understand ourselves through the process of self-examination, we understand ourselves in a self-evident way in the family, society, and state in which we live. The focus of subjectivity is a distorting mirror.'[49] History is central, however, for that in which we live and understand ourselves is handed over to us from the time which precedes us. Gadamer's formulation is a little misleading, however, in saying that we *understand* ourselves in this way. Since our situatedness affects us long before we can express this linguistically, and affects us in ways we are not aware of, the main point is rather that we are situated and live situated in a self-evident way.

That we are conditioned by the past does not mean that we are limited by it. The process of forming knowledge and understanding could not start at all if we had no ideas, beliefs and conceptions, and these come, according to Gadamer, from the tradition we already belong to. Our situatedness is hence not a limitation, but

---

42 Hans-Georg Gadamer, *Truth and Method*, trans. Joel Weinsheimer and Donald G. Marshall (New York, 1989).

43 Ibid., p. 200.

44 Ibid., p. 276.

45 Ibid., p. 282.

46 Ibid., p. 300.

47 Ibid., p. 301.

48 Ibid., p. 276. Translation of Hans-Georg Gadamer, *Gesammelte Werke: Band I: Hermeneutik I: Wahrheit und Methode: Grundzüge einer philosophischen Hermeneutik* (Tübingen, 1986), p. 281: '... gehört die Geschichte nicht uns, sondern wir gehören ihr'.

49 Gadamer, *Truth and Method*, p. 276. Translation of Gadamer, *Wahrheit und Methode*, p. 281: 'Lange bevor wir uns in der Rückbesinnung selber verstehen, verstehen wir uns auf selbstverständliche Weise in Familie, Gesellschaft und Staat, in denen wir leben. Der Fokus der Subjektivität ist ein Zerrspiegel.'

contributes positively to the process of understanding.[50] This process starts not from nowhere, but from where we, as knowledge formers, are:

> Prejudices are not necessarily unjustified and erroneous, so that they inevitably distort the truth. In fact, the historicity of our existence entails that prejudices, in the literal sense of the word, constitute the initial directedness of our whole ability to experience. Prejudices are biases of our openness to the world. They are simply conditions whereby we experience something – whereby what we encounter says something to us. This formulation certainly does not mean that we are enclosed within a wall of prejudices and only let through the narrow portals those things that can produce a pass saying, 'Nothing new will be said here.' Instead we welcome just that guest who promises something new to our curiosity.[51]

If we pay attention to the fact that different persons live in different families, societies, states, and above all historical situations, we become less inclined to believe that everybody *must* have the same questions and interests, and *must* approach what is to be investigated with the same or no prejudgements. Here, we have instead seen that entering the process of forming knowledge and understanding involves giving a certain priority to one's own prejudgements. Since they contribute positively to this process, they should be brought along when we are trying to understand something – that is, we should not try to forget them or be neutral in relation to what is to be understood, but let what is to be understood develop our prejudgements.[52] In this sense, commitment, embodiment, upbringing and being situated in society and history are not obstacles to knowledge, true beliefs, rationality and the like, but on the contrary, conditions for them in the role they play in our lives.

Heidegger also stressed that reasoning is never presuppositionless.[53] Gadamer moreover credits Heidegger explicitly for having explicated the circular structure of understanding.[54] To both Heidegger and Gadamer, it is important that our situatedness

---

50 See, for example, Gadamer, *Truth and Method*, pp. 268–9.

51 Hans-Georg Gadamer, *Philosophical Hermeneutics*, trans. David E. Linge (Berkeley, CA, 1976), p. 9. Translation of Hans-Georg Gadamer, *Kleine Schriften I: Philosophie Hermeneutik* (Tübingen, 1967), p. 106: 'Vorurteile sind nicht notwendig unberechtigt und irrig, so daß sie die Wahrheit verstellen. In Wahrheit liegt es in der Geschichtlichkeit unserer Existenz, daß die Vorurteile im wörtlichen Sinne des Wortes die vorgängige Gerichtetheit all unseres Erfahren-Könnens ausmachen. Sie sind Voreingenommenheiten unserer Weltoffenheit, die geradezu Bedingungen dafür sind, daß wir etwas erfahren, daß uns das, was uns begegnet, etwas sagt. Gewiß heißt das nicht, daß wir, durch eine Mauer von Vorurteilen eingefriedet, nur das durch die enge Pforte lassen, was seinen Paß vorweisen kann, auf dem steht: hier wird nichts Neues gesagt. Gerade der Gast ist uns willkommen, der unserer Neugier Neues verheißt.' When Gadamer writes '… Vorurteile im wörtlichen Sinne des Wortes …', he refers to the fact that the German word *Vorurteil* is a compound of *vor* and *Urteil*. To retain this when translating into English, translating *Vorurteil* as 'prejudgement' could be considered.

52 Gadamer, *Truth and Method*, pp. 267–9.

53 Heidegger, *Being and Time*, pp. 191–2 (150).

54 Gadamer, *Truth and Method*, p. 266.

should not be understood as a trap, but that it is the starting point for development. We have already seen this in Gadamer's writing 'Instead we welcome just that guest who promises something new to our curiosity.'[55] Heidegger stresses that the hermeneutic circle is not a limitation, but on the contrary, what makes change possible:

> But if we see this circle as a vicious one and look out for ways of avoiding it, even if we just 'sense' it as an inevitable imperfection, then the act of understanding has been misunderstood from the ground up. ... What is decisive is not to get out of the circle but to come into it in the right way.[56]

Later in this chapter, and in the next, this theme of change will be developed in more detail.

Embodiment

Heidegger does not make the embodiment of Dasein explicit. In the following, I will therefore say something about that aspect.

It is important to notice that when we here talk about the subject as embodied and the like, this is not to be understood as an empirical hypothesis about the physicality of thought, a hypothesis which has been or could be confirmed by scientists. Embodiment in the sense in which we talk about it here can be made obvious long before such hypotheses are confirmed or even formulated. Embodiment in the sense we talk about it here is a matter of how the world shows itself to each one of us, and could hence also be pointed out to those who believe that each one of us has a soul which survives physical death.[57] However, if somebody actually believes that she has no body, she need not be convinced by the arguments below – but that is not their purpose.[58]

One way of arguing for embodiment in this sense is to argue like Charles Taylor. He formulates a transcendental argument to argue for the conception of the subject as embodied agency.[59] The argument starts from the fact that perception is basic to us

---

55 Gadamer, *Philosophical Hermeneutics*, p. 9. Translation of Gadamer, *Kleine Schriften I: Philosophie Hermeneutik*, p. 106: 'Gerade der Gast ist uns willkommen, der unserer Neugier Neues verheißt.'

56 Heidegger, *Being and Time*, pp. 194–5; italics removed. Translation of Heidegger, *Sein und Zeit*, p. 153: '*Aber in diesem Zirkel ein vitiosum sehen und nach Wegen Ausschau halten, ihn zu vermeiden, ja ihn noch nur als unvermeidliche Unvollkommenheit »empfinden«, heißt das Verstehen von Grund aus mißverstehen. ... Das Entscheidende ist nicht, aus dem Zirkel heraus-, sondern in ihn nach der rechten Weise hineinzukommen.*'

57 Since embodiment in the sense we talk about it here could be pointed out to those who believe that each one of us has a soul which survives physical death, those who hold this belief combine it either with a belief in the resurrection of the body or in reincarnation, or with an insistence on the mystery of that belief, that it is beyond human understanding.

58 In similarity to Heidegger's and Gadamer's arguments.

59 Taylor, *Philosophical Arguments*, pp. 21–4.

as subjects. That this is so could be seen by noting that to be a subject is to be aware of a world. One can, of course, be aware of a world in many ways, but perception is basic because it is always there as long as one is aware, and because it is the foundation of other ways of being aware – for example, thinking.

The argument thus starts from the fact that perception is basic to us as subjects. Our perceptual field has an orientational structure, a foreground and a background, an up and a down, and must have one to be what it is. This orientational structure shows that the perceptual field is essentially that of an embodied agent. This could be seen by studying the up–down directionality of the field. This directionality is related to how one would move, stand and act in the field. It is as a bodily agent functioning in a gravitational field that 'up' and 'down' have meaning for me. The conclusion is not that we happen to be embodied agents, that we are embodied agents as a matter of contingent empirical fact, but that we are embodied agents essentially. Thus we do not call something which is not an embodied agent 'subject'.

That some religious believers talk about God as a subject without a body makes no difference to this. Our different ways of talking about God are dependent on our different ways of talking about ourselves. Saying that God is a subject without a body is thus a derived way of talking about being a subject. Furthermore, it would be better to say that the category 'subject' does not quite fit God than to talk about God being a subject without a body, and thereby to point out that what it more exactly means to say that God is, is what religious persons would call a mystery.

A philosopher who has especially emphasized embodiment and is referred to by Taylor is Maurice Merleau-Ponty. What he points out above all is that the body is not an object, something which stands in a relation to us, in a relation which is similar to the relation in which objects in the external world stand to us.[60] The body is rather '… on the side of the subject; it is our *point of view on the world* … Our body is not in space like things; it inhabits or haunts space.'[61] Here I will mention two of Merleau-Ponty's arguments for this. Firstly, he takes the example of somebody stamping on a nail and hurting her foot. In such a case, the foot is not the cause of an unlocalized awareness of pain, as if the only difference between the nail and the foot is that the latter is nearer to us. Instead, we say in such a case that the foot hurts or that the pain comes from the foot.[62] Secondly, external objects are moved by us and we move our bodies. However, in the first case we move them with, for example, our hands, but in the second case we move the body directly. Thus, the body is not

---

60 See, for example, Maurice Merleau-Ponty, *Phenomenology of Perception*, trans. Colin Smith (London, 1962), pp. 92 and 198; Maurice Merleau-Ponty, 'An Unpublished Text by Maurice Merleau-Ponty: A Prospectus of His Work', trans. Arleen B. Dallery, in James M. Edie (ed.), *The Primacy of Perception and Other Essays on Phenomenological Psychology, the Philosophy of Art, History and Politics* (Evanston, IL, 1964), p. 5.

61 Merleau-Ponty, 'An Unpublished Text', p. 5. Translation of Maurice Merleau-Ponty, 'Un inédit de Maurice Merleau-Ponty', *Revue de Métaphysique et de Morale*, 67 (1962): 403: '… du côté du sujet, il est *notre point de vue sur le monde* … Notre corps n'est pas dans l'espace comme les choses : il l'habite ou le hante …'.

62 Merleau-Ponty, *Phenomenology of Perception*, p. 93.

an external object which we first have to find in order to move it, but is what makes our moving things possible.[63]

Of course, such arguments as Taylor and Merleau-Ponty have formulated need not convince somebody who, for example, actually believes that she has no body. The purpose of the arguments is not to convert such a skeptic, but to point out what is easily forgotten when thinking about philosophical problems. In philosophy the subject has often been understood, explicitly or implicitly, as a pure mind or as an independent reason, as *res cogitans*.[64] The subject has then been understood as something that, so to speak, inhabits the body and looks out. What is then forgotten is the embodiment of perception. When for example seeing something, which seems to be the privileged way of perceiving here, one turns in the direction of what is to be seen, moves one's eyes to see the whole surface, and perhaps turns the thing around with one's hands to see the back of it. This is not done as if the mind used the body as an instrument for perception, as if using one's body is but one of many possible ways of perceiving, and that we can choose a way of perceiving where we do not have to use our bodies at all. Rather, seeing something *is*, in an important sense, turning towards it, moving one's eyes, and so on. These body movements are in most cases not done consciously, but as an integral part of the whole process of perception. That body movements are involved in perception tends to be forgotten precisely because they are so natural that they are not noticed.

It must be noticed that talking about sense data, as in phenomenalism, is not a way of taking embodiment into account. There is nothing in the concept of 'sense data' that shows that these appear to us by means of the body. On the contrary, one of the points of the concept of sense data is that they can be understood without taking their way of appearance into account. Therefore, sense data can, in principle, appear without the body, and according to the phenomenalist, it is thus not necessary to take the body into account when understanding knowledge. Here, I have pointed out, however, that our knowledge is connected to the ways we live in the world and deal with it, ways which would not be what they are if we were not embodied.

---

63 Ibid., p. 94.

64 It must be noticed, however, that not even Descartes, whom this seems to apply to more than anybody else, separates the soul from the body in such an extreme way as is often believed. In his *Meditations on First Philosophy*, he writes:

> Nature also teaches me, by these sensations of pain, hunger, thirst and so on, that I am not merely present in my body as a sailor is present in a ship, but that I am very closely joined and, as it were, intermingled with it, so that I and the body form a unit. If this were not so, I, who am nothing but a thinking thing, would not feel pain when the body was hurt, but would perceive the damage purely by the intellect, just as a sailor perceives by sight if anything in his ship is broken. Similarly, when the body needed food or drink, I should have an explicit understanding of the fact, instead of having confused sensations of hunger and thirst. (René Descartes, *The Philosophical Writings of Descartes: Volume II*, trans. John Cottingham, Robert Stoothoff and Dugald Murdoch (Cambridge, 1984), p. 56)

Being embodied is in one sense a limitation, since it means, for example, that one can only be at one place at a time, that one cannot see every side of an object simultaneously, and that there is a limitation to how much one can learn during one's lifetime. This does not mean, however, that being embodied is an obstacle to knowledge in the role it plays in our lives – it is in fact a condition for it. It would only be possible to deny this if it were possible to refer to a way of attaining knowledge which was completely independent of perception, or if there were unembodied perception.

Wittgenstein, Davidson and Interaction

When it comes to the issue of situatedness in society, we can use what has already been said in Chapter 2. There we saw, with the help of Wittgenstein, that being able to follow a rule need not be understood as being a matter of stating how the rule should be interpreted, nor does linguistic competence need to be understood as the ability to give definitions for the meanings of words and being able to state syntactical rules. One can understand the ability to follow one particular rule or the ability to use one particular word in this way, but when such an understanding has a claim to generality, it is defective, since the ability to give definitions and state rules already presupposes the ability to follow rules and use words. In one way, being able to follow rules and communicating are simply things we do. We acquire these abilities by learning, for example by learning to play games and speak. Such learning presupposes, of course, that we are beings who can learn such things.

In the same way, abilities such as being rational, being able to give reasons and evaluating argumentation, and being able to distinguish true from false beliefs, need not be understood as abilities which are simply there, but as abilities we acquire by learning. In fact, if learning were not needed, if the ability to evaluate argumentation, for example, were innate, that would mean that evaluating argumentation would be as rational an activity as physical growth. In order to account for the *rationality* of evaluating argumentation, it is hence necessary, firstly, to take intersubjectivity into account,[65] and secondly, to notice that our failures here are something we, at least partly, are responsible for ourselves – that is, that one's ability to evaluate argumentation is something one can improve.

That these abilities are acquired by training should not, however, be understood as if we acquired them by means of explicit training, as if it was already meaningful to apply the word 'rational' to what we as new-born do, and that all that was needed was refinement – that would be a confusion akin to the one Wittgenstein attributes to Augustine in the beginning of *Philosophical Investigations*.[66] Instead, we can point to the fact that we are simply born into, being brought up in and living in a world where there already are people who act in specific ways, ways which are called rational.

---

65 This will be done below and in Chapter 5.
66 Wittgenstein, *Philosophical Investigations*, p. 2e (§ 1).

What this learning effects is a certain agreement in action, against which we talk about something being right or wrong, true or false, correct or incorrect. Since we learn to reason by means of simple forms of reasoning and show that we have learnt to reason by reasoning ourselves,[67] there would not be anything like reasoning if there were disagreement about these simple forms.[68] Such an agreement is primarily an agreement about what reasoning practically is, and not merely an agreement about the definition of reasoning. That this is so can be seen if one notices that it makes no sense to talk about two persons being in agreement concerning a definition if this agreement *never* shows itself in practice.[69]

Since to be reasonable and rational is something we learn by being born into, being brought up in, and living in our world, we can say, with Richard Bernstein: '... we belong to tradition, history, and language before they belong to us'.[70] What is considered reasonable and rational is in that sense neither arbitrary, since we do not choose here, nor is it subjective: we are born into a world where people already act in rational ways, and we are dependent on them to learn to act rationally ourselves.

That we are situated means furthermore that the subject is not a *tabula rasa* at the start. This does not mean, however, that we have to say that loads of things are innate in the strict sense. The important point is that we are born into a world and a society which have existed long before us. We are born into a world and a society where there are already established ways of doing things.

Thus we have here an additional way in which commitment, embodiment, upbringing and being situated in society and history are not obstacles to knowledge, true beliefs, rationality and the like, but on the contrary, conditions for them in the role they play in our lives.

The suggestion that being situated in society is not an obstacle to, but on the contrary, a condition for knowledge, true beliefs, rationality and the like in the role they play in our lives can be further underlined by noticing how Wittgenstein, in *Philosophical Investigations*, shows some of the problems of supposing that there could be a necessarily private language.[71] One of the problems is that there is no way of distinguishing between right and wrong in such a language: '... whatever is going to seem right to me is right. And that only means that here we can't talk about "right"'.[72] Wittgenstein's argument is not that we cannot trust our memory, and that we therefore cannot be sure that we use a particular word in the private language in

---

67 Ibid., pp. 70e–71e (§ 208); Wittgenstein, *Remarks on the Foundations of Mathematics*, pp. 320–21, 327, 420–21 (§§ VI:17, VI:25, VII:59).

68 Wittgenstein, *Lectures on the Foundations of Mathematics*, p. 102.

69 Wittgenstein, *Philosophical Investigations*, p. 75e (§ 242), Wittgenstein, *Remarks on the Foundations of Mathematics*, p. 343 (§ VI:39).

70 Bernstein, *Beyond Objectivism and Relativism*, p. 167. Bernstein alludes here to Gadamer, *Truth and Method*, p. 276.

71 See, for example, Wittgenstein, *Philosophical Investigations*, pp. 75e, 78e–79e, 85e (§§ 243, 258, 260, 293).

72 Ibid., p. 78e (§ 258): '... richtig ist, was immer mir als richtig erscheinen wird. Und das heißt nur, daß hier von "richtig" nicht geredet werden kann'.

the same way every time. Wittgenstein's argument is rather that in such a language, there would be no other criteria for something being right than its seeming to be right for the person in question, which means that she can do whatever she likes. The private language would hence not be what we call a language, which means that the person who really wants to use the phrase 'private language' would never find anything which would make her satisfied. That it is possible to talk with oneself may entice one into believing that a private language is possible, but talking with oneself is something we do in a world and a life in which we talk with others, are together with others, and so on. Although Wittgenstein is not discussing here whether the existence of other persons is a necessary condition for the existence of every kind of language, we can say that the ways in which we are actually talking are internally related to the fact that these ways of talking are primarily prevalent in interaction with other persons.

That the concepts of right and wrong, in the role they play in our lives, presuppose interaction with other people is an important point for Donald Davidson, but his arguments are a little different than Wittgenstein's. Davidson's starting point is the question of how the contents of words are determined. Davidson asks what explains the fact that it seems natural to say that a person who says 'table' in the presence of tables is responding to tables. Why not say that her responses are not to tables, but to patterns of stimulations of her nerve endings? After all, the patterns of stimulation presumably produce the response every time, while tables produce it only under favourable conditions. According to Davidson, the answer to this question is that it is we interpreters who find different tables similar and the person's responses to tables on different occasions similar. The kinds of objects or events which we find it natural to say that the person responds to are then the objects or events we naturally find similar which are correlated with responses from the other person which we find similar. This Davidson calls a form of triangulation, where three relations are important: the relation between the other person and tables, the relation between us and tables, and the communicative relation between us and the other person. Without these relations there would be no answers to the question of what a concept is a concept of, of what a word means, and this goes for the language of the other person, as we have just seen, as well as for our own language, since a person cannot determine the content of her words in complete isolation.[73]

The reason why a person cannot determine the content of her words in complete isolation is that being able to distinguish between right and wrong presupposes the ability to distinguish between what is to go on as before and what is not to go on as before. If I point to different noses and you say 'nose' every time, I am able to fix a content to your utterance of 'nose'. Occasional mistakes are then possible: if you go on as before (say 'nose' when I point to a nose, and do not say 'nose' when I do not point to a nose), you can be said to be right – in cases when I point to a nose and you say something different, you are wrong. In each case, I thus find the stimulus

---

73 Donald Davidson, *Subjective, Intersubjective, Objective* (Oxford, 2001), pp. 117–20. See also ibid., pp. 129–30, 201–3, 212–14.

similar and the response similar (you are then right), or dissimilar (you are then wrong). This does not mean that every correlation of things in the world with your utterances is necessarily correct – all it means is that it is only possible to apply the concept of making a mistake when interpersonal communication has created a space for its application. Communicatively isolated, there is no way for you to fix what your words mean in a way which makes it possible for you to distinguish between cases when you go on as before and cases when you do not go on as before, in the sense explained above.[74]

The way Davidson argues here is misleading, however, intimating that communication is best understood as a matter of correlating somebody's responses with appropriate circumstances, and in that way formulating hypotheses about the meaning of what she is saying, and this will be more obvious in the next chapter. However, Davidson's point is correct: words outside *any* communicative use do not have what we call meaning. It is in the context of a speaker, a hearer and something they have in common which can be spoken about that it makes sense to say that a word means something.

As a matter of precaution, I want to emphasize that what I have been doing here is only pointing out some relations between us as interacting beings and language, without discussing whether we actually are interacting or not. Hence, the above argument should not be understood as an argument which is supposed to show a convinced solipsist that she is wrong.

Some Consequences of Leaving the Demand for Universality Behind

In this chapter, I have, in some different ways, suggested that commitment, embodiment, upbringing and being situated in society and history are not obstacles to knowledge, true beliefs, rationality and the like, but on the contrary, conditions for them in the role they play in our lives. This implies that the demand for universality is confused in two different ways. Firstly, if the demand for universality is understood as a demand for a view from nowhere, the problem is simply that the phrase 'view from nowhere' does not stand for anything. A person who wants to find a view from nowhere will never find anything which will satisfy her – as soon as she, being a person, has attained a specific view, this view is not a view from nowhere.

Secondly, the demand for universality can be understood as a demand that every statement must be argued for by means of conclusive arguments, appreciated by, in principle, everybody – arguments which show that the belief in question follows from other beliefs which have already been proven in this way or are self-evident. The problem here is that a vast number of beliefs we hold – beliefs which we do not regard as problematic – cannot be argued for in this way. The demand for universality invites conservatism then, since there seems then not to be much of a difference between one's present beliefs and suggested new beliefs (it is not possible

---

74   Ibid., p. 129; Donald Davidson, *Truth, Language, and History* (Oxford, 2005), pp. 124–5.

to argue for any of them in the way the demand for universality demands), and one can then as well stick to the old ones.[75] Furthermore, the words 'knowledge', 'true beliefs', 'rationality' and the like play an important role in our lives. This role is dependent on our mode of being, on us as committed, embodied and situated beings. Commitment, embodiment, upbringing and being situated in society and history are hence not obstacles to knowledge, true beliefs, rationality and the like, but on the contrary, conditions for them in the role they play in our lives, as we have seen. What separates us from others, what in a way makes universal agreement hard to arrive at, are hence not obstacles to, but on the contrary conditions for knowledge, true beliefs, rationality and the like in the role they play in our lives.

If we moreover focus on the theme of progress, which I will talk about further below, the idea of a definite stopping-place where all possibilities for further development are exhausted, a stopping-place which we can actually recognize as a stopping-place when we have reached it, is not useful. It is not useful since it is doubtful whether we can understand what a situation in which all possibilities for further development are exhausted would be like. For us, existence has to do with, among other things, meeting problems, making improvements, and developing. To live in a situation where there is no place for such things is then hard to imagine. Therefore, if such a situation is possible, it lies so far away from where we are that it is merely a theoretical possibility, which means that we do not have to take it into account when we focus on the importance of progress.

That there are other opinions and ways of living therefore does not delegitimize ours, and generally it is advisable to start from where we are. This has sometimes been called ethnocentrism, a term which is a little misleading, but what it *stands for* deserves to be discussed.

Ethnocentrism

Richard Rorty has used the term 'ethnocentrism' frequently, and I will contrast what has been said here with his position. His starting point is this dilemma: either you stick to your liberal ideas even when you meet people who do not share them and admit that it is ethnocentric to do so, or you give up your liberal ideas when you do not succeed in showing others the superiority of these ideas.[76] Rorty's answer is that we should accept ethnocentrism. Thus, when Rorty uses the term 'ethnocentrism' to signify '… that we have to start from where we are …',[77] '… an inescapable

---

75 Cf. Michel Eyquem de Montaigne, *The Essays of Michel Eyquem de Montaigne*, trans. Charles Cotton (Chicago, IL, 1952), p. 276; Chaïm Perelman, *The Realm of Rhetoric*, trans. William Kluback (Notre Dame, IN, 1982), p. 157.

76 See Richard Rorty, *Objectivity, Relativism, and Truth: Philosophical Papers Volume 1* (Cambridge, 1991), pp. 203 & 207–8.

77 Ibid., p. 29.

condition – roughly synonymous with "human finitude" …'[78], he is fairly close to what I have been saying. Ethnocentrism is thus right in the sense that it is not wrong, generally speaking, to privilege, in the sense in which we are using the word here, your own opinions and way of living, although it can be wrong in some concrete cases, for some concrete reasons. As Rorty says: '… the fact that nothing is immune from criticism does not mean that we have a duty to justify everything'.[79] Another correct point in Rorty's ethnocentrism, an empirical and contingent point, is that we cannot have a fruitful discussion with everybody, that we cannot justify our beliefs to everybody.[80] This is an important point, which we will come back to in Chapter 6.

Rorty's use of the term 'ethnocentrism' is, for many reasons, problematic, however. I will mention two reasons here. Firstly, the term 'ethnocentrism' is problematic when it is used to refer to a particular group, a particular *ethnos*. Rorty says, for example: '… we must, in practice, privilege our own group, even though there can be no noncircular justification for doing so. … To be ethnocentric is to divide the human race into the people to whom one must justify one's beliefs and the others.'[81] The problem is that Rorty is talking about groups, where he ought to talk about beliefs. Rorty is right if we interpret him as saying that irrespective of how I evaluate the beliefs of the others, it is as the person *I* am, with the beliefs *I* have, that I encounter the beliefs of the others, not as a neutral subject without any beliefs or purposes.[82] Talking about groups is problematic, however. Such talk may be innocent, if the criterion according to which persons are divided into different groups concerns whether they act in similar ways or not, whether they hold the same beliefs or not. The problem is, however, that the criterion Rorty implicitly uses is another: 'our own group' is here, for example, an ethnic group, a religious community or a political movement, and hence, according to Rorty, it is to *such* groups we must remain loyal.[83]

Secondly, Rorty's argumentation for ethnocentrism is problematic. For him, ethnocentrism is a consequence of leaving behind a representational view of knowledge. Rorty says that '… an antirepresentationalist view of inquiry leaves one without a skyhook with which to escape from the ethnocentrism produced by

---

78 Ibid., p. 15. 'Human finitude' is an expression which has to be used carefully. It does not mean that to start from where we are, is something which some better species than us does not have to do, that is it does not mean that if we only were able to improve our cognitive abilities we would not need to start from where we are.

79 Rorty, *Objectivity, Relativism, and Truth*, p. 29. Cf. Wittgenstein, *Philosophical Investigations*, p. 84e (§ 289); Wittgenstein, *Remarks on the Foundations of Mathematics*, p. 406 (§ VII:40).

80 Rorty, *Objectivity, Relativism, and Truth*, pp. 30–31.

81 Ibid., pp. 29–30.

82 Cf. Hilary Putnam, *Realism with a Human Face* (Cambridge, 1990), p. 26.

83 To be fair to Rorty, it must be mentioned, however, that he on one occasion says that he has not distinguished distinctly enough between ethnocentrism as an inescapable condition and as reference to a particular political group; Rorty, *Objectivity, Relativism, and Truth*, p. 15.

acculturation …'[84]. He presumes, however, that representationalism was our only opportunity to escape ethnocentrism, but of course, it is not impossible *a priori* for us to acquire beliefs which differ considerably from our previous beliefs.[85] This does not happen often, however, so understood as an empirical claim, Rorty's saying is right. Therefore it is in most cases right to say with Rorty, although the word 'only' should be dropped and 'no such' exchanged for 'not much':

> We can only hope to transcend our acculturation if our culture contains (or, thanks to disruptions from outside or internal revolt, comes to contain) splits which supply toeholds for new initiatives. Without such splits – without tensions which make people listen to unfamiliar ideas in the hope of finding means of overcoming those tensions – there is no such hope.[86]

The same goes for the following saying by Rorty: '… to say that we must work by our own lights, that we must be ethnocentric, is merely to say that beliefs suggested by another culture must be tested by trying to weave them together with beliefs we already have.'[87] Rorty is right in saying that there is no other way of testing other beliefs than by trying to weave them together with beliefs we already have. This should not, however, be understood as if we *must* test other beliefs – beliefs can be adopted without testing them.

The problem with Rorty's argumentation is hence that he now and then presumes that beliefs are and should be acquired by a process which is at least similar to justification in the respect that it makes new beliefs continuous with the old. Sometimes it seems, however, as if Rorty does not see it as generally impossible for somebody to leave the group she belongs to or to adopt an alien belief without weaving it together with beliefs she already has – that is, that a 'revolutionary' change is possible. However, that is not possible for people who belong to the group Rorty belongs to, and Rorty can therefore, from the necessity of ethnocentrism, draw the political conclusion that reformist politics is the only type possible for him and those in his group:[88] 'Our community – the community of the liberal intellectuals of the secular West – wants to be able to give a *post factum* account of any change of view. We want to be able, so to speak, to justify ourselves to our earlier selves.'[89] Giving reasons *post factum*, to our earlier selves, is almost always possible, however, as Kuhn has shown.[90] A person who still believes what we once believed perhaps does not find these reasons good, however, but that does not *always* matter. Whether such a person finds these reasons good or not cannot *always* be decisive for us, so Rorty

---

84   Ibid., p. 2.
85   By saying this, I do not say that escaping ethnocentrism means getting in contact with 'Reality'. It is such a philosophical idea that Rorty repudiates in the above quote.
86   Ibid., pp. 13–14.
87   Ibid., p. 26. See also ibid., p. 212.
88   Ibid., pp. 29 & 212–3.
89   Ibid., p. 29.
90   Kuhn, *The Structure of Scientific Revolutions*, pp. 137–8 & 166–7.

can hardly claim that we should *never* break with the group we belong to, or that doing so is *always* irrational, not even when the beliefs of this group have developed continuously out of a liberal culture.

We have now seen two respects in which Rorty's use of the term 'ethnocentrism' is problematic. Ethnocentrism is right, however, as I have said, when it signifies that it is not wrong, generally speaking, to privilege, in the sense in which we are using the word here, your own opinions and way of living. The general reason for this is that I have an obligation to give up a belief only if I myself have a reason for giving it up. A person who has a specific belief and knows that there are counter-arguments to her belief, counter-arguments which many think are strong, but does not understand these arguments, is then not obliged to give up her belief. One could say, however, that she is obliged to try to understand these arguments. However, it is possible for her to give reasons why she should not try to understand some arguments in a particular case, for example by saying that she has no time for it. Such reasons will probably often be *ad hoc*, but they are not always bad. What this shows is that it is impossible to give a *general* answer to the question of when a belief should be given up. Perhaps this is a pity, but on the other hand, the belief that some sort of algorithm for solving all political, ethical, existential and religious problems exists agrees badly with the ways such problems manifest themselves, and the role they play, in our lives.

Since I have an obligation to give up a belief only if I myself have a reason for giving it up, it does not suffice that others have such reasons. There is hence a tension between two beliefs only if these beliefs are beliefs of the same person, but not if these beliefs are simply there. That this is so is due to an important asymmetry: the relation I have to my own beliefs is different from my relation to the beliefs of others. My own beliefs are, in a sense, not the beliefs of anybody. There is therefore a difference between judging between a belief of person A and a belief of person B (in a case where I have no belief on the issue), and judging between a belief of person A and a belief of my own. In both cases, it is as the person I am, with the beliefs I have, that I judge the beliefs. This means that the relation between the two beliefs which are to be judged is not the same in the latter case as in the first case: in the first case the two beliefs are in the beginning on an equal footing, but in the second case this is not so. If I should take the same attitude towards my own beliefs as I do towards the beliefs of others, I would only in some cases be able to make up my mind regarding them, since I would have too little to start from to be able to make a rational decision.[91] Making someone give up a belief must therefore either be to make her give up the belief in spite of the fact that an obligation to give it up is not there, or to give her reasons for giving it up by connecting to beliefs she already holds, or to combine these two ways.[92]

----

91 Cf. Simon Thompson, 'Richard Rorty on Truth, Justification and Justice', in Matthew Festenstein and Simon Thompson (eds), *Richard Rorty: Critical Dialogues* (Cambridge, 2001), p. 43.

92 This will be developed further in Chapter 6.

This asymmetry is, strangely enough, missed by Rorty. Often, he says things like the following:

> As someone whose sense of moral identity is tied up with the need to go beyond the boundaries of my own group, I can recuperate the notion of *hinaus bemühen soll*, though perhaps not in a way that Habermas would find adequate. For I can say that I could not live with myself if I did not do my best to go beyond the borders in question. In that sense, I am morally *obliged* to do so, but only in the same sense that a Nazi who could not live with himself if he spared a certain Jew is under a moral obligation to kill that Jew.[93]

Rorty uses here the words 'in the same sense' without noticing that there is an important difference between the two cases: that he is right and the Nazi is wrong. Rorty probably has no reasons which would convince the Nazi, and saying that one is right and the Nazi is wrong then adds nothing to the already existing conflict. This does not entail, however, that one should refrain from saying that one is right and the Nazi is wrong. Refraining from saying this seems to be a consequence of Rorty's emphasis on our historical and cultural contingency, but if we take our contingency seriously, we will see that the reverse is true: as the beings we now are, we can only restrain ourselves from saying that the Nazi is wrong by suppressing the persons we are. It makes no difference to this that we, when we imagine ourselves being born and living in other historical circumstances, can come to see that if that were the case, we would perhaps have a different attitude towards Nazism. That we are interested in imagining ourselves in precisely these historical and cultural circumstances is due to the fact that we do not understand such persons, since they were unbelievably wrong. Our actual attempts to try to enter into the life of Nazis are hence, in fact, due to our conviction that they were wrong, and Rorty overlooks that this is the case.

One consequence of what Rorty calls ethnocentrism is that reason, if we for the moment use that word, is not impartial. Of course, one of the purposes of rational evaluation of different beliefs is to evaluate them without being too much committed to any of them. 'Too much' is not the same as 'not at all', however. Since commitment, embodiment, upbringing and being situated in society and history are not obstacles to, but on the contrary, conditions for knowledge, true beliefs, rationality and the like in the role they play in our lives, rational evaluation and the like are dependent on where we are situated. Motivating why we do as we do is thus only possible to a certain extent. There is no 'deep' philosophical justification of why we do as we do. Such justification is not needed for us to do what we do. All we need to do what we do, we have gained by means of upbringing and training. Just by living in a society which has existed long before us, we adopt ways of being, thinking, speaking and doing. When arguments are demanded of us for why we do as we do, we need not be able to give such arguments, and consequently, we need not give such arguments. This means, conversely, that others need not give arguments to us when we demand

---

93 Richard Rorty, 'Response to Jürgen Habermas', in Robert B. Brandom (ed.), *Rorty and His Critics* (Malden, 2000), p. 61. Rorty here refers to Jürgen Habermas, 'Rortys pragmatische Wende', *Deutsche Zeitschrift für Philosophie*, 44 (1996): 739.

arguments of them. In a situation where somebody does something wrong, this is especially disturbing, since it can easily be felt that here, the other *must* give arguments for what she does. For such a demand to have any force, however, we have to be able to show her something that at least indicates that what she does is wrong. This means that showing this precedes the demand for arguments. In Chapter 6, I will discuss how we can try to show this, but here I want to say simply that when someone demands arguments of us for why we do as we do, we need not be able to give such arguments, and this does not generally delegitimize our ways of doing what we do.

MacIntyre and Traditions

At this point, I want to call attention to the differences between what I just have said and Alasdair MacIntyre's discussion of traditions, in order to anticipate a possible misunderstanding of what I have been trying to say here. Part of MacIntyre's problem is that there are many alternative answers to the question about the character of rationality, which results in conflicts which are particularly difficult to handle, since a disagreement about rationality is a disagreement about how one should proceed in order to solve this disagreement.[94] In order to understand this problem, a prerequisite to solving it,[95] MacIntyre talks about rational enquiry as embodied in traditions, where standards of rational justification develop and change.[96] Within a tradition, there are common criteria in the form of overlapping problems and overlapping understandings of progress, and it is therefore possible to compare and evaluate previous and later thinkers in the tradition with each other.[97]

The problem with MacIntyre's reasoning is firstly that it is not clear how different traditions are to be distinguished.[98] MacIntyre says that a tradition is not some sort of community, but rather some sort of continuity in debate and enquiry.[99] To say that persons A and B reason differently because they belong to different traditions is then not informative, for the concept 'tradition' can only be used to explain these connections and differences between persons if it were possible to detect traditions independently of how the traditions differed regarding rationality. If this is so, MacIntyre has not helped us to understand the problem better, as he said he would. If MacIntyre would say that a tradition is something which could be detected independently of its understanding of rationality, however, the hypothesis that this

---

94 Alasdair MacIntyre, *Whose Justice? Which Rationality?* (London, 1988), pp. 2 and 4.

95 Ibid., pp. 9–10.

96 Ibid., p. 7.

97 Ibid., p. 328.

98 Amy Allen claims that this is not only unclear, but that it is extremely difficult for MacIntyre to demarcate a sharp boundary between one tradition and the next. Allen argues, however, in another way than I do. See Amy Allen, 'MacIntyre's Traditionalism', *The Journal of Value Inquiry*, 31 (1997): 522–3.

99 MacIntyre, *Whose Justice? Which Rationality?*, pp. 12 and 327.

something could explain our differences regarding rationality would be a doubtful empirical hypothesis. It is, of course, true that there are different cultures and the like, but these are not so distinctively separated from each other as MacIntyre thinks. Our lives are rather lived where many different 'traditions' – if the word is to be understood as something which could be detected independently of its understanding of rationality – cross and intermingle, so debates between them take, in most cases, a much less confrontational character.

Secondly, MacIntyre's examples of traditions in *Whose Justice? Which Rationality?*, Aristotelianism, Augustinian Christianity, the Scottish 'common sense' tradition and modern liberalism are not what I am after. When we grow up, we learn how to reason, but this is not done in relation to philosophical traditions of this kind, unless in a very indirect way.

Thirdly, it seems as if MacIntyre says that you should remain faithful to your tradition.[100] Of course, there can be reasons for this in some cases, but there are hardly any good arguments for why you should take that attitude generally.

Rationality without the Demand for Universality

As we saw above, the demand for universality distorts the character of rationality, by overlooking how rationality is connected to our situatedness. In a case of vast disagreement it is mostly not possible to reconcile the disagreement by using such words as 'rational' or 'reasonable',[101] so saying in such a situation to somebody that she is irrational hardly helps us reconciling the disagreement, but merely makes the disagreement visible in another way. The word 'rational' has important functions in our lives, however, but so far, not much has been said here about how rationality could be understood without the demand for universality. As a beginning of doing that, I will point at some uses of the word 'rational' which are interesting and illuminating,

---

100 Ibid., pp. 393–4.

101 I do not distinguish between 'reasonable' and 'rational'. Those who do, use 'rational' as the more abstract and philosophical, connected to mathematics, proofs, principles, coherence, consistency, necessity, the *a priori*, the unchanging, and the like, whereas 'reasonable' has a more practical touch; see Paul Ricoeur, *From Text to Action: Essays in Hermeneutics, II*, trans. Kathleen Blamey and John B. Thompson (London, 1991), p. 188. This distinction between rational and reasonable has its background in a distinction between instrumental/technical rationality (*Zweckrationalität*) and a rationality, called reasonability, which has to do with values and is sensitive to the context. As has already been seen and will be seen, I argue that technical rationality, understood as a set of formulated principles or the like, is insufficient in the sense that it cannot by itself determine how it is to be applied in concrete cases or when it has to be developed or changed, which means that such a distinction is unhelpful. This means that it is not possible to uphold a sharp distinction between 'reasonable' and 'rational', and the distinction is then useful only for limited purposes. Jürgen Habermas makes the same point, but argues in another way than I do; see Jürgen Habermas, *The Philosophical Discourse of Modernity: Twelve Lectures*, trans. Frederick Lawrence (Cambridge, MA, 1987), pp. 315–16.

without claiming that these are the only ways in which this word is used. Thus, what I say below does not exhaust the meaning of 'rationality'.

To ask whether a belief is rational or irrational is at least to ask whether one has the right to hold the belief. The question is, however, when you have that right and when you do not have it. One way to answer that question is to say that you have it when you are able to motivate to those around you as to why you have come to believe what you believe. It is here not necessary that they become convinced of what you believe. It is rather a question of making them still respect you, although you have changed in some respects: making them see that you are the same person as before, that you have not been cheated, and so on. Rationality is thus here a matter of integrating the person you are now with the person you once were. Since we can belong to several communities and have different people around us, it is possible that some say that your holding a certain belief is rational, whereas others say that it is irrational, although the belief and the motivation are the same.

This way of using 'rational' is an example of a more general way of using the word. To be rational is here to do things in the way they are to be done, for example to find out what time it is by looking at a watch and not by just guessing.[102] In the above example, where I discussed the acquisition of beliefs, to be rational was to acquire beliefs in the way beliefs are to be acquired.

This way of using 'rational' is only of use, however, when you and the person you are talking to start out from the same view of how beliefs are to be acquired.[103] If you do not, you will hardly be able to motivate your beliefs in a way which she will appreciate. The word 'rational' can also be used in situations where you and the person you are in disagreement with start out from different views of how beliefs are to be acquired, however. In such situations, to say that the other is irrational does not add anything to the disagreement, though – that is, using words such as 'rational' or 'irrational' is not helpful in reconciling the disagreement. In order to secure a fruitful discussion in such a situation, you must work for some kind of mutual understanding first.

However, is not the word 'rational' also used in order to effect changes in our present ways of doing things? Do we not want to do things in a more rational way? It thus seems like I have left out something important, and more therefore needs to be said concerning rationality.

---

102 See Pär Segerdahl, *Språkteorier och språkspel: Fem moderna språkteorier ur en Wittgensteininspirerad synvinkel* (Lund, 1998), pp. 162–3.

103 This is not to say that the view which you and your interlocutor start out from necessarily is your view. It suffices that this view is your interlocutor's, and that you assume it for the sake of argument in order to show her what you want to show. Cf. Wouter H. Slob, *Dialogical Rhetoric: An Essay on Truth and Normativity after Postmodernism* (Dordrecht, 2002), pp. 97–8; Jeffrey Stout, *Democracy and Tradition* (Princeton, NJ, 2004), pp. 73–5.

The Importance of Dissatisfaction

Our wish for universality, in the sense in which the word has been used in this chapter, originates and remains because of our desire for change and progress. Moreover, we believe and know that we make progress, at least occasionally and to some extent. Even if we are situated, does humanity at its best nevertheless not have the ability to free itself from its situatedness, whether often or very seldom? Or is it not at least important to entertain the wish and the endeavour to free oneself from one's situatedness, as this is our only hope?

It is especially important to address these questions of change and progress in relation to religious beliefs. Let me give two examples. It does not suffice to point to the difficulty of convincing others of the superiority of democracy and say that religious belief is as epistemologically unproblematic as the belief in democracy.[104] Nor does it suffice to say that since there are no philosophical arguments which are interesting and substantial as well as universally convincing, it is no problem that there are no conclusive and universally convincing arguments for or against the claim that God exists.[105] Of course, if there are no such arguments in general, the demand for such arguments when it comes to the belief that God exists is pointless. This does not mean that the absence of such arguments is no problem, however. It is on the contrary important to see that there is a problem here, a problem which is not unique to the belief that God exists. The reasons why it does not suffice to say these two things are then, firstly, that although you are unable to show everybody the superiority of democracy as well as unable to show everybody that your beliefs on religious questions are right, this does not mean that the attempt to convince others should be given up. Of course it would be great to have an argument which would convince everybody that what you consider bad really is bad, and it is thus a practical problem that we have no such arguments in the case of democracy or in the case of religion. If we had, we would get rid of loads of problems as if by a stroke of magic. If we give up this attempt, we end up legitimizing not only our own beliefs, but also beliefs of others which strike us as horrible (unless we define 'religious' in some peculiar way, everybody finds *some* religious belief horrible). Secondly, exclusively defending one's own beliefs results in the opportunity of changing one's own beliefs, and so making progress, getting lost. Here, I will focus on the latter of these two problems, saving the former for Chapter 6. Hence, my point is that although religious beliefs are not epistemologically problematic, as has been shown in previous chapters, this does not mean that they could not be problematic in other respects, so the discussion must continue.

---

104 Jerome Gellman, for example, argues in this way. See Jerome Gellman, 'Religious Diversity and the Epistemic Justification of Religious Belief', *Faith and Philosophy*, 10 (1993): 350–51.

105 Mikael Stenmark argues in this way. See Mikael Stenmark, 'The End of the Theism–atheism Debate?', *Religious Studies*, 34 (1998): 267.

Ethnocentrism, meaning that the existence of other opinions and ways of living does not delegitimize ours and that a change of beliefs always starts from where we are, can become a trap if it is not combined with an emphasis on our resources for development, that there is an aspect of development in our notion of rationality.[106] Up until now, the way of using the word 'rational' we have concentrated upon has been when it is used to draw our attention to how things are done when they are done in the way they are to be done. The word 'rational' can be used in another context, however, when it is a question of changing the way things are done, rather than doing them in the usual way.

This aspect of development can on the one hand be described as something normal,[107] on the other as something which cannot be captured by formalizable rules or argumentative procedures.[108] On the one hand, it can be described as something normal: when we exceed and evaluate different activities, we do this as a matter of doing something the way it is to be done, by doing it in the light of other objectives. These procedures of evaluation can in their turn be evaluated, and when we do this, we do it again in the light of more overarching objectives. The word 'rational' here does not guide our evaluations, but we call the improved activity which is the result of the evaluation rational.[109] On the other hand, this aspect of development can be described as something which cannot be captured by formalizable rules or argumentative procedures: when we try to make things better, this is not always done in such a systematic way. Sometimes we just feel that something is wrong, without being able to say exactly what. This feeling may then be a starting point for a change in our present way of doing things. This work for change need not be systematic – it can be a matter of just trying out different things and seeing what happens. Sometimes this leads to a failure, but sometimes it makes one satisfied. The new way of doing things then replaces the old one, and we may speak of progress, since the new way is better, but it need not be possible to say exactly what its being better consists of. The important point here is that being rational is not just doing things in the way they are to be done, but can also be to try to do something new and better in such an unsystematic way.[110] The new and better may be called a more rational way of doing things than the old one, but this need not be said with reference to a set of criteria of rationality which is unaffected by the change.

Of course, many factors can account for why we do things in new ways. One such factor is technical development, which causes new ways of acting. We cannot use only such 'outer' factors to describe change, however, since the technical development itself is a result of human activity. Central here is the feeling of dissatisfaction: things

---

106 Cf. Thompson, 'Richard Rorty on Truth, Justification and Justice', p. 35.
107 See Segerdahl, *Språkteorier och språkspel*, pp. 164–5.
108 See Kompridis, 'So We Need Something Else for Reason to Mean': 285.
109 See Segerdahl, *Språkteorier och språkspel*, pp. 164–5.
110 See Kompridis, 'So We Need Something Else for Reason to Mean': 282–6.

are not as good as they could be, we must try to make them better.[111] Exactly in what respects things are not as good as they could be and in what direction things are to be changed are not given, however – this is a central area of disagreement.

One factor in the change for new ways of doing things is thus ourselves. That we are situated does not mean that we have no resources for changing the situation.[112] Therefore, to be situated does not mean to be stuck in one place for ever. This is not a matter of freeing oneself from one's situatedness, but of freeing oneself from particular situations. In the same way as our present situation is not anything which has been here for ever, but is a result of previous developments, we are moving away from our present situation towards new ones.

That being dissatisfied is an important characteristic of human beings does not mean that a situation where all resources for change are exhausted is necessarily impossible. However, what we mean by rationality is closely connected to change. If there were no critical aspect to rationality, it would not be what we call rationality, and this aspect must therefore not be forgotten when trying to describe rationality.

---

111 There could be said to be a Faustian element to the understanding of rationality elaborated here, which to some would make it problematical. 'Faustian' is then said to be the proper description of the spirit of Western culture, a culture striving for permanent economic growth by means of domination of nature, which leads to ecological problems. See, for example, Georg Henrik von Wright, 'Dante between Ulysses and Faust', in Monika Asztalos, John E. Murdoch and Ilkka Niiniluoto (eds), *Acta Philosophica Fennica 48: Knowledge and the Sciences in Medieval Philosophy. Proceedings of the Eighth International Congress of Medieval Philosophy, Volume I* (1990), p. 8. Marshall Berman, *All That Is Solid Melts Into Air: The Experience of Modernity* (New York, 1982), pp. 75–85, contains many different examples of this way of understanding the word 'Faustian'. This reading of Goethe's *Faust* (Johann Wolfgang von Goethe, *Faust, Parts One and Two*, trans. George Madison Priest (Chicago, IL, 1952)) can be summed up shortly in the following way.

Faust makes a pact with Mephistopheles: in this world, Mephistopheles will be Faust's servant, in the next, Faust will be Mephistopheles's. Mephistopheles promises Faust that he will experience joy and pleasures, but Faust does not believe that he will ever be satisfied: 'If to the moment I shall ever say: / "Ah, linger on, thou art so fair!" / Then may you fetters on me lay, / Then will I perish, then and there!'; ibid., p. 41. At the end of the play, Faust is leading a project of diking in land from the sea, and when he sees people at work on this project, he begs the moment to linger on and dies; ibid., p. 281. However, his soul is saved by angels, since 'Who e'er aspiring, struggles on, / For him there is salvation'; ibid., p. 290.

In one sense, there could be said to be a Faustian element to the understanding of rationality elaborated here: being rational is being unable to settle down anywhere except in the work for improvement of the human situation. This does not mean that this understanding of rationality is bound up with the problematic side of Faustianism, however. That the ability to be dissatisfied, which makes progress (whatever we mean by that word) possible, at the same time can give rise to the opposite of progress means that we can never stop questioning, that we can never rest assured that we now are on the secure road towards complete happiness – the ability to be dissatisfied also has an important role to play here.

112 Cf. Hilary Putnam, *Realism and Reason: Philosophical Papers, Volume 3* (Cambridge, 1983), p. 240.

Nikolas Kompridis stresses how such an oblivion drains reason of utopian energy, since reason is then no longer understood in terms of individual and cultural human emancipation, which implies that we can no longer make sense of attempts to change ourselves and the world as a rational activity.[113] Using the term 'reason' here obscures the matter, however, since it may lead one to believe that we all have a distinctive faculty which leads us towards a common goal, and that irreconcilable conflicts are not possible. However, it is possible to formulate Kompridis's point without using this word.

Rationality without Criteria

The understanding of reason which drains it of utopian energies is, according to Kompridis, the understanding according to which reason is governed by rules or is a matter of applying criteria laid down in advance. This understanding drains reason of utopian energies because it makes rational, comprehensive change impossible. This shows, however, that a change of central beliefs cannot be deduced, is not a matter of applying criteria. When we change some central beliefs, we can call this a rational process without our being able to show those that stick to the beliefs we once had that the ones we now have are better than the old beliefs. Instead of understanding what it is to be rational as only a matter of deducing and applying criteria, Kompridis stresses our capacity for transformation by means of creativity and imagination.[114]

Furthermore, if being rational is expressed criterially, in explicit rules, this would impose a limitation to our notion of rationality, a limitation which is quite alien to the idea of rationality.[115] To say that being rational is a matter of applying criteria laid down in advance means that there are definite limitations to what rationality could be, limitations set in advance which cannot be overcome, at least not rationally. The creative and innovative aspects of rationality are then lost.[116]

Therefore trying to develop lists of factors, accounting for when the movement from some central beliefs to other central beliefs is a rational progress, in cases where the latter cannot be deduced from the former by means of criteria,[117] is at best theoretically interesting and practically of significance heuristically, and at worst dangerous. What is central is not such factors, but the creative aspect of rationality, which at best is unaffected by these factors, at worst fettered. Such factors would, in the perspective of the creativity of rationality, only be of interest retrospectively, as a matter of theoretically giving an account of what has already been done.

---

113 Kompridis, 'So We Need Something Else for Reason to Mean': 273.

114 Kompridis, 'So We Need Something Else for Reason to Mean': 282–3 and 288. Cf. also Michael Rosen, 'The Role of Rules', *International Journal of Philosophical Studies*, 9 (2001): 373–4 and 380–81.

115 Cf. Kompridis, 'So We Need Something Else for Reason to Mean': esp. 282–3. Cf. further Putnam, *Reason, Truth and History*, p. 111–13.

116 Cf. Rosen, 'The Role of Rules': 380.

117 As Taylor (*Philosophical Arguments*, pp. 43–53) and Kompridis ('So We Need Something Else for Reason to Mean': 276) try to do.

Prospectively, such factors may fetter the creative aspect of rationality: it is possible that we in future cases find that we have to do things which are not in accord with any of these factors. Hence, every expression of rationality may sooner or later need to be questioned, in the name of rationality itself.

There is also a second problem with understanding rationality criterially, a problem which has already been hinted at in Chapter 2. When discussing Wittgenstein's remarks on following rules, I pointed out that rules cannot state how they are to be applied and thus guarantee that a person who understands the rule always applies it in the right way.[118] If there were a rule for how a specific rule is to be applied, we would need another rule for how this rule is to be applied, and so on *ad infinitum*. Formal terms cannot therefore describe rationality exhaustively. Of course, rules can be formulated, and formulations can be made more clear, to rule out some specific misunderstandings. What Wittgenstein objects to is the idea that the ability to speak, count and so on can be analysed exhaustively in terms of rules, the idea that we are *guided* by such formalizable rules, the idea that such rules could *explain* how we know what the right application of a rule is. The reason why this idea does not hold is that no matter how carefully we formulate such a rule, such a formulation can never eliminate the possibility of its being misunderstood and misapplied.[119]

Being rational is thus, among other things, to be able to apply rules in new cases in the right way. This ability is not a matter of automatic or mechanical operation, as if the application were a matter of deduction. It is rather a matter of sound judgement. Gadamer writes:

> ... the ordering of life by the rules of law and morality is incomplete and needs productive supplementation. Judgement is necessary in order to make a correct evaluation of the concrete instance. ... Every judgement about something intended in its concrete individuality (e.g., the judgment required in a situation that calls for action) is – strictly speaking – a judgment about a special case.[120]

---

118 Rather, the reverse is true: we say that a person understands the rule when she applies it in the right way. See Wittgenstein, *Remarks on the Foundations of Mathematics*, pp. 192 and 317 (§§ III:66 and VI:15).

119 See Wittgenstein, *Philosophical Investigations*, pp. 63–9 (§§ 185–202).

120 Gadamer, *Truth and Method*, pp. 38–9. Translation of Gadamer, *Wahrheit und Methode*, pp. 44–5: '... ist die Durchordnung des Lebens durch die Regeln des Rechts und der Sitte eine unvollständige, der produktiven Ergänzung bedürftige. Es bedarf der Urteilskraft, die konkreten Fälle richtig einzuschätzen. ... Jedes Urteil über ein in seiner konkreten Individualität Gemeintes, wie es die uns begegnenden Situationen des Handelns von uns verlangen, ist streng genommen ein Urteil über einen Sonderfall.' Gadamer exaggerates: every situation that calls for action is, of course, not so unique that the judgement required must be characterized as a judgement about a special case. However, Gadamer's point is not affected by this.

Gadamer is, of course, not the first to have realized that rules need application, which in its turn cannot be governed by further rules. In Gadamer's case, the influence comes mainly from Aristotle and Kant. See Aristotle, *The Nicomachean Ethics*, pp. 101–2, 105, 107–8 (1139a and 1140a–1141b); Kant, *Critique of Pure Reason*, p. 268 (A 133/B 172).

This second problem (concerning application of rules in new cases) with understanding rationality criterially is connected to the first (concerning how rules set limits to change): the difference between new and creative ways of talking and acting (which I focused on above) and old and conventional ones (which I focus on here) is a matter of degree, since to act conventionally can require some creativity when it is done in new circumstances. However, the creativity of rationality which I focused on above cannot be captured by the rules which are in focus here. In the cases I focus on here, the acting is in accord with already existing ways of acting, and acting in that way requires sound judgement, but in the cases above, new ways of acting were established.

There is also a third problem with understanding rationality criterially. John McDowell objects to the idea of our being guided by formalizable rules and explicit criteria by saying that no matter how thoughtful one was in formulating the rule, cases could turn up in which a mechanical application of the rule would strike one as wrong, and this not because one had changed one's mind.[121] The important point is that every rule may have exceptions.[122] Although no completely new way of acting must be established in such a case, it is possible that the acting which the rule suggests when interpreted in the right way – an interpretation which cannot be captured by rules – strikes one as wrong, which means that the rule needs modification. Of course, rules cannot be given for how rules should be modified – if they could, that would not be a matter of modification; no modification would then be needed.

Conclusion

That we are situated means that a *completely* impartial and value-free perspective is not possible. If one pays attention to this fact, one becomes less inclined to believe that it *must* be possible to reconcile every disagreement, and hence also less inclined to adopt a relativist position – that is, less inclined to give up making the distinction between true and false in a certain context. According to the demand for universality, every statement has to be argued for by means of conclusive arguments, arguments which show that the statement in question follows from other statements which have already been proven in this way or are self-evident. These arguments must be appreciated by, in principle, everybody. To be rational is then to only hold beliefs which can be shown to be correct in this way. However, we have seen how commitment, embodiment, upbringing and being situated in society and history are not obstacles to knowledge, true beliefs, rationality and the like, but on the contrary, conditions for them in the role they play in our lives. This means that what separates

---

121 John McDowell, *Mind, Value, and Reality* (Cambridge – London, 1998), p. 58.

122 Cf. Donald Davidson, *Problems of Rationality* (Oxford, 2004), p. 42, where he writes that principles can have exceptions, exceptions which cannot be enumerated on a finite list. If all exceptions could be enumerated on a finite list, no principle would have exceptions: it would then be possible to replace every principle which seemed to have exceptions with an exceptionless, but more complicated, principle.

us from others, what in a way makes universal agreement hard to arrive at, are not obstacles to, but on the contrary conditions for knowledge, true beliefs, rationality and the like in the role they play in our lives. Therefore, the conception of rationality connected to the demand for universality distorts the character of rationality. This means that being rational does not imply that you necessarily have to be able to show someone with other beliefs that you are right.

At the same time, however, I have tried to retain what was good in the demand for universality. This has been done mainly be stressing the importance of dissatisfaction and its connection to rationality. It is hence important to think from the perspective of others, to bear in mind that they whom we call irrational can say the same thing about us. However, thinking from the perspective of others is done from the position which is inhabited by *us*. The point is thus that we need both aspects: we need to listen to others and be open to what they have to say, since this could make us change our minds and make improvements, but we also need to be able to say that they are wrong or irrational, even in situations where they can say the same thing about us and we cannot show them that we are right. My discussions of rules entail that there are no general rules for when we ought to be open to others and when we ought not to be open to others, among other reasons, since if we had to follow a particular set of rules, rational comprehensive change would be impossible. This would be impossible since a comprehensive change includes a change of the rules, which means that the change cannot be guided by rules.

In this chapter, my discussion has mainly been conducted in terms of rationality. As has been obvious, the question of truth has also come to the surface now and then: I have, for example, claimed that being rational does not imply that you have to be able to show someone with other beliefs that your beliefs are true. That the question of truth has come to the surface now and then is not so strange, since rationality and truth are closely linked. I will here only mention two connections: firstly, to be rational when, for example, answering the question 'What time is it?' is to do things in the way they are to be done – that is, look at a watch and thereafter answer the question. A true answer is one which accords with the result one would have obtained if one did things in the way they are to be done – that is, if one did things in the rational way, in this case an answer which accords with the result one would have obtained if one looked at a watch.[123] Secondly, to be rational is to be attentive to mistakes and to try to eliminate possible sources of error. This is connected to the use of 'true' when we use it in saying such things as 'I believe so, but it is perhaps not true.'

Moreover, the focus on the distinction between true and false makes it possible for us to say *something* about many contexts at the same time. Of course, how the distinction between true and false is made differs from context to context, so a further analysis has to enter into more specific details. However, in so far as we do talk about true and false in different contexts, these different uses of the words 'true' and 'false' are not totally isolated from each other, and an analysis of the concept

---

123 Segerdahl, *Språkteorier och språkspel*, p. 162.

of truth can therefore be helpful in our attempt to understand what it takes to have a fruitful discussion in different contexts, but we must not believe that we arrive at an essence of the concept of truth by means of such an analysis.

For these reasons, in the next chapter I will analyse the concept of truth in its connection to my general problem. This discussion will underline additionally what I have said here, that one can rightly say that one is right and that somebody else is wrong without being able to show this to her. The discussion will thus primarily aim to show that it is possible to understand the concept of truth without the demand for universality. Furthermore, it will be shown that it is possible to understand the concept of truth without appealing to a specific non-trivial criterion of truth, since that would lead to the same problems I have pointed at here in connection with rules. This understanding of the concept of truth must not distort what it is supposed to be an understanding of, and for that reason I will concentrate on the aspect of the concept of truth which seems to be hard to retain without the demand for universality, the objectivity of truth – that is, the fact that the truth of most beliefs is independent of my believing them to be true.

Chapter 5

The Objectivity of Truth

In this chapter, I will show that it is possible to give an account of the concept of truth, and that the call to change and progress which I suggested at the end of the last chapter is connected to it, without the demand for universality. The distinction between believing that something is true and its being true is therefore to be upheld, as far as it can be upheld, without presupposing that it is possible to place oneself in an external position where one is liberated from one's commitment, body, upbringing and society, a position from where we can compare what we believe with what is true, and in that way change our beliefs in the right direction. For reasons explicated in the last chapter, this account of the concept of truth must not be given by appealing to a specific non-trivial criterion of truth. To show that this is possible, I will use Donald Davidson as a conversational partner. I will begin by giving an extensive background to Davidson's understanding of the objectivity of truth, concentrating on his idea of radical interpretation. After having explicated Davidson's understanding of the objectivity of truth, I will discuss it, as well as its consequences, critically.

Radical Interpretation: Background

To understand Davidson's discussion of the concept of truth, I believe it is helpful to start with his idea of radical interpretation. When Davidson introduces this idea for the first time,[1] it is in the context of a discussion of theories of meaning. That Davidson introduces the concept in order to shed some light upon linguistic meaning is crucial for understanding it. As becomes all the more evident in later papers, such as 'A Nice Derangement of Epitaphs',[2] meaning is here not to be seen *in abstracto*, unrelated to context and person. Davidson therefore writes the following:

> … when we talk of what words mean, what names name, what it is for an utterance to be true, we must start with cases where communication succeeds, by which I mean occasions on which an audience interprets a speaker's words as the speaker intends and expects those words to be interpreted. Unless there are such occasions, talk of meaning is empty. How we use the notion of meaning in cases where a speaker's intentions are for one or

---

1   Davidson, *Inquiries into Truth and Interpretation*, p. 27. Davidson is still using Quine's term 'radical translation' here.

2   Davidson, *Truth, Language, and History*, pp. 89–107.

another reason frustrated seems to me relatively unimportant as long as we keep cases distinct.[3]

Radical interpretation is thus a way to shed some light upon communication, upon what is necessary for successful communication.[4]

The main reason behind this way of understanding meaning is that philosophical accounts of meaning have always been given with the intention of saying something about communication, but have often failed to do so because of a tendency to see language as a system of conventions and rules, expressed in dictionaries and grammar-books. (Why such accounts are a failure will be explained in a moment.) Davidson, however, directs our attention to uses of language which might seem to be bizarre, but which are nonetheless not hard to understand: 'The plane will be landing momentarily', 'He wented to the store.'[5] What these sayings draw our attention to is our ability to interpret words we have never heard before, something which is an important part of linguistic competence, and a philosophical account of meaning must therefore take that ability into account. Davidson gives an example:

> Take proper names. In small, isolated groups everyone may know the names everyone else knows, and so have ready in advance of a speech encounter a theory that will, without correction, cope with the names to be employed. But even this semantic paradise will be destroyed by each new nickname, visitor, or birth.[6]

That Davidson here uses the word 'theory' is misleading, since he does not intend to say that we actually know or have such theories, merely that our ability to interpret can be described as the possession of a theory.[7] In a moment, I will say a little more about Davidson's misleading formulations.

What Davidson is interested in is, as I have said, what is necessary for linguistic communication, and his conclusion from the discussion presented above is that a common language, in the sense of shared rules and conventions, is not necessary for communication, for the simple reason, to sum up, that '... almost no two people share all words. Even during a conversation, each is apt to use words the other did not know before the conversation began, and so cannot belong to a practice the speakers shared in detail ...'.[8] This is not, however, to say that there are no reasons

3   Donald Davidson, 'Reply to Andreas Kemmerling', in Ralf Stoecker (ed.), *Reflecting Davidson: Donald Davidson Responding to an International Forum of Philosophers* (Berlin, 1993), p. 117.

4   Davidson, *Truth, Language, and History*, p. 115.

5   The examples are taken from ibid., p. 115.

6   Ibid., p. 99.

7   Davidson, *Problems of Rationality*, p. 131; Davidson, *Truth, Language, and History*, pp. 95–6 and 112–13.

8   Davidson, *Truth, Language, and History*, p. 115.

for speaking as others speak or as oneself has spoken in the past,[9] only that this is not necessary for successful communication.

Radical interpretation now comes in as a way of giving an account of how we can come to understand what somebody is saying in cases where we do not know what her words mean.[10] Radical interpretation is here not something which stands out from learning from experience in general:

> ... we have erased the boundary between knowing a language and knowing our way around in the world generally. ... There is no more chance of regularising, or teaching, this process [the process of interpreting somebody's speech] than there is of regularising or teaching the process of creating new theories to cope with new data in any field – for that is what this process involves.[11]

Before going into Davidson's account of radical interpretation, something ought to be said about what Davidson claims this account shows. Firstly, Davidson does not say that radical interpretation must be possible – that is, he does not exclude the possibility of other ways of getting to know what somebody means, only that radical interpretation is possible, which he tries to show.[12] Secondly, Davidson does not think that in everyday life, we constantly reflect on what others mean, and formulate theories of interpretation. Davidson is not interested in answering the question of what we actually do when we come to understand the speech of others, but is interested in the philosophical question of what is necessary and sufficient for such understanding.[13] Thirdly, it might seem that what Davidson is saying is defective in the same way as the confused way of thinking about rules I discussed, with the help of Wittgenstein, in Chapter 2. There, we saw that the thought that we *always* interpret rules is confused, since that entails that following rules is impossible. Instead we saw, as Wittgenstein says:

---

9   See Davidson, 'Reply to Andreas Kemmerlin', p. 119; Donald Davidson, 'Reply to Peter Pagin', in Urszula M. Żegleń (ed.), *Donald Davidson: Truth, Meaning and Knowledge* (London, 1999), p. 73; Akeel Bilgrami, 'Norms and Meaning', in Ralf Stoecker (ed.), *Reflecting Davidson: Donald Davidson Responding to an International Forum of Philosophers* (Berlin, 1993), p. 134.

10   Also, in all the usual cases where the way the other speaks causes no problem, but we understand her without reflecting upon how we come to understand what she is saying, radical interpretation is, according to Davidson, relevant. If it is asked *how* you know that you understand what the other is saying, radical interpretation can provide a way to answer this question. Hence: 'All understanding of the speech of another involves radical interpretation'; Davidson, *Inquiries into Truth and Interpretation*, p. 125.

11   Davidson, *Truth, Language, and History*, p. 107.

12   Donald Davidson, 'Reply to Jerry Fodor and Ernest Lepore', in Ralf Stoecker (ed.), *Reflecting Davidson: Donald Davidson Responding to an International Forum of Philosophers* (Berlin, 1993), pp. 77–8; Davidson, *Problems of Rationality*, pp. 31 and 35.

13   Davidson, *Problems of Rationality*, pp 131–3; Davidson, *Truth, Language, and History*, pp. 111–12 and 324.

...that there is a way of grasping a rule which is *not* an *interpretation*, but which is exhibited in what we call 'obeying the rule' and 'going against it' in actual cases. Hence there is an inclination to say: every action according to the rule is an interpretation. But we ought to restrict the term 'interpretation' to the substitution of one expression of the rule for another.[14]

However, Davidson uses 'interpretation' in a different way to Wittgenstein. For Davidson, an interpretation of an expression is not another expression: somebody who understands an expression is simply said by Davidson to possess an interpretation, no matter how this understanding manifests itself. Of course, we need words to describe the understanding – that is, the interpretation – of an expression, but these words are not the interpretation.[15] Another way to express this is to point to the fact that a T-sentence – that is, a sentence of the form '*s* is true if and only if *p*', which we will talk about more later – is not about relating two different sentences, but about giving the truth condition of an object-language sentence. This must, of course, be done in some language, but this language is a meta-language – that is, not something on the same level as the object-language. Fourthly, Davidson uses the word 'theory' in a way which is more confusing than helpful.[16] What is important to remember is that when Davidson talks about a hearer having a theory of interpretation, he does not intend to say that the hearer knows such a theory, merely that her interpretations are in accord with a theory.[17]

The big problem with Davidson's way of reasoning is his misleading formulations, which we have already seen when it comes to words such as 'interpretation' and 'theory'. Here is another example: '... when we talk of what words mean ... we must

---

14 Wittgenstein, *Philosophical Investigations*, p. 69e (§ 201): '... daß es eine Auffassung einer Regel gibt, die *nicht* eine *Deutung* ist; sondern sich, von Fall zu Fall der Anwendung, in dem äußert, was wir "der Regel folgen", und was wir "ihr entgegenhandeln" nennen. Darum besteht eine Neigung, zu sagen: jedes Handeln nach der Regel sei ein Deuten. "Deuten" aber sollte man nur nennen: einen Ausdruck der Regel durch einen anderen ersetzen.'

15 Davidson, *Truth, Language, and History*, pp. 112–13.

16 See Richard Rorty, 'Response to Donald Davidson', in Robert B. Brandom (ed.), *Rorty and His Critics* (Malden, 2000), p. 75. Rorty compares here, in a satirical way, Davidson's project with a scientist formulating the physiological and physical knowledge which would be necessary and sufficient for riding a bike. To talk about the theoretical knowledge which would be necessary and sufficient for understanding the speech of others could thus be misleading. For my purposes the structure of such a theory, that the theory is a theory of truth in Tarski's style, is not very important, since it is possible to make the points I want to without going into the details of this structure.

17 Davidson, *Problems of Rationality*, p. 131; Davidson, *Truth, Language, and History*, pp. 95–6 and 112–13. It is, of course, possible that even though Davidson says that he does not believe that we actually formulate theories of interpretation, but merely that we speak and understand in accord with a theory, he is still held captive by the idea that in our language use, some kind of theory construction takes place. See Martin Gustafsson, 'Systematic Meaning and Linguistic Diversity: The Place of Meaning-theories in Davidson's Later Philosophy', *Inquiry*, 41 (1998): 449.

start with cases where communication succeeds, by which I mean occasions on which an audience interprets a speaker's words as the speaker intends and expects those words to be interpreted'.[18] In order to avoid the risk of confusion, 'communication' should not be understood exclusively as conveying information, but as linguistic acting in general. Furthermore, 'intends' and 'expects' should not be understood as indicating that there is necessarily something which is in the head of the person who speaks when she speaks. What 'intention' means here is only that there is an answer to the question, 'what did you mean when you said p?'. Therefore, what I am going to do in the following is to point out how Davidson's idea of radical interpretation can be illuminating, without being committed to his way of formulating this idea.

Furthermore, what must be noticed is that the philosophical question about what meaning is can be about different, although related, things. Hence what Davidson does is not to give answers to all the questions that hide behind the phrase 'What is meaning?' One can thus very well agree with Davidson, but nevertheless say that there is another use of the word 'meaning' (and related words), which makes it possible to say, for example, 'When person A said x she meant y, but x does not mean y.' What Davidson says is that it is not necessary for successful communication that there be this form of meaning-in-a-language-such-as-English, and he is, of course, right in stressing that what a word means in a specific language, such as English, is not written in heaven, but is dependent on how people actually use expressions to communicate.

The point of the last two paragraphs in relation to radical interpretation is this. There is a basic level in language which is not to be distinguished from how we know our way around in the world generally. It is possible here to learn to speak not in the sense of learning a new foreign language, but in the sense of learning specific ways of acting linguistically. From these ways of acting linguistically, systems – that is, languages such as English – can be constructed for certain purposes, for example for the purpose of teaching foreigners a language they do not know. Within such systems, there are norms for correct and incorrect linguistic behaviour, but these norms are dependent on how we act linguistically, and these norms are not necessary – that is, we can diverge from them and nevertheless be understood. When two persons who both know the language speak with each other, talking about intention in order to explain meaning is not necessary. Talk about intentions comes up, for example, when there is something which is hard to understand, perhaps because some sentence is grammatically incomplete, or when something is hinted at which makes it necessary to read between the lines.

Radical Interpretation

Radical interpretation is, as I have already said, what a hearer is involved in when she tries to understand the speech of another, without prior knowledge of what the

---

18 Davidson, 'Reply to Andreas Kemmerling', p. 117.

words the speaker uses mean. The evidence for a theory, in Davidson's sense, of interpretation must therefore be available to someone who does not know how to interpret the utterances the theory is designed to cover.[19]

In 'Truth and Meaning',[20] Davidson argues that a theory of truth along the lines of Tarski's truth definitions, but modified in some ways, would be enough to provide us with an answer to the question of what it is for words to mean what they do.[21] A theory of meaning can thus be formulated as a theory which for every sentence *s* of the object-language entails a sentence (a so-called T-sentence) of the form '*s* is true if and only if *p*.' *p* is here any[22] meta-language sentence which is true if and only if *s* is true.[23] The T-sentences – for example, '"Es regnet" is true if and only if it rains' – are not the theory, but are entailed by the theory, and a theory of meaning can thus be tested by testing whether the T-sentences are true or not. The question then is what is evidence for the truth or falsity of T-sentences, for example '"Es regnet" is true if and only if it rains', or for that matter '"Es regnet" is true if and only if it snows.'

One problem with Davidson's theory of meaning is that it only deals with sentences that have truth-values, and not with interrogations and imperatives, for example.[24] This is not necessarily a fundamental problem for Davidson's account of radical interpretation, however. Firstly, if you are trying to understand the speech of another without prior knowledge of what the words she uses mean, you will no doubt have to interpret sentences with truth-values, even if there are also other sentences which must be interpreted. The sentences with truth-values are therefore important when interpreting the speech of another, and the interpretation of these sentences will be helpful when interpreting sentences without truth-values. Secondly, Davidson hints that concentrating on sentences with truth-values simplifies the process of interpretation, since the attitude of holding a sentence true is an attitude which is fairly simple to identify even before one is able to interpret *what* the speaker holds true,[25] but whether that is correct or not is an empirical question which should be investigated.

As I have already said, the evidence for the truth or falsity of T-sentences must be available to someone who does not know how to interpret the utterances the theory which the T-sentences are entailed by is designed to cover. Of course, the evidence cannot be that the T-sentence corresponds with what is stated in a dictionary – what we are after is what serves as evidence for the dictionary. The evidence for the truth or falsity of T-sentences is instead that the speaker whose language the theory which the T-sentences are entailed by is designed to cover holds various sentences true at

---

19 Davidson, *Inquiries into Truth and Interpretation*, p. 128.

20 Ibid., pp. 17–36.

21 Ibid., p. xv.

22 There are some restrictions on which sentences could replace *p*. See ibid., pp. xvi, 26, 173–9.

23 Ibid., p. 134.

24 Davidson hints that he is aware of this problem in Davidson, *Truth, Language, and History*, p. 167.

25 Davidson, *Inquiries into Truth and Interpretation*, pp. 134–5.

certain times and under specified circumstances.[26] The evidence for the truth of a T-sentence like '"Es regnet" is true if and only if it rains' is then that the sentence 'Es regnet' is held true by the speaker whom you want to interpret in those circumstances and at those times when you hold 'It rains' true. The T-sentence is entailed by a theory of meaning, so the evidence for the T-sentence is, indirectly, evidence for a theory of meaning.

Of course, the speaker may be wrong – that is, she may sometimes hold a sentence true which at this moment and in this circumstance is not true, so radical interpretation is about getting a best fit between sentences and circumstances.[27] Davidson formulates this interpretative principle in different ways on different occasions. In the essay 'Radical Interpretation', he talks about 'maximizing agreement'.[28] This is not to be taken literally, however, since sentences are infinite in number, but is to be understood as a matter of making the speaker right as often as possible,[29] so Davidson adopts the expression 'optimizing agreement' instead.[30] He also emphasizes that different sorts of agreements and disagreements have differing importance:

> Disagreement about theoretical matters may (in some cases) be more tolerable than disagreement about what is more evident; disagreement about how things look or appear is less tolerable than disagreement about how they are; disagreement about the truth of attributions of certain attitudes to a speaker by that same speaker may not be tolerable at all, or barely.[31]

Probable and explicable mistakes must also be taken into account.[32] The final formulation of what is called the principle of charity is that it is the intelligibility of the speaker which should be maximized.[33] It can be noticed here that this principle is not necessarily bound to sentences with truth-values, even if it is so for Davidson. The reason why this principle is necessary when interpreting will be discussed in the next section.

---

26 If one wants to include sentences without truth-value, one can thus, in an un-Davidsonian way, say that the evidence for the truth of an interpretation of a particular sentence is a matter of how, where and when the sentence to be interpreted is used by those whose utterances one wants to understand.

27 Davidson, *Inquiries into Truth and Interpretation*, pp. 135–6.

28 Ibid., p. 136.

29 Ibid.

30 Ibid., p. 169.

31 Ibid.. See also Davidson, *Problems of Rationality*, p. 157.

32 Davidson, *Inquiries into Truth and Interpretation*, pp. 136 and 282.

33 Ibid., p. xix.

The Principle of Charity as a Condition for Interpretation

To talk about 'charity', as Davidson does, is a little misleading. Charity is a virtue which we can try to develop, whereas charity here is not an option, but a condition for interpretation.[34] This means that an uncharitable interpretation is not conceivable, since it would not be what we call an interpretation. An interpretation, as we use the word, is hence charitable. What Davidson does is to show why this is so.

According to Davidson the radical interpreter must in the basic cases make the speaker right, according to the standards of the interpreter, on most cases.[35] ('Basic' and 'most' are used here to point to what I have already said: that disagreement about theoretical matters is often more tolerable than disagreements about what is more evident, that disagreement about how things look or appear is less tolerable than disagreement about how they are, and so on.) The main reason for this is the interdependence of belief and meaning. In the normal case, we can infer what someone believes from her utterances, since we can then assume that we know what the words she uses mean, but this is exactly what we cannot assume in the case of

---

34 Davidson, *Inquiries into Truth and Interpretation*, p. 197; Davidson, *Problems of Rationality*, pp. 72–3.

35 When it comes to religious belief, it sounds strange to say that an interpretation must make the other right, according to the standards of the interpreter, on most cases. Davidson's philosophy would sound strange if it entailed that all beliefs, including religious beliefs, were mainly right. However, Davidson uses the phrases 'in the basic cases' and 'on most cases'. This means that wrong beliefs can be detected, but only on the basis of other, true beliefs. Two persons can hence disagree about something if they have enough in common for their disagreement to make sense. Therefore, two persons can be in disagreement about whether it is meaningful to ask God to forgive one for one's sins if they are in agreement on what it is to ask somebody for forgiveness, and so on.

That wrong beliefs can be detected, but only on the basis of other, true beliefs, is a fact that critics of religious belief have often been aware of, and they have therefore tried to formulate naturalistic interpretations of religion in order to make sense of the disagreement. Such naturalistic interpretations are meant to show how religious beliefs arise from true beliefs which are not religious.

For examples of how Davidson's philosophy has been used in the philosophy of religion, see Terry F. Godlove, *Religion, Interpretation, and Diversity of Belief: The Framework Model from Kant to Durkheim to Davidson* (Cambridge, 1989); Hans H. Penner, 'Why Does Semantics Matter?', in Nancy K. Frankenberry and Hans H. Penner (eds), *Language, Truth, and Religious Belief: Studies in Twentieth-century Theory and Method in Religion* (Atlanta, GA, 1999); Nancy K. Frankenberry, 'Pragmatism, Truth, and the Disenchantment of Subjectivity', in Nancy K. Frankenberry and Hans H. Penner (eds), *Language, Truth, and Religious Belief: Studies in Twentieth-Century Theory and Method in Religion* (Atlanta, GA, 1999); Catherine M. Bell, '"The Chinese Believe in Spirits": Belief and Believing in the Study of Religion', in Nancy K. Frankenberry (ed.), *Radical Interpretation in Religion* (Cambridge, 2002). There is a problematic tendency in some of these, however, most obvious in Penner ('Why Does Semantics Matter', pp. 497–8), who writes that if Davidson's theory of truth is correct, the consequence is that religion is a system of propositional beliefs, beliefs differentiated from other beliefs solely by their reference to superhuman beings.

radical interpretation. Nor can we infer what the words someone uses mean from her utterances unless we know her beliefs, and making detailed sense of a person's beliefs cannot be done independently of making sense of her utterances.[36] Davidson's idea is then:

> ... to solve the problem of the interdependence of belief and meaning by holding belief constant as far as possible while solving for meaning. This is accomplished by assigning truth conditions to alien sentences that make native speakers right when plausibly possible, according, of course, to our own view of what is right. What justifies the procedure is the fact that disagreement and agreement alike are intelligible only against a background of massive agreement.[37]

Thus the principle does not rest on a charitable assumption about human intelligence that might turn out to be false[38] – if it did it would be an option and not a condition, as I explained above. What it rests on, according to Davidson, is, as was said above, the fact that disagreement and agreement are intelligible only against a background of massive agreement. What this means is that two persons could only be said to disagree, and hence also to agree, if there is something which they have in common which they disagree *on* – that is, there must be a common co-ordinate system on which to plot the different points of view.[39] A belief, whether the interpreter finds it to be true or false, relies for its identification on other beliefs, beliefs which the interpreter holds true.[40]

This is especially obvious when it comes to perceptual beliefs. The speaker can, of course, hold some false perceptual beliefs, and we must take probable and explicable mistakes into account, but these must be exceptions for there to be anything like interpretation, since we interpret sentences by identifying the circumstances in which they are uttered:[41] '... the interpreter interprets sentences held true (which is not to be distinguished from attributing beliefs) according to the events and objects in the outside world that cause the sentence to be held true'.[42] Of course, these true beliefs need not be held by the speaker explicitly, only implicitly. The same goes for logical entailments, where occasional mistakes by the speaker are possible, but general

---

36 See Davidson, *Inquiries into Truth and Interpretation*, pp. xviii, 27, 134–5, 142–4, 195. Of course, we can come to know some of what a person believes without her saying anything. For example, if a person tastes something and immediately spits it out, she probably finds the taste horrible. However, such an interpretation is dependent on some sort of principle of charity too: if it were not, there would not be anything which could explain why someone spitting out something indicates that she finds the taste horrible.

37 Ibid., p. 137.

38 Ibid.

39 Ibid., p. 184.

40 Davidson, *Subjective, Intersubjective, Objective*, p. 195.

41 See Davidson, *Problems of Rationality*, p. 48.

42 Davidson, *Subjective, Intersubjective, Objective*, p. 150.

errors remove every reason for attributing language and beliefs to the speaker.[43] The examples I will give in a moment will show how this is supposed to work.

Basically, the problems with giving reasons for the principle of charity are similar to the problems with giving reasons for induction. Induction seems to rest on the assumption that nature is uniform, that what happens now will happen in the future and so on – an assumption that might turn out to be false. This is not correct, however. If we did not use induction, there would not only be nothing like science, but nothing like learning from experience at all, which means that in such a case, it makes no sense to talk about seeing that nature is not uniform. That nature is uniform is at most a precondition for induction, not a reason for it. The same goes for interpretation: that human beings are similar is at most a precondition for interpretation and communication, not a reason for it. The relation between charity and interpretation is hence not optional, but conceptual, which, in a way, is a rejection of the meaningfulness of the question of why interpretation has to be charitable. That the relation is conceptual means that an uncharitable interpretation is not conceivable, since it would not be what we call an interpretation. An interpretation, as we use the word, is charitable.

When introducing one example of his idea, Davidson says: 'The way this problem [the problem of the interdependence of belief and meaning] is solved is best appreciated from undramatic examples.'[44] One advantage of the examples is also that they free us, at least partly, from Davidson's misleading way of formulating his ideas. I will therefore present some of Davidson's examples. The first one is this:

> If you see a ketch sailing by and your companion says, 'Look at that handsome yawl', you may be faced with a problem of interpretation. One natural possibility is that your friend has mistaken a ketch for a yawl, and has formed a false belief. But if his vision is good and his line of sight favourable it is even more plausible that he does not use the word 'yawl' quite as you do, and has made no mistake at all about the position of the jigger on the passing yacht. We do this sort of off the cuff interpretation all the time, deciding in favour of reinterpretation of words in order to preserve a reasonable theory of belief.[45]

What this example shows is, firstly, what it means to say that a false belief relies for its identification on other, true, beliefs: if you interpret your friend as having a false belief, you interpret him as having made a mistake about the position of the jigger on the passing yacht, and that presupposes that he believes that a yacht is passing, that he believes that it has a jigger, and so on. Secondly, the example shows what it means to take probable and explicable mistakes into account: whether the second interpretation (different uses of words and a true belief) is to be preferred to the first (the same use of words but a false belief) depends on whether his vision is sufficiently good and his line of sight sufficiently favourable to make the second interpretation more probable than the first. Thirdly, the example shows that the border between the

43 Davidson, *Inquiries into Truth and Interpretation*, p. 137.
44 Ibid., p. 196.
45 Ibid.

two cases (on the one hand the same use of words but a false belief, on the other hand different uses of words and a true belief) is not sharp. Of course, the friend could also be said to be wrong in the case of different uses of words and a true belief, since in that case he probably does not know how the words 'yawl' and 'ketch' are used.

The second example, also an example of how beliefs rely for their identification on other, true, beliefs, is this:

> I can believe a cloud is passing before the sun, but only because I believe there is a sun, that clouds are made of water vapour, that water can exist in liquid or gaseous form; and so on, without end. No particular list of further beliefs is required to give substance to my belief that a cloud is passing before the sun; but some appropriate set of related beliefs must be there. If I suppose that you believe a cloud is passing before the sun, I suppose you have the right sort of pattern of beliefs to support that one belief, and these beliefs I assume you to have must, to do their supporting work, be enough like my beliefs to justify the description of your belief as a belief that a cloud is passing before the sun.[46]

These beliefs – for example, the belief that there is a sun – which we must have in common are, as the example shows, often so self-evident that it is possible that we never formulate them for ourselves. However, if we attribute the belief that a cloud is passing before the sun to someone, our interpretation, irrespective of whether we think that the belief is true or false, must rely on some set of such beliefs even if neither we nor the speaker ever formulate these beliefs. Of course, this set of beliefs need not include such scientific beliefs as Davidson mentions in this example.

The third example is this:

> Each time a mouse appears nearby in good light and with the speaker oriented in the direction of the mouse, etc., the speaker utters what sounds to the interpreter like the same expression: 'Ratón'. When lighting is poor or the speaker inattentive, the response is less firmly correlated with mouse appearances. I think that unless there is a host of evidence against such an interpretation, the competent interpreter will take the speaker to mean by his words, and to believe, that there is a mouse present. What recommends this interpretation is the fact that the presence of a mouse has apparently in each case caused the speaker intentionally to utter the same expression, 'Ratón', and to utter it in an affirmative spirit.[47]

This example shows how beliefs rely for their identification on what causes them – that is, rely on the common environment. Of course the speaker may be wrong on some occasions, some more probable than others, as the example shows, and the interpreter's interpretation may of course be wrong or over-simplified. However, charity is a condition for interpretation in the sense that an interpretation which has no relation to the common environment would be completely arbitrary, and the speaker and the interpreter must therefore have many beliefs in common in order to disagree.

---

46 Ibid., p. 200.
47 Davidson, *Subjective, Intersubjective, Objective*, p. 196.

The fourth and last example is this:

> Let someone say ... 'There's a hippopotamus in the refrigerator'; am I necessarily right
> in reporting him as having said that there is a hippopotamus in the refrigerator? Perhaps;
> but under questioning he goes on, 'It's roundish, has a wrinkled skin, does not mind being
> touched. It has a pleasant taste, at least the juice, and it costs a dime. I squeeze two or
> three for breakfast.' After some finite amount of such talk we slip over the line where it
> is plausible or even possible to say correctly that he said there was a hippopotamus in
> the refrigerator, for it becomes clear he means something else by at least some of his
> words than I do. The simplest hypothesis so far is that my word 'hippopotamus' no longer
> translates his word 'hippopotamus'; my word 'orange' might do better.[48]

Here we have another example of what it means that a false belief relies for its
identification on other, true, beliefs. The example also shows in a good way that the
border between interpreting the speaker as holding a false belief, or as holding a true
belief but using the word 'hippopotamus' in a peculiar way, is not sharp. This means
that a clear line between synthetic false sentences about the world, and sentences
which are false since their words are used in a non-standard way ('A hippopotamus
is roundish, has a wrinkled skin, does not mind being touched, has a pleasant taste,
and costs a dime', for example), is not to be drawn. Thus a *sharp* analytic/synthetic-
distinction cannot be upheld (but some form of this distinction may be upheld),[49] but
there are, of course, mistakes which are more probable and less probable. At some
points, there are two possible interpretations: 'the speaker holds a false belief' and
'the speaker holds a true belief but uses the word "hippopotamus" in a peculiar way'
– that is, we have a case of indeterminacy of interpretation.[50]

The Impossibility of Massive Error

That a condition for interpretation is that we maximize the intelligibility of the speaker
means that we cannot come to find the speaker being massively wrong, as we have
seen. However, Davidson wants to make a stronger point: it is not only impossible
for an interpreter to *find* a speaker being massively wrong, but even impossible for
a speaker to *be* massively wrong. Davidson gives the following argument for this
claim:

> Why couldn't it happen that speaker and interpreter understand one another on the basis of
> shared but erroneous beliefs? This can, and no doubt often does, happen. But it cannot be
> the rule. For imagine for a moment an interpreter who is omniscient about the world, and

---

48 Davidson, *Inquiries into Truth and Interpretation*, pp. 100–101.

49 Davidson's rejection of this distinction is more radical than this, but his rejection is
made against a background of a Carnapian way of understanding the distinction. See Davidson,
Inquiries into Truth and Interpretation, pp. 187–9; Davidson, *Subjective, Intersubjective,
Objective*, pp. 144–5 and 195.

50 See also Davidson, *Subjective, Intersubjective, Objective*, p. 80.

about what does and would cause a speaker to assent to any sentence in his (potentially unlimited) repertoire. The omniscient interpreter, using the same method as the fallible interpreter, finds the fallible speaker largely consistent and correct. By his own standards, of course, but since these are objectively correct, the fallible speaker is seen to be largely correct and consistent by objective standards.[51]

Davidson perhaps believed that this thought experiment was uncontroversial, but there are many problems with it.[52] Firstly, this interpreter is obviously not omniscient in the literal sense of the word, since this interpreter needs to use the same method of interpretation as we ordinary interpreters. Secondly, it is not self-evident that the notion of omniscience is intelligible. However, Davidson's critics have not seen that an omniscient interpreter, in any sense of the word, is not needed to come to his conclusion, and that this conclusion is a consequence of Davidson's way of seeing truth and meaning in general. The reasons for the conclusion is rather what I have already mentioned: what a sentence (the linguistic representative of a belief) of a speaker means is determined by the circumstances in which it is held true by the speaker (by what in the world causes the speaker to hold it true) and by its relation to other beliefs;[53] false beliefs get their content from true beliefs, so if our errors are numerous, there is much we are right about.[54] If it were possible for a speaker to determine what her words mean in complete isolation from other persons and the world, the relation to the common environment would not be needed for her words to have meaning, and she could then be massively wrong about the world. According to Davidson, however, '… the contents of sentences … [are] given by what could be picked up in the learning process …'.[55] Therefore, we are, in the basic cases, mostly right.[56] However, this conclusion is not, to be sure, reached by way of an argumentation which complies with the sceptic's demands on the argumentation. What Davidson shows is rather that if you see meaning and truth in the way he does – a way of seeing which there are, of course, good reasons for – then scepticism cannot get off the ground.[57]

---

51 Ibid., pp. 150–51. See also Davidson, *Inquiries into Truth and Interpretation*, p. 201.

52 See, for example, Edward Craig, 'Davidson and the Sceptic: The Thumbnail Version', *Analysis*, 50 (1990): 213; Richard Foley and Richard Fumerton, 'Davidson's Theism?', *Philosophical Studies*, 48 (1985): 84–5; A.C. Genova, 'The Very Idea of Massive Truth', in Lewis Edwin Hahn (ed.), *The Philosophy of Donald Davidson* (Chicago, IL, 1999), 177–8.

53 Davidson, *Inquiries into Truth and Interpretation*, pp. 168 and 201; Davidson, *Subjective, Intersubjective, Objective*, p. 200.

54 Davidson, *Problems of Rationality*, p. 5.

55 Donald Davidson, 'Reply to A.C. Genova', in Lewis Edwin Hahn (ed.), *The Philosophy of Donald Davidson* (Chicago, IL, 1999), p. 192.

56 For a similar argument, see Wittgenstein, 'Philosophy', p. 193.

57 See Davidson, 'Reply to A.C. Genova', p. 192; Donald Davidson, 'Reply to Barry Stroud', in Lewis Edwin Hahn (ed.), *The Philosophy of Donald Davidson* (Chicago, IL, 1999), p. 162; Davidson, *Subjective, Intersubjective, Objective*, p. 157; Davidson, *Problems of Rationality*, pp. 5–6.

However, that we are not massively wrong does not mean that there are not many things we can learn. Firstly, there are many issues which we have no beliefs on, and consequently no false beliefs on. Secondly, we can learn new practices, which make new beliefs possible, and the number of possible practices is endless. Learning the clock, for example, makes new true (and false) beliefs possible, but as has already been said, it makes no sense to say that we are generally wrong when it comes to saying what time it is.

The Relation to the World and to Other Persons

As we have seen, according to Davidson, the contents of words and sentences are determined by the things and events in the world that cause them, which means that we must not only be taken to be mainly right in the basic cases, but actually *are* mainly right in these cases. Here, I want to focus on this relation to the world, which is of great importance for Davidson.

This world which we cannot be massively wrong about is not a world understood in terms of, for example, sense data. On the contrary, the world consists of such objects we talk about – for example, tables, wolves and snow. Davidson does not have a world underlying the world of familiar objects, an underlying world which the familiar world is an interpretation of or our language might distort.[58] The main reason for this is that it is only possible to be wrong, and hence also right, about a public world, and that the world of familiar objects is the public world we all stand in relation to. Davidson can therefore conclude that:

> In giving up dependence on the concept of an uninterpreted reality, something outside all schemes and science, we do not relinquish the notion of objective truth – quite the contrary. … In giving up dualism of scheme and world, we do not give up the world, but re-establish unmediated touch with the familiar objects whose antics make our sentences and opinions true or false.[59]

That being wrong, and thereby also being right, presupposes interaction with other persons and the common world is an important point for Davidson. In Chapter 4, I gave an account of his reasons for this. Davidson argues that without the three relations between us interpreters, the person whose utterances we want to interpret and the common environment, there would not be any answers to the question what a concept is a concept of, what a word means, and this goes for the language of the other person as well as for our own language. Communicatively isolated, there is no way for you to fix what your words mean in a way which makes it possible for you to distinguish between cases when you go on as before, and cases when you do not go on as before.

---

58 Davidson, *Inquiries into Truth and Interpretation*, p. 185.
59 Ibid., p. 198.

Davidson on the Objectivity of Truth

The distinction between right and wrong, true and false, has appeared repeatedly in our discussion of Davidson. The basic importance of this distinction is that without appreciating it, we cannot be said to have beliefs. Davidson writes:

> ... to have a belief it is not enough to discriminate among aspects of the world, to behave in different ways in different circumstances; a snail or a periwinkle does this. Having a belief demands in addition appreciating the contrast between true belief and false, between appearance and reality, mere seeming and being.[60]

The point here is not that being able to make mistakes is a condition for having beliefs. It is thus not a counter-argument to Davidson's argument to say that a sunflower can make a mistake by turning towards an artificial light as if it were a sun without the sunflower having beliefs. Even if we accept that it makes sense to talk about sunflowers making mistakes, this is not a counter-argument to Davidson's argument, since the sunflower can then only make mistakes, but it does not appreciate the contrast between true belief and false, to use Davidson's formulation.[61]

To appreciate the contrast between true belief and false is to appreciate the objectivity of truth. Davidson has explicated this aspect of the concept of truth in slightly different ways, some of them, as we will see, a little misleading. The misleading way of explicating this aspect is to say that appreciating the objectivity of truth means that I am aware that I can be mistaken or that my beliefs may be wrong.[62] Why this is misleading, I will explain later on. The better formulation is that appreciating the objectivity of truth means that I am aware of the fact that the truth of most beliefs (apart from beliefs such as 'I have a belief') is independent of my believing them to be true.[63] Here, it is, of course, important to remember that the independence is only on the level of singular beliefs. Massive errors are not possible, so being believed and being true is not completely independent, for enough beliefs must be true in order to give content to the false beliefs.[64]

However, it is not only the relation to the world that is the source of the objectivity of truth. The source of this aspect of the concept of truth is the process of triangulation

---

60 Davidson, *Subjective, Intersubjective, Objective*, p. 209. See also Davidson, *Problems of Rationality*, pp. 4 and 54–5.

61 Davidson, *Subjective, Intersubjective, Objective*, p. 209.

62 See ibid., pp. 104, 129, 209. For other misleading formulations, see Davidson, *Problems of Rationality*, p. 10: '... someone who has a belief ... knows that that belief may be true or false'; and pp. 54–5: 'For a creature to have a concept ... it requires that the creature be able to classify things it *believes* fall under the concept while aware that it may be making a mistake.'

63 See Donald Davidson, *Truth and Predication* (Cambridge/London, 2005), p. 42; Davidson, *Subjective, Intersubjective, Objective*, pp. xiii, 104, 129, 209; Donald Davidson, 'Externalisms', in Petr Kotatko, Peter Pagin and Gabriel Segal (eds), *Interpreting Davidson* (Stanford, 2001), p. 1; Davidson, *Problems of Rationality*, pp. 42 and 141.

64 Davidson, *Subjective, Intersubjective, Objective*, p. 214.

– that is, both the relation to the world and the communicative relation to other persons are needed to give an account of the objectivity of beliefs, as we have already seen. Davidson can therefore say: 'The ultimate source (not ground) of objectivity is, in my opinion, intersubjectivity. If we were not in communication with others, there would be nothing on which to base the *idea* of being wrong, or, therefore, of being right, either in what we say or in what we think.'[65] Communicatively isolated, there is no way for you to fix what your words mean in a way which makes it possible for you to distinguish between cases when you go on as before and cases when you do not go on as before.

It is important to notice that Davidson's account of the concept of truth means that the predicate 'is true' is not only applicable to empirical beliefs.[66] That it is possible to distinguish between true and false in a specific context therefore does not presuppose that the subject matter in question is empirical or quasi-empirical, only that claiming and denying is possible in this context, and that the truth of the beliefs is independent of anyone believing them to be true. That the truth of the beliefs is independent of anyone believing them to be true means that we can imagine ourselves believing what we now deny, for instance due to hallucinations or a disease. For our purposes, this is of immense importance, since this makes it possible to talk about true and false religious beliefs, without this talk about true and false religious beliefs entailing a commitment to a general ontological thesis concerning existence and reality. Hence, when I talk about true and false religious beliefs, or about true and false moral beliefs, this is done with reference to this understanding of truth, which must be borne in mind, and does not involve any further ontological ideas. Since Davidson's way of explicating the objectivity of truth is partly misleading, however, we will discuss this subject some more.

The Objectivity of Truth

That there is a difference between us thinking something is true and this really being true goes without saying. The reason is simply that using 'true' without making this distinction is not how we use 'true' – if we did, the word 'true' would be unnecessary and pointless.[67] Hilary Putnam has an interesting argument, which Davidson now and then refers to, which relies on this feature of our concept of truth.[68] Putnam's point is that 'is true' can never be substituted by any other predicate P – for example, 'is believed by us to be true' – since it is always possible to find a statement S such that S might have the property P and still not be true. In this sense, 'true' is indefinable.

To be attentive to the difference Putnam stresses, the difference between us thinking that something is true and this really being true is about being more careful

---

65 Ibid., p. 83; Davidson, *Problems of Rationality*, pp. 5–6.

66 See ibid., pp. 39–57, for a discussion of the truth and objectivity of value judgements.

67 Cf. Wittgenstein, *Philosophical Investigations*, p. 78e (§ 258).

68 See Hilary Putnam, *Meaning and the Moral Sciences* (London, 1978), pp. 108–9.

and looking out for mistakes. Although you have been careful, you should know that a mistake might be there nevertheless.[69] It does not suffice, however, to be careful. When we examine whether a mistake has been made, whether we have been careful enough, we make this examination by comparing what has been done with our idea of how it should be done. There may be better ways of doing things, however, so this idea of how things should be done must also be questioned. The distinction between us thinking something is true and this really being true thus also serves, in a way, as a reminder of the fact that there may be other ways of doing things which could be better, and 'true' therefore has an important critical, or 'cautionary', function, by reminding us of the fact that we are often in need of critical thinking. This is connected to the aspect of development in our notion of rationality I elaborated in the last chapter.

Mistakes Are Not Always Possible

Two conclusions which are often drawn from Putnam's argument are that there is always room for error,[70] and that there is no final goal for human development.[71] In the following, I will discuss these conclusions, in order to explicate the objectivity of truth and arrive at a better understanding of this aspect of the concept of truth than Davidson's, starting with the first conclusion. The example Putnam discusses is 'The rug is green',[72] and a definition of 'is true' which makes it impossible that we see wrong – for example, a definition which equates 'is true' and 'is believed by us to be true' – is, of course, wrong. The problem is to what extent errors are possible, however. It is, of course, possible that the rug seems to be green, but when I look at it in better light, I see that it is actually blue. However, let us imagine that we have a rug which seems to be green, that different persons look at it in different lights and all find that it is green, but that someone says that it is always possible that we all are wrong, that the rug may actually be blue. Would such a saying make sense? Is there not a limitation to the possibility of error?

According to Wittgenstein, there is such a limitation. His discussion of this limitation concerns principally mathematics, but can as well be applied to sayings such as 'The rug is green', as we will see below. The starting point here is well

---

69 There are cases when this difference plays a more important role, for example when the past is discussed in a court of law. In such cases, carefulness may not be enough, for what really happened can in fact be unattainable. However, that the past in a particular case is unattainable gets its importance from the fact that this case stands out from all other cases where what has happened is attainable. In these latter cases, what we say about the past is not only beyond all reasonable doubt, but in fact simply expresses how it was. That the case where the past is unattainable is a special case shows itself in the fact that we can find this disturbing, and hence different from the normal case.

70 Ibid., p. 108.

71 Richard Rorty, *Truth and Progress: Philosophical Papers, Volume 3* (Cambridge, 1998), p. 22.

72 Putnam, *Meaning and the Moral Sciences*, p. 108.

known: if we ask for the meaning of an expression, a good way of answering the question is to look and see how the expression is used. This means that the meaning of mathematical words, such as 'multiplication', is not independent of how they are used. Another way of expressing this is by saying that there is an internal relation between a rule and its application. Thus if you are asked to square 12 and do not answer '144', you have not squared 12, since what we call following the rule is defined by reference to the result of the operation.[73] To say that it is possible that we have always been wrong in saying that $12 \times 12 = 144$ is then to rely on a notion of multiplication which could be spelled out independently of any application, a notion according to which what following the rule means is determined independently of the result of the operation. To say that such a notion is precisely what Giuseppe Peano was able to formulate[74] is not a tenable counter-argument, since the question can then be asked again: does it make sense to talk about understanding Peano's axioms and definitions independently of their application? Furthermore, this axiomatization is dependent on how we usually multiply, in order to be an axiomatization of multiplication and not of something else. In this context, Wittgenstein says the following in connection to a saying by Bertrand Russell:[75]

> Russell said, 'It is possible that we have always made a mistake in saying $12 \times 12 = 144$.' But what would it be like to make a mistake? Would we not say, 'This is what we do when we perform the process which we call "multiplication". 144 is what we call "the right result"'? Russell goes on to say, 'So it is only probable that $12 \times 12 = 144$.' But this means nothing. If we had all of us always calculated $12 \times 12 = 143$, then that would be correct – *that* would be the technique.[76]

To see what Wittgenstein is driving at here, let us imagine that someone looked over the basic arithmetical propositions and saw that if we do what we in other cases do when we multiply, one of the derivations is incorrect, for example that $12 \times 12 = 143$. The problem with this thought experiment, according to Wittgenstein, is that it takes for granted that 'what we in other cases do when we multiply' has a meaning which is determined independently of specific multiplications, that what it means in this particular case (when the factors are 12 and 12) to do what we in other cases do when we multiply is self-evidently decided beforehand. Of course, it is possible to say that $12 \times 12 = 143$ is now going to be the correct multiplication, in order to stress some kind of similarity in the system of multiplication, but such a change

---

73 Wittgenstein, *Remarks on the Foundations of Mathematics*, p. 319 (§ VI:16); Baker and Hacker, *Wittgenstein: Rules, Grammar and Necessity*, p. 149.

74 See Giuseppe Peano, 'The Principles of Arithmetic, Presented by a New Method', trans. Jean van Heijenoort, in Jean van Heijenoort (ed.), *From Frege to Gödel: A Source Book in Mathematical Logic, 1879–1931* (Cambridge, 1967), pp. 94–6.

75 Cf. Bertrand Russell, *The Collected Papers of Bertrand Russell, Volume 10: A Fresh Look at Empiricism, 1927–42* (London, 1996), p. 12.

76 Wittgenstein, *Lectures on the Foundations of Mathematics*, p. 97. Cf. Wittgenstein, *Remarks on the Foundations of Mathematics*, p. 199 (§ III:73).

would have such vast consequences for how multiplication is learnt and used that multiplication would no longer have the same role in our lives, would no longer be the same thing.

Another reason behind Wittgenstein's discussion here is that there are internal relations between rules and facts about the world – that is, if we imagine the world to be different, certain rules would no longer be what they now are. One such fact about the world is regularities in our behaviour. If we did not agree in our applications of the rule, the rule would not have the point it now has:

> The whole thing is based on the fact that we *don't* all get different results. That's why it was so absurd to say 12 × 12 = 144 may be the wrong result. Because the agreement in getting this result is the justification for this technique. It is one of the agreements upon which our mathematical calculations are based.[77]

This does not mean, however, that we never disagree in this type of mathematical matters, but the important point is that such disagreements are exceptions.

This does not imply that what is correct, right and true is what is normal, that human agreement decides what is correct, or that the majority decides what is right. What the rule manifests is, on the contrary, what is correct. That a human agreement is necessary here is only a precondition, not a part of the content of what we say when we say something.[78] Human agreement thus decides not what is correct in an already existing technique, but is just a precondition for such a technique, as I stressed in Chapter 2.

The important point is that no matter what rules we have, they must be followed in most cases for the activity to exist as constituted by these rules. Mistakes can therefore only be exceptions.[79] This is not something which only goes for mathematics. We cannot be wrong generally when we talk about colours, for example.[80] What colour words mean is, as in mathematics, connected to how they are used, so there is a limitation to the possibility of error also concerning 'The rug is green.' The number of examples is endless.[81] If we make mistakes, these are corrected by us doing the

---

77 Wittgenstein, *Lectures on the Foundations of Mathematics*, p. 102. That the agreement is the *justification* of the technique is misleadingly put, however. Justification takes places in a technique which itself has no justification, only preconditions, without which the technique would not be what it now is, as Wittgenstein rightly says on many occasions; see, for example, Wittgenstein, *Remarks on the Foundations of Mathematics*, p. 365 (§ VII:9), and Wittgenstein, *Lectures on the Foundations of Mathematics*, p. 107.

78 Wittgenstein, *Remarks on the Foundations of Mathematics*, pp. 323 and 365 (§§ VI:21 and VII:9).

79 See Wittgenstein, *Philosophical Investigations*, p. 193e, and Wittgenstein, *Lectures on the Foundations of Mathematics*, p. 25.

80 See Wittgenstein, *Philosophical Investigations*, p. 193e.

81 Wittgenstein says, for example: 'The language-game that operates with people's names can certainly exist even if I am mistaken about my name, – but it does presuppose that it is nonsensical to say that the majority of people are mistaken about their names'; Wittgenstein, *On Certainty*, p. 83e (§ 628).

same thing again, but now probably more carefully and more observant of possible sources of error. There is a limit, however, where corrections of mistakes stop being corrections and become changes of the practice itself, by referring to other objectives (or by not referring to any objectives at all). For such a new variant of a practice to be a *variant* and not something completely different, it must, in the basic cases, mostly agree with the old one. It seems therefore to be an exaggeration to say that what is true is unreachable, that we never have the truth in our hands. A distinction has to be made between what we think is true and what is true, but that does not mean that they never coincide.

Certainty and the Objectivity of Truth

Thus it is misleading to say that appreciating the objectivity of truth means that I am aware that I can be wrong, that having a belief means that I know it may be true or false, that having a concept means being able to classify things I believe fall under the concept while aware that I may err, as I said above. This means further that the objectivity of truth does not presuppose that I can always be wrong. That idea is another way of saying that truth is unreachable, an idea which is problematic, as we have seen. Although Davidson says that appreciating the objectivity of truth means that I am aware that I can be wrong and the like,[82] this idea can be argued against, using Davidson's own philosophy. Since Richard Rorty expresses himself in the same way and for Davidsonian reasons, I will in the following discussion use both his and Davidson's formulations and arguments.

Davidson and Rorty argue that truth cannot be strictly reduced to any other concepts (such as justification).[83] The reason for this is Putnam's argument which I described above: we can always non-trivially ask, about any x which truth is supposed to be reducible to: is a belief that is x true?[84] Apart from the endorsing and disquotational use of 'true', there is therefore also a cautionary use of it, a use we employ when we want to emphasize that even if a belief is as justified as can be, it may not be true.[85] Davidson: 'We know many things, and will learn more; what we will never know for certain is which of the things we believe are true.'[86] Rorty:

---

82 See Davidson, *Subjective, Intersubjective, Objective*, pp. 104, 129, 209; Davidson, *Problems of Rationality*, pp. 10 and 54–5.

83 Davidson, *Truth and Predication*, p. 55; Davidson, *Subjective, Intersubjective, Objective*, p. 155; Davidson, *Truth, Language, and History*, pp. 20–21; Rorty, *Objectivity, Relativism, and Truth*, pp. 50, 127, 153; Rorty, *Truth and Progress*, pp. 3, 21.

84 Davidson, *Subjective, Intersubjective, Objective*, p. 156; Rorty, *Objectivity, Relativism, and Truth*, p. 127; Rorty, *Truth and Progress*, pp. 21–2; Putnam, *Meaning and the Moral Sciences*, pp. 108–9.

85 Rorty, *Objectivity, Relativism, and Truth*, p. 128; Rorty, *Truth and Progress*, pp. 21–2; Rorty, 'Universality and Truth', in Robert B. Brandom (ed.), *Rorty and His Critics* (Malden, 2000), p. 4; Rorty, 'Response to Jürgen Habermas', p. 57.

86 Donald Davidson, *Truth, Language, and History*, p. 6.

... we can ... add, after any assertion we or others make, 'But of course somebody someday (maybe we ourselves, today) may come up with something (new evidence, a better explanatory hypothesis, etc.) showing that that assertion was not true.' This is an example of 'true's' cautionary use. ... There is, to be sure, something unconditional about truth. ... But the unconditionality in question does not provide a *reason* for the fact that the cautionary use of 'true' is always apropos. To say that truth is eternal and unchangeable is just a picturesque way of *restating* this fact about our linguistic practices.[87]

Many of these formulations are mistaken: to say that we will never know for certain which of the things we believe are true is only possible if we are blind to the role and function of knowing and certainty in our lives. To say that the cautionary use of 'true' is always apropos entails that it would be meaningful for someone to say to me, 'But of course somebody someday (maybe you yourself, today) may come up with something (new evidence, a better explanatory hypothesis, and so on) showing that your belief that you are right now sitting in front of your computer is not true', a saying which is pointless,[88] except if said in certain circumstances. If somebody would say, 'I doubt that you are right now sitting in front of your computer', it would be hard to know what to make of what she was saying, it would even be hard to say what her saying meant.[89] Therefore, although truth cannot be strictly reduced to any other concept (such as justification), we cannot *always* non-trivially ask, about any x truth is supposed to be reducible to 'Is a belief that is x true?' Putnam's argument should instead be formulated in this way: for any x, there could always be some occasions where we can ask non-trivially 'Is a belief that is x true?'

Furthermore, Rorty is right when he says that the unconditionality of truth does not provide a *reason* for the cautionary use of 'true'. However, to talk about the unconditionality of truth is not a picturesque way of restating our willingness to change our minds, as Rorty claims. This willingness is rather a primitive reaction in our talk of truth and falsity, in our using 'truth' in this way. That we do talk about truth in this way is conceptually dependent on our general willingness to change our minds. If we were not willing to change our minds, if we did not live lives in which we try to do things in better ways, to talk about the unconditionality of truth would not make any sense. Talking about the unconditionality of truth is something we do only in some philosophical contexts, and we would not do this if we did not, in all kinds of different contexts, talk about the importance of having a general willingness

---

87 Rorty, 'Response to Jürgen Habermas', p. 57.

88 It could be said here that it is precisely those beliefs whose possible falsity we cannot imagine which we should question – that a belief appears to be self-evident is an indication of its ideological nature; see Louis Althusser, *Lenin and Philosophy and Other Essays*, trans. Ben Brewster (London, 1971), pp. 161 and 163–4. That may be true, but such a questioning is hardly a matter of showing that such beliefs are simply false. Rather, what should be done in such a case is to show that a particular belief, although in itself true, may be one-sided if not combined with other beliefs, or that which true beliefs are actually expressed or emphasized in a particular society reveals something about that society, or that the fact that a particular belief is true in a particular society shows that this society ought to be changed.

89 Cf. Duncan Richter, *Wittgenstein at His Word* (London/New York, 2004), p. 92.

to change one's mind. The unconditionality of truth thus need not be understood as a metaphysical absolute, but can be understood simply as a way of formulating our general willingness to change our minds, a willingness which is conceptually primary.

In Chapter 4, I gave an account of Heidegger's description of human beings as always living in a world which is basically familiar to them. Hence, according to this understanding, our beliefs are not about something which is more independent of us than this familiar world, but are precisely about this world, and Davidson and Rorty agree with this. Within this picture of our relation to the world, two aspects need to be taken in consideration. Firstly, and this aspect is probably what makes Rorty talk about a cautionary use of 'true' and Davidson about the objectivity of truth: a belief is not true simply for the reason that we believe it. We are now and then wrong. We are able to improve our knowledge. We do not say, 'I knew p, but p was false.' Secondly: although there always is a logical possibility that a particular belief is wrong, we know many things, and know them for certain. The possibility of being wrong is often only a logical possibility,[90] which means that there need not always be a current possibility of errors – that is, there are many beliefs about which it is pointless to say, 'It is possible that this belief is false.'[91] This means – and this is the central point – that appreciating the objectivity of truth is not to be aware that you can be wrong, that your beliefs may be wrong, but to be aware of the fact that the truth of most beliefs is independent of your believing it to be true. To say that my belief that I am right now sitting in front of my computer may be false is pointless, but since an error is logically possible, I can imagine myself sitting here and believing falsely, which shows that the truth about beliefs about me sitting in front of my computer is not dependent on my believing them. In *that* sense, we can imagine ourselves believing what we now deny. This logical possibility does not show a current possibility, however. The thought experiment must therefore appeal to extreme circumstances (hallucinations, for example) in order to be conceivable. That such extreme exceptional cases are precisely extreme exceptional cases shows that they stand out from the usual cases, get their status as extreme exceptional cases from them, and in order to become conceivable, require a narrative (for example, a reference to disease).

Davidson and Rorty are hence right when they say that most of our beliefs are true, but when they emphasize the cautionary use of 'true' too strongly in the way I showed above, they overlook that there are many utterances which we need not be cautioned about, utterances we know are true.[92] The scepticism which lurks behind

---

90 Davidson expresses himself in a way which shows that he is aware of this. See, for example, Davidson, *Truth, Language, and History*, pp. 6–7; Davidson, *Subjective, Intersubjective, Objective*, pp. 206–7.

91 Cf. Jürgen Habermas, *Truth and Justification*, trans. Barbara Fultner (Cambridge, 2003), p. 39.

92 Cf. Wittgenstein, *On Certainty*, p. 83e (§ 625): '… these rules of caution only make sense if they come to an end somewhere'.

Davidson's and Rorty's formulations is problematic for the same reason relativism is: scepticism cannot make a distinction between 'being true' and 'is believed to be true'. According to the sceptic, saying that something is true is impermissible, which means that the distinction between 'being true' and 'is believed to be true' is never put to practical use.

The Truth as the Final Goal of Inquiry

The other conclusion often drawn from Putnam's argument is that there is no final goal for human development. Since 'is true' can never be substituted by any other predicate, the cautionary use of 'true' is always meaningful, therefore truth cannot be a final goal for human development, since this is not a goal which is reachable.[93] Davidson:

> Since it is neither visible as a target, nor recognizable when achieved, there is no point in calling truth a goal. Truth is not a value, so the "pursuit of truth" is an empty enterprise unless it means only that it is often worthwhile to increase our confidence in our beliefs, by collecting further evidence or checking our calculations.[94]

This motivation of why the truth is not the final goal of inquiry is confused, however, as I will show, but this does not mean that the truth is the final goal of inquiry. Firstly, I will therefore explain why the truth is not the final goal of inquiry. The truth can be supposed to be a goal on the level of practices, on the level of sentences, or both. I will examine these two possibilities in this order.

When we improve a particular practice, this is not done with the truth as the goal. Talking about true and false answers to the question 'What time is it?' makes sense. In so far as a practice makes it possible for us to answer such a question correctly, the practice is adequate, but it is not 'true': practices are not true or false; beliefs, sentences and the like are.

Also, when we come to sentences, there is nothing like 'distance from the truth': the sentence is either true or not true, not something in between. We can, of course, aim to produce true sentences and clear away false ones, but this means only that we draw away from falsehood. There is namely no limit to the number of true sentences, among other reasons because if we have a finite set of true sentences, we can always produce new ones by talking about this set, and because the number of new practices, and thus also new sentences, is endless. If we demarcate a specific subject matter, however, there might be a limit to the number of true sentences that could be said on the subject matter in question. Only in such a case, producing true sentences and

---

93 Davidson, *Truth, Language, and History*, pp. 6–7; Rorty, *Truth and Progress*, pp. 3–4 and 22; Richard Rorty, *Philosophy and Social Hope* (London, 1999), p. 82; Rorty, 'Universality and Truth', pp. 2, 7, 27; Richard Rorty, 'Response to Akeel Bilgrami', in Robert B. Brandom (ed.), *Rorty and His Critics* (Malden, 2000), p. 262.

94 Davidson, *Truth, Language, and History*, pp. 6–7.

clearing away false ones can be said to be a matter of coming closer to the truth, if we want to use that phrase.

The picture of us drawing nearer to the truth as a final goal is thus a bad picture of what motivates inquiry on the whole. A motivation need not be formulated in terms of a final goal, however. Many human activities are a matter of doing things better, for example faster, than they were done before, and here we are not striving for a final goal, so inquiry could be compared to such activities. In such cases, we are not striving towards the impossible as if it were a limit in the mathematical sense, for example by trying to do things in no time, but we are trying to do better than we have done previously, for example by trying to do things faster than before.

Truth can therefore be called a goal of a specific inquiry, but it is not the final goal of inquiry on the whole. The suggestion that we should stop seeing the truth as the final goal of inquiry can be motivated in different ways, however, also in ways which are problematic, for example by referring to Putnam's argument. Rorty, for example, says that: 'The trouble with aiming at truth is that you would not know when you had reached it, even if you had in fact reached it. But you *can* aim at ever more justification, the assuagement of ever more doubt.'[95] Rorty is wrong in an important way here. He seems to be stuck with the picture of truth as something mystic, a picture he ought to help us get rid of.[96] Rorty is, of course, right in reminding us of the fact that in cases of disagreement, we cannot turn to the truth as a neutral arbiter which shows who is right. In cases of disagreement, what we can do is to try to justify our belief to the persons we disagree with. Recognizing our disagreement presupposes that we agree on many things, however, and on this level of agreement, the truth is not out of reach. When justifying a belief, for example, we can ask whether it is true that the belief is justified. It is here possible for Rorty to say that the question is not about whether it is true that the belief is justified, but about whether this, in its turn, is justified, in that way pushing the question about justification to another level. Such new levels can always be found, but Rorty overlooks that we at some point do not seek for any more justification, but believe that we in fact have the truth, that we say something true and do not feel the need to found this in further justifications. This does not mean that truth here is defined in terms of justification or in terms of our belief that we have the truth. Just as saying that my saying that I am right now sitting in front of my computer may be false is pointless, saying that we may be wrong in such cases is pointless.

This may seem to be an astounding conclusion, but it is a consequence of what I have already written about the limitation to the possibility of error. The epistemological

---

95 Rorty, *Philosophy and Social Hope*, p. 82.

96 Rorty has in recent writings begun to formulate his point in ways which are not problematic in this sense. He says, for example: 'Philosophers, like everybody else, should seek to justify their beliefs. "True" is the commendatory adjective we apply to beliefs we think better justified than their competitors. So in an obvious sense we could not cease to seek for truth as long as we seek to justify our beliefs to one another'; Richard Rorty, 'Response to Molly Cochran', in Matthew Festenstein and Simon Thompson (eds), *Richard Rorty: Critical Dialogues* (Cambridge, 2002), pp. 201–2.

tradition has regarded the world as something alien, as something we have problem getting to know, as something distant. Philosophers like Wittgenstein and Heidegger have, in different ways, inspired us to get rid of such a way of looking at the world. The world is, on the contrary, what we always already talk about and are in. Long before we intellectualize our relation to the world by trying to get knowledge about it, we are active in it. Truth is therefore not something strange we cannot attain. On the contrary, we know in most cases whether something is true or not, and what we believe that we know is, in fact, in most cases true, even when we do not justify our beliefs.

Correspondence and Coherence

In the context of a discussion of the objectivity of truth and our – and our language's – relation to the world, the question of the relation of this discussion to correspondence and coherence theories of truth naturally comes up. What these theories are about is giving an account of what it means to say that a sentence is true, as well as what it is that makes a true sentence true.

Davidson argues against attempts to give reductive or analytic definitions of truth, as we have seen above. This does not mean that he thinks that nothing can be said about truth. On the contrary, Davidson says, for example, that '... the truth of an utterance depends on just two things: what the words as spoken mean, and how the world is arranged'.[97] and he thinks that Aristotle's characterization of truth, 'To say of what is that it is not, or of what is not that it is, is false, while to say of what is that it is, or of what is not that it is not, is true',[98] is a good characterization of truth.[99] Davidson's objection to definitions of truth is rather an objection to attempts to explain truth by trying to find something which truth is the same as and which is clearer and easier to understand, and the problem with such attempts is that truth already is as clear a concept as could be:[100]

---

97 Davidson, *Subjective, Intersubjective, Objective*, p. 139.

98 Davidson, *Truth, Language, and History*, p. 21. See Aristotle, *Metaphysics: Books Γ, Δ and E*, trans. Christopher Kirwan (Oxford, 1993), p. 23 (1 011b).

99 Davidson, *Truth, Language, and History*, pp. 22–4.

100 Here, one could compare Davidson's objection to attempts to give reductive definitions of truth to Frege's argument against the same thing:

Now it would be futile to employ a definition in order to make it clearer what is to be understood by 'true'. If, for example, we wished to say 'an idea is true if it agrees with reality' nothing would have been achieved, since in order to apply this definition we should have to decide whether some idea or other did agree with reality. ... Truth is obviously something so primitive and simple that it is not possible to reduce it to anything still simpler. (Gottlob Frege, 'Logic', in Michael Beaney (ed.), *The Frege Reader* (Oxford, 1997), p. 228)

... truth is as clear and basic a concept as we have. Tarski has given us an idea of how to apply the general concept (or try to apply it) to particular languages on the assumption that we already understand it; but of course he didn't show how to define it in general (he proved, rather, that this couldn't be done).[101]

Although Davidson objects to the general project of giving explanations of truth, he tries also to show what are the shortcomings of theories of truth such as the correspondence theory. The main problem with this theory, according to Davidson, is that it fails to do what it sets out to do – namely, to explain truth – for it does not manage to say in a non-trivial way what sort of thing it is that makes a true sentence true, what entities it is that true sentences corresponds to:

> The trouble lies in the claim that the formula has explanatory power. The notion of correspondence would be a help if we were able to say, in an *instructive* way, which fact or slice of reality it is that makes a particular sentence true. No one has succeeded in doing this. If we ask, for example, what makes the sentence 'The moon is a quarter of a million miles away' true, the only answer we come up with is that it is the fact that the moon is a quarter of a million miles away.[102]

One of the main sources of the correspondence theory is that we in fact compare our beliefs with reality in order to find out whether they are true or not, by, for example, performing experiments. What Davidson denies is not that we perform experiments, only that this is to be analysed as involving non-propositional evidence – that is,

---

Here, Frege is not showing that it is impossible to construct a language by substituting 'is true' in our language, when it appears, with 'agrees with reality'. What he gives an example of is, however, that 'is true' in our language has a more basic use than potential definitional expressions, that it does not become clearer when defined.

101 Davidson, *Subjective, Intersubjective, Objective*, p. 155. See also Davidson, *Truth and Predication*, p. 55; Davidson, *Subjective, Intersubjective, Objective*, p. 139; Davidson, *Truth, Language, and History*, pp. 20–21. What Tarski says on this subject can be seen in Alfred Tarski, 'The Semantic Conception of Truth and the Foundations of Semantics', *Philosophy and Phenomenological Research*, 4 (1944). Tarski proved that the concept of truth cannot be defined in general, in the sense that a language which contains semantic terms such as the term 'true' referring to sentences of this language is inconsistent (since it makes, for example, the antinomy of the liar possible). To avoid this, Tarski distinguishes between object-language and meta-language when it comes to the definition and use of the concept of truth, which means that the concept of truth cannot be defined *in general*; Tarski, 'The Semantic Conception of Truth and the Foundations of Semantics': 348–51. One way to counter what Tarski is saying is to say that 'true' is not a semantic concept, by referring to how 'true' is usually used (see Peter F. Strawson, 'Truth', *Analysis*, 9 (1949): 85), but in that case there is no need for a general definition of truth in the first place (see Strawson, 'Truth': 97).

102 Davidson, *Truth, Language, and History*, p. 5. See also Davidson, *Truth and Predication*, pp. 39–41; Davidson, *Subjective, Intersubjective, Objective*, pp. 70 and 155. Cf. Rorty, *Objectivity, Relativism, and Truth*, p. 6: '... "we use 'atom' as we do, and atomic physics works, because atoms are as they are" is no more enlightening than "opium puts people to sleep because of its dormitive power"'.

evidence that is not a form of belief.[103] The relation between the non-propositional – that is, the happenings in the world – and the propositional – that is, our beliefs – cannot be evidential, so Davidson suggests that it is to be seen as causal: 'Sensations cause some beliefs and in *this* sense are the basis or grounds of those beliefs. But a causal explanation of a belief does not show how and why the belief is justified.'[104] As I have already said, according to Davidson, most of our beliefs are right, which means that despite all of the justificatory relations there are among beliefs, our beliefs could not be out of touch with the world. Truth is thus neither epistemic (since for any x, there could always be some occasions where we can ask non-trivially 'Is a belief that is x true?'), nor radically non-epistemic (since the world cannot be radically different to how we believe it is).[105] Davidson's conclusion is then:

> Nothing, no *thing*, makes sentences or theories true ... *That* experience takes a certain course, that our skin is warmed or punctured, that the universe is finite, these facts, if we like to talk that way, make sentences and theories true. But this point is put better without mention of facts. The sentence 'My skin is warm' is true if and only if my skin is warm.[106]

The problem, which the correspondence theory of truth is supposed to be an answer to, is how my beliefs, understood as private objects of the mind, can say something true about an outside world. If we understand beliefs in another way, however, as determined by the relations between myself, my interlocutor and our common world, this problem does not arise, and we do not need to talk about correspondence, representations and facts or states of affairs making sentences true.[107]

John McDowell has criticized Davidson's way of describing our relation to the world in this way. The criticism is that, as McDowell says: 'Davidson's picture depicts our empirical thinking as engaged in with no rational constraint, but only causal influence, from outside.'[108] That rational constraint is needed is easily seen: without such constraint, it would make no sense to talk about what we should think, as opposed to what we do think.[109] The question whether our thinking according to Davidson is not only causally constrained but also rationally constrained must, however, be answered in the affirmative, and McDowell's criticism is thus misplaced.[110] According to Davidson, being wrong and right, appreciating the objectivity of truth, and being rational all presuppose interaction with other persons. In the process of triangulation – that is, standing in a mutual relationship to other

---

103 Davidson, *Subjective, Intersubjective, Objective*, pp. 164–5.
104 Ibid., p. 143. Cf. Rorty, *Objectivity, Relativism, and Truth*, p. 120.
105 Davidson, *Subjective, Intersubjective, Objective*, p. 156.
106 Davidson, *Inquiries into Truth and Interpretation*, p. 194.
107 Davidson, *Subjective, Intersubjective, Objective*, p. 46.
108 John McDowell, *Mind and World* (Cambridge, 1994), p. 14.
109 Ibid., p. 68.
110 Cf. Donald Davidson, 'Reply to Roger F. Gibson', in Urszula M. Żegleń (ed.), *Donald Davidson: Truth, Meaning and Knowledge* (London, 1999), p. 135.

persons and to a common world – talking about rationality makes sense. What McDowell fails to see is that this social dimension is needed,[111] which means that without adding this dimension, McDowell's own way of giving an account of the way we are rationally constrained fails. McDowell is, of course, right in that causality alone cannot provide a rational constraint, but as we have seen, causality is not all there is for Davidson. Davidson's account of the way we are rationally constrained would, however, be unsatisfying if one would like such constraint to come from outside humanity, for example from some sort of God's Eye point of view, but this is probably not what McDowell is after.

That Davidson objects to the correspondence theory does not mean that he advocates a coherence theory of truth. The problem with the latter theory is that what we mean when we say that something is true is not that it is justified – that is, we can non-trivially ask 'Is a belief that is justified true?':

> Any further attempts [apart from Tarski's] to explain, define, analyze, or explicate the concept will be empty or wrong: correspondence theories, coherence theories, pragmatist theories, theories that identify truth with warranted assertability (perhaps under 'ideal' or 'optimum' conditions), theories that ask truth to explain the success of science, or serve as the ultimate outcome of science or the conversations of some élite, all such theories either add nothing to our understanding of truth or have obvious counterexamples. ... Putnam's comparison of various attempts to characterize truth with the attempts to define 'good' in naturalistic terms seems to me ... apt. It also seems to apply to Putnam's identification of truth with idealized warranted assertability.[112]

The specific problem with epistemic theories such as the coherence theory is that they reduce reality to so much less than we believe it is and talk about it as being.[113]

I would like to add, however, that it is confused to believe that a theory such as the correspondence theory of truth is simply wrong. This theory would not be so popular as it is if it did not connect to obvious aspects of our relation to reality. 'Representation' and 'correspondence', in the sense they are used in philosophy, are certainly not words we usually use, but they are connected to patterns of thought which are so self-evident that talk about representation and correspondence could in fact be said to be empty truisms:[114] obviously, much of what we say is about reality. Thus what we ought to do is to get rid of confused philosophical ideas, by coming to understand that expressions such as '"p" says how things are in reality' and even '"p" is true since it says how things are' are unproblematic in the sense that they do

---

111 See Robert Brandom, 'Perception and Rational Constraint', *Philosophy and Phenomenological Research*, 58 (1998): 373; Martin Kusch, *Knowledge by Agreement: The Programme of Communitarian Epistemology* (Oxford/New York, 2002), pp. 111–12.

112 Davidson, *Subjective, Intersubjective, Objective*, pp. 155–6. This criticism of Putnam is not entirely fair. See Putnam, *Realism with a Human Face*, pp. vii–viii.

113 Davidson, *Truth and Predication*, p. 34; Davidson, *Subjective, Intersubjective, Objective*, p. 178.

114 Cf. Gordon P. Baker and Peter M.S. Hacker, *Scepticism, Rules and Language* (Oxford, 1984), pp. 125–6.

not compel us to hold these philosophical ideas, and thus need not be given up, at least not for that reason.[115]

This can also be expressed by saying that in many cases, '"p" is true' and '"p" says how things are in reality' mean the same thing. This is so only for some sentences, however, for not every sentence is understood as being about reality in the strict sense. This means that among all sentences, there are both such that are about reality and such that are not. This is only a matter of how we use different sentences and what we say about them, however, not a matter of ontology in any 'deeper' sense.

Rorty, who appreciates Davidson's rejection of the correspondence and the coherence theory of truth, has only recently[116] realized that his dismissive attitude towards such common sayings as the above was ill-founded, and his description of this realization is interesting. What he has realized is that being critical of the attempt to define truth as accurate representation of the intrinsic nature of reality does not mean denying that true sentences get things right:

> … there are certain word–world relations which are *neither causal nor representational* – for instance, the relation 'true of' which holds between 'Snow is white' and snow, and the relation 'refers to' which holds between 'snow' and snow. These relations, however, do not hold between that sentence and what philosophers like to call 'reality as it is in itself,' but only between those expressions and snow.[117]

What this means, and here I think that Rorty would disagree, is that we can use all the familiar expressions like correspondence, representation, reference, getting the facts right, the world making true sentences true and the like, as long as we do not believe, or draw conclusions as if we believe, that these sayings add something to the saying that a specific sentence is true, or that they explain or give us knowledge about what it means for a sentence to be true.[118] That we can ask non-trivially 'Is a belief that is justified true?' shows that justification and truth cannot be identified. The question 'Is a belief that gets the facts right true?' cannot be asked non-trivially, however (the same goes for other expressions, such as 'corresponds with the world', which can be substituted for 'gets the facts right'), which shows that these expressions can be

---

115 Cf. Alice Crary, 'Wittgenstein's Philosophy in Relation to Political Thought', in Alice Crary and Rupert Read (eds), *The New Wittgenstein* (London, 2000), p. 124. There is an obvious similarity between what I say here and what John McDowell says in, for example, John McDowell, 'Towards Rehabilitating Objectivity', in Robert B. Brandom (ed.), *Rorty and His Critics* (Malden, 2000). There is a difference, however, in that McDowell seems to think that the world provides us with some sort of norms – see Rorty's criticism in Richard Rorty, 'Response to John McDowell', in Robert B. Brandom (ed.), *Rorty and His Critics* (Malden, 2000), pp. 125–6; Rorty, 'Response to Bjørn Ramberg', in Robert B. Brandom (ed.), *Rorty and His Critics* (Malden, 2000), p. 376 – an impression which, among other things, is occasioned by McDowell's not very helpful rhetoric (for example, 'being answerable to the world').

116 See Rorty, 'Response to Bjørn Ramberg', pp. 374–6.

117 Ibid., p. 374.

118 Cf. Wittgenstein, *Philosophical Grammar*, pp. 161–2 (§ I:112).

identified with 'is true'. However, and this must be borne in mind, 'truth' is not, for the reason Davidson gives, analysed when these expressions are used. It is rather what these expressions mean which can be explicated using the simple and clear predicate 'is true'.

Conclusion

As we have seen, the word 'true' has two important uses: an endorsing use, and a cautionary use. None of these uses points at a particular criterion of truth. This is important since, as I showed in the last chapter, a criterial understanding of rationality and truth makes rational, comprehensive change impossible, unless these criteria are trivial. Hence, that Davidson rejects both the correspondence theory and the coherence theory of truth is crucial in this context. The openness towards the new is jeopardized if one sticks to a criterial understanding, but here the openness has been retained by means of stressing the cautionary use of 'true'.

Especially important is that the distinction between believing that something is true and this being true has been upheld, without presupposing that it is possible to place oneself in an external position where one is liberated from one's commitment, body, upbringing and society, a position from where we can compare what we believe with what is true and in that way change our beliefs in the right direction. To improve your own beliefs and question the beliefs of others in a fruitful way is consequently not done by invoking the demand for universality, but by discussing concretely and taking into consideration what is already believed. It is now necessary to go into detail about how this could be done, which I will do in the next chapter.

Chapter 6

How Is Fruitful Discussion Possible?

I have now shown that it is possible to talk about right and wrong, true and false, even in situations where there is no way to reconcile the conflict or disagreement once and for all (times and persons). If you can never rightly say that somebody is wrong, you cannot say that not-p is false (p being your belief). You cannot then say that p is true – that is, you cannot say that p. This means that you cannot voice your own opinion – the disagreement would not be allowed to be put into words. The consequence of believing that you can never rightly say that somebody is wrong is thus problematic. A simplified way of realizing that you can sometimes rightly say that somebody is wrong, even in situations where you are not able to show this to the person in question, is by noticing that it does not follow from the fact that there is no common measure with which the different opinions can be measured that they all are equally good.[1] This does not follow, since saying that they are equally good presupposes a measure, and since this measure cannot be a common measure, it is not self-evident. To see that there is a disagreement presupposes, however, that there is an agreement on another level, as I have also shown.

The demand for arguments which are appreciated by, in principle, everybody, a demand I have rejected as unreasonable, springs out of the genuine need to prevent conflicts which cannot be reconciled by means of an argumentative encounter – a conflict would be easily reconciled if we could find arguments relevant for the disputed question, arguments appreciated by everybody. Since that need is a genuine need, we must show what can actually be done to reconcile conflicts. We must therefore return to our main question: How is fruitful discussion of religious beliefs possible? This question must now be answered, starting with the observation that there is no guarantee that such discussion is always possible. We would have a guarantee that such a discussion is always possible only if what I have called rationalistic discussion[2] were possible. Here, I am first going to give some examples of the failure of rationalistic discussion, examples more concrete than those I have previously given, and then begin to discuss the above question.

Before going into the discussion, some clarifications ought to be made. The following discussion does not presuppose that conversation is *always* good, that

---

1 Cf. Dewi Zephaniah Phillips, *Introducing Philosophy: The Challenge of Scepticism* (Oxford, 1996), p. 105.

2 What characterizes such a discussion is that it is universal – that is, that it starts from certain putative universal norms and rules for argumentation, and shows from these that a certain belief is rational.

agreement is *always* good, that when you disagree with somebody, you must *always* try to convince her, that you *always* have to say that somebody who differs from you is wrong. What is presupposed is only that conversation is *sometimes* good, that agreement is *sometimes* good, and so on. When somebody differs from you, you can react in many different ways: sometimes you try to understand the other and nothing more, sometimes you do not do anything at all, and sometimes you do something different, like trying to show the other person that she is wrong. It is the last reaction we will deal with here. For that reason, the importance of self-criticism, which has been stressed in earlier chapters, will not play a major role here.

The Failure of Rationalistic Discussion

Rationalistic discussion is only possible if everybody reasons in the same way, or if there are some arguments which are agreed to be good and some agreed to be bad which could be used to come to an agreement on beliefs which are under discussion.[3] The general problem here is that ways of reasoning, about which there is at least widespread agreement, are hard to apply in concrete cases and are seldom decisive – the universality of a specific criterion comes at the price of its being vague, unspecific and relatively useless.[4] Such criteria are too unspecific and vague to show that a specific religious belief, for example, is to be believed or abandoned. In the following, I will give some examples of arguments, criteria and the like which could be said to be universal,[5] and show the problem in using them in concrete cases.[6]

---

3   This means that somebody who claims that such discussion is always possible must deal with the problem of how to show people she regards as being wrong that they are wrong, both as a practical as well as a theoretical problem.

4   See Gavin D'Costa, 'Whose Objectivity? Which Neutrality? The Doomed Quest for a Neutral Vantage Point from Which to Judge Religions', *Religious Studies*, 29 (1993): 81. Cf. Perelman, *The Realm of Rhetoric*, p. 27; Michael Walzer, *Thick and Thin: Moral Arguments at Home and Abroad* (Notre Dame, IN, 1994), pp. 2–4.

5   I will in most cases not discuss whether they are universal or not, because they are in most cases of little use, no matter what.

6   What I will say in the following also has consequences for universalism in ethics. It could, of course, be said that to act in a morally responsible way is to act in a way in which one thinks anyone should act if she was in the same situation. The problem is, however, that what 'same' means here is not at all clear. One way to make the distinction between same and different in this context is to say that every situation is, in one sense, the same – that is to say, that acting in a morally responsible way is to act in accordance with a principle which should by followed by everybody always and everywhere. (Cf. Immanuel Kant, *Practical Philosophy*, trans. Mary J. Gregor (Cambridge, 1996), pp. 73 and 164.) The problem is then that such a principle, in order to be universal, is relatively vague and unspecific, and consequently rules out few possible actions. Cf. Georg Wilhelm Friedrich Hegel, *Hegel's Philosophy of Right*, trans. T.M. Knox (Oxford, 1952), pp. 89–90 and 253–4; Georg Wilhelm Friedrich Hegel, *Natural Law: The Scientific Ways of Treating Natural Law, Its Place in Moral Philosophy, and Its Relation to the Positive Sciences of Law*, trans. T.M. Knox (Philadelphia, PA, 1975),

The first suggestion for universal criteria that often come up is logical criteria. Such criteria are only decisive if a person contradicts herself in an obvious way, however – the hard thing in most cases is to show that there is a contradiction. This first suggestion points at something important, however: there is a close connection between logic and argumentation, in the sense that somebody who argues illogically can hardly be said to argue at all. Moreover, if somebody seems to be breaking the laws of logic constantly, this casts doubt on our interpretation of what she is saying, which means that in the case where the interpretation is correct, disagreements are only possible against a background of massive agreement on, among other things, the basic principles of logic.[7] These two observations do not, however, provide us with universal criteria which guarantee that fruitful discussion of religious beliefs is always possible. Logical criteria are merely of use to rule out beliefs which are self-contradictory (and even that can be difficult), but cannot show which of two mutually contradictory beliefs is to be believed.[8] Thus we have here another type of problem concerning universal criteria than the general problem I talked about above.

Another suggestion is that basic concepts of substance, person, time, space, identity and the like are common to us all as humans.[9] If such concepts should guarantee the possibility of rationalistic discussion, they must be understood as universal criteria which can be used as starting points when arguing, but then the general problem is prevalent here: since they are too vague and unspecific, then most conflicts would be unaffected.

Could it not then be said that certain criteria are fixed in language on the whole,[10] or in certain social practices, such as disputing or arguing, or in ethical discourse?[11]

---

pp. 77–9. Another way to make the distinction between same and different in this context is to say that every situation is unique. The principle which could then be said to be followed is distinct and clear, but does not say anything about how somebody should act in other cases.

7　Davidson hints on some occasions (Davidson, *Problems of Rationality*, pp. 47 and 49–51; see also ibid., pp. 36, 195–7, 218–19) that this fact guarantees the possibility of fruitful discussion. This seems to be an exaggeration of the prospects for such a discussion, however. From the fact that a disagreement is only possible against a background of massive agreement, without which there is no answer to the question of what the disagreement is a disagreement *on*, it does not follow that this background contains criteria which can always (or in the most cases) fruitfully be used to reconcile the disagreement.

8　For that reason, Kant warns against using logic, which is only a canon for judgement, as an organon for producing seemingly objective assertions. See Kant, *Critique of Pure Reason*, p. 198 (A61/B85).

9　See Erica Appelros, *God in the Act of Reference: Debating Religious Realism and Non-realism* (Aldershot, 2002), pp. 37–8.

10　Karl-Otto Apel claims that certain universal ethical norms are presupposed *a priori* in all rational argumentation; Karl-Otto Apel, *Towards a Transformation of Philosophy*, trans. Glyn Adey and David Frisby (London, 1980), p. 257. However, these norms are presupposed not only in such social practices, but in all meaningful acting and speaking; ibid., p. 269. These norms commit everyone who has acquired communicative competence to, for example, strive for solutions which respect the interests of the collective, and not only one's own interests; ibid., p. 278.

11　See, for example, Seyla Benhabib, *Situating the Self: Gender, Community and Postmodernism in Contemporary Ethics* (Cambridge, 1992), pp. 31–3; Habermas, *Truth and*

Criteria fixed in language in general, on the one hand, must, if they are to guarantee the possibility of rationalistic discussion, be criteria similar to those we have already mentioned – that is, criteria which somebody cannot constantly refrain from satisfying without at the same time making it impossible for others to understand what she is saying. The problem then is that those beliefs which we want to show are wrong are beliefs we do understand. Criteria fixed in language are criteria which are supposed to show that certain things are wrong *just by* being said or written. It is obvious, however, that there are many things which are false, but false for other reasons than that they are said or written, and it is these things we are interested in.

Criteria fixed in social practices, on the other hand, seem then to be more promising. The idea here is that some things cannot be disputed, since they are presupposed when disputing, or that some things cannot be argued against, since they are presupposed when arguing. This idea is partly correct: the practice we call argumentation is distinguished from other practices by being engaged in, in a particular way. If somebody does something else, we do not call what she does 'arguing'. Moreover, if one of the interlocutors in a discussion does certain things or says certain things, their discussion breaks down completely. If somebody, for example, *constantly* says, when the other interlocutor formulates a counter-argument, 'That was not what I meant', the discussion breaks down sooner or later. It is thus possible for philosophers like Apel, Benhabib and Habermas to give informative specifications of what can and cannot be said or done in a discussion, both in relation to what we call 'arguing' as well as in relation to what it takes for a discussion to break down. However, if such specifications are understood as attempts to base what arguing is and what it is not in something more universal or *a priori*, they are problematic for reasons stated above and below.

When this idea is used as a way of bringing forth universal criteria, there are therefore some problems with it. Firstly, even if 'arguing' and related words in the way we use them are to some extent related to norms such as mutual respect, this does not mean that we cannot imagine other possibilities in the context of convincing others when it comes to the use of words such as 'arguing'. For example, in authoritarian societies, reference to one's own authority can for some persons be counted as an argument for a belief, and respect is then not mutual, but one-way.[12] Moreover, such norms as mutual respect are not of much use anyway: the general problem (such criteria are unspecific and vague) is also a problem here.

The second problem with the idea of informative specifications of what practices such as argumentation and discussion involve, specifications understood as bringing

---

Justification, pp. 105–8. For Benhabib, the principles presupposed in all ethical discourse are the principles of universal moral respect and egalitarian reciprocity; for Habermas, they are publicity and inclusiveness, equal rights to engage in communication, exclusion of deception and illusion, and absence of coercion.

12 If you, faced with the possibility of such a situation, say that the one who refers to her authority is not arguing at all, you hint at the fact, which I will come back to a little later, that the practice of argumentation is dependent on beliefs which are not argued for or against in the practice itself, beliefs which are not necessary, but contingent.

forth universal criteria, is that we do not have to be involved in these social practices. Somebody can very well say 'p' without claiming that she is arguing that p. This is not simply an extreme possibility: there are, for all of us, people with whom we do not discuss certain things. There is also a possibility, for all of us, that there are people with whom we even *ought not* to discuss, since we ought not to respect them in the sense that discussing with them demands.[13] Moreover, since the concept of discussion excludes certain persons from those who are able to discuss, and certain issues and beliefs from being taken up in the discussion, it may in some situations be good to abstain from discussing in order not to conform to an order of things which one would like to change.

Another possible way to argue for universal criteria is to say that certain beliefs, for example moral or religious beliefs, are better, more rational and the like, since they are more natural, in the sense that people are more easily convinced by them. You could, for example, say that the opinions of a Nazi today can be explained psychologically and sociologically, and that it is possible to make a Nazi give up her ideology by incorporating her in normal society, whereas most of us would not be convinced Nazis just because we lived among such people. Of course, there is some truth in this, but which conclusions we ought to draw from such facts is not self-evident. The argument that Nazism is irrational since it is unnatural is close to saying that Nazism is wrong since we who are not Nazis are more skilled persuaders, and hence is close to saying that might makes right. The only way for the Nazi to strengthen her case would then be to become more fanatical, and this would not be the development we had wished. Moreover, to argue from what is now normal is problematic, since it precludes changes of this normality, a change which is sometimes needed.

A further way of arguing is to say that although there are too few universal criteria, and those we have are not of much use in this context, there are many things which are not actually questioned by anybody, even if they could be questioned, and that these things can be of use. Charles Taylor, for example, claims that we never face people who unconfusedly and undividedly reject our most basic moral intuitions.[14] Taylor says that it seems as if we have experienced such people, the Nazis above all, but in fact they tried to argue from principles which are similar to our own, which means that their conclusions were obviously confused.[15] The problem with Taylor's way of arguing is that although it is possible to say that the Nazis did not reject our most basic moral intuitions unconfusedly and undividedly, this does not help us when it comes to showing them that they are wrong. It seems a little too naïve to think that a Nazi's political views are simple mistakes, which could be shown to her to be wrong by starting from her fundamental dispositions towards good and right.

The suggestion that it is always possible to find a mediator or a third party who can resolve the disagreement is another problematic one. It presupposes that it is always

---

13 See Dewi Zephaniah Phillips, *Philosophy's Cool Place* (Ithaca, NY, 1999), pp. 74–5.
14 Taylor, *Philosophical Arguments*, p. 35.
15 Ibid.

possible to find a person both of the parties of the disagreement have confidence in, and that if such a person is found, both of them will necessarily accept her verdict.

We can now conclude by saying that it is reasonable to assume that there are too few things which everybody is agreed on, and that those things everybody is agreed on are not of much use when it comes to reconciling conflicts. If there were lots of useful universal criteria, fruitful discussion would always be possible and we would not have to ask which kind of criticism really makes a difference and which not. That this question is an obviously important one shows that we already know that rationalistic discussion – that is, a discussion where we start from certain putative universal norms and rules for argumentation, and show from these that a certain belief is rational or irrational – is in many cases not possible. The idea of rationalistic discussion seems to underestimate the difficulty of reconciling conflicts, a difficulty which shows itself repeatedly when it comes to concrete cases. The only thing we can say seems to be that we should always *try* to argue with concrete others, by finding something we have in common with them and starting our argumentation there,[16] or by, for the sake of argument, assuming some of their beliefs.[17] The decisive point is whether we can find some beliefs, not necessarily beliefs we have in common, in the other person which we can connect to, in order to show her what we want to show. Of course, we can still try to convince *everybody*, but this is in many cases not done by aiming at everybody at the same time, but by aiming at particular persons and groups, until everybody has been convinced. However, the attempt to find some beliefs we can connect to in others to show them what we want to show can, in particular cases, turn out to be hopeless.

This conclusion, that there is no guarantee that a fruitful discussion is always possible, may be hard to accept. One feels like saying that in some way or other, it *must* always be possible to discuss, since in order to be able to live together in a society, we have to overcome our disagreements, at least be reaching a compromise.[18] However, even if compromises are often important, they are not necessary. Communities, for example societies and organizations, can manage to live with vast disagreements for years, sometimes with good consequences, sometimes with disastrous ones. Moreover, the saying that we have to overcome our disagreements in order to be able to live together can make us forget the possibility that some things can be so important that one would rather see the community broken up than make a compromise on that matter, especially since there is nothing in the nature of compromises which guarantees that they are always reached by means of a fair and democratic process.

---

16 See ibid., p. 36.

17 Cf. Slob, *Dialogical Rhetoric*, pp. 97–8; Stout, *Democracy and Tradition*, pp. 73–5.

18 See Hannah Arendt, *Between Past and Future: Eight Exercises in Political Thought* (New York, 1968), p. 220; Benhabib, *Situating the Self*, p. 9.

The Limitations of Argumentation

As we have come to see, we have no guarantee that it is always possible to reconcile a conflict by means of arguments. What we can do, if we restrict ourselves to argumentation, is to hope and try. In situations where it turns out that argumentation is not possible, it may be tempting to say that all we can do is to learn to live with the disagreements. That this is all we can do when we do not succeed in showing others by means of arguments what we want to show, is true, however, only if there is merely one way of showing that somebody is wrong: by means of arguments. What I will try to show in the following is that this is not so – that there are other ways of showing a person that she is wrong than by means of arguments. Expressed in another way, what I will try to show is that the possibility of argumentation presupposes a certain agreement, an agreement which cannot be attained by means of argumentation, but can be attained in other ways. Of course, that there are other ways of showing somebody that she is wrong does not mean that in all cases where you cannot show somebody by means of arguments that she is wrong, you can show her that she is wrong in other ways. The possibility of irreconcilable conflicts is consequently not denied here.

It is not so strange that philosophers are inclined to think that there is only one way of showing and that argumentation is always possible. Showing by means of arguments is what scientists do, and in so far as philosophers have tried to imitate them, they have seen philosophy as primarily a matter of analysis and argumentation. The results of such imitation have sometimes been good, but this strategy might conceal the fact that argumentation cannot show us everything which can be shown, that this way of showing presupposes another. Some of these other ways of showing are, in fact, an important part of philosophy.

In order to show that there are other ways to show somebody that she is wrong than by means of arguments, I will begin by trying to attain a more extensive understanding of disagreements which prove impossible to reconcile by means of argumentation. The word 'argumentation' has been used here to indicate a way of linguistically convincing others, convincing by pointing out to the one who is to be convinced that something follows or does not follow from things she already believes. The word 'argumentation' also includes convincing by conducting scientific experiments, in so far as the one who is to be convinced is clear, in advance, about what should happen in the experiment in order that she will change her mind on the issue which is under dispute.

Understanding Disagreements which are Argumentatively Irreconcilable

Disagreements which prove impossible to reconcile by means of argumentation are, if we use the above understanding of 'argumentation', disagreements about what could show that something is wrong, about what arguments are relevant and what not, about what arguments are good and what not, and so on. Relating to the discussion of the concept of truth in the last chapter, we can sum up this type of disagreement by calling it a disagreement concerning how the distinction between true and false is to be made in a certain context. Hence, argumentation presupposes a common way of making the distinction between true and false in the specific context,[19] otherwise it would just be a matter of two persons repeating their different opinions in front of each other. This agreement on how the distinction between true and false is to be made in a certain context can only be reached by means of argumentation if there is an agreement on how the distinction between true and false is to be made when it comes to the question of how different ways of making the distinction in this context are to be evaluated. Therefore, all such agreements cannot be reached by means of argumentation.

But are there really different ways of making the distinction between true and false? In one way, we have already answered that question. Chapter 2 showed that the distinction between true and false is made in different ways in different contexts – that is, that which arguments are relevant and which are not and which arguments are good and which are not is not the same when discussing religious questions as when discussing scientific ones, when discussing moral questions as when discussing mathematical ones, for example. The same chapter showed that our ways of talking about pain and induction are not based on hypothetical reasoning, but that the different ways the distinction between true and false is made in these different contexts are rooted in the diverse ways we deal with the world around us.

The import of the above question is, however, different. Is it possible that *in* a certain context there are different ways of making the distinction between true and false? This is a question which cannot be answered in a general way. Whether the distinction between true and false can be made in just one or in several ways in a specific context depends primarily on whether or not we regard departures from our way of making the distinction between true and false in this context as a matter of incompetence. If somebody systematically reasons differently in mathematics, for example, we say that she is not doing mathematics, that she must learn how to do it, and the like. When it comes to moral questions, this is not so. Here, if somebody systematically reasons differently, that is not generally seen as a matter of incompetence (but it is, of course, often regarded as false reasoning). In this context, different ways of making the distinction between true and false are therefore possible. That this is so indicates not necessarily that the context of morals is defective as compared to mathematics – the difference between them is internally related to the different roles they play in our lives.

However, there is always *some* limitation to how the distinction between true and false in a specific context can be made in order to still be a way of making this distinction or still concern this context. For that reason, the phrase 'systematically reason' was used above. For something to be a way of making the distinction between true and false in a certain context, it must make mistakes possible – otherwise there

---

19 This common way of making the distinction between true and false can be established by one of the interlocutors assuming, for the sake of argument, the way the other makes the distinction between true and false.

would be no difference between being right and thinking one was right – which means that anything cannot be a way of making the distinction between true and false. This means that a way of making the distinction between true and false must be visible, to all of us, as precisely a way – that is, as something regular – and what is regular and what is not is not determined by the individual. Hence, firstly, although the distinction between true and false in many contexts can be made in different ways, there is a limitation to the diversity. Secondly, it is not meaningful to think that we are generally wrong, since if our way of making the distinction between true and false in a specific context is visible as a way, we are right in at least the basic cases.[20] Furthermore, the distinction between true and false cannot be made anyhow in, for example, a moral context, otherwise it would not be a question of morals any more.[21] This means that different ways of making the distinction between true and false in a moral context must have *some* similarities in order to be ways of making the distinction between true and false in a moral context.

These two senses in which there are limitations to how the distinction between true and false can be made in a specific context are conceptual. Such conceptual limitations must be distinguished from normative limitations one might want to set up. Remember that here, we are not discussing which ways of making the distinction between true and false are legitimate and which not, but are only pointing at the conditions for something *being* a way of making this distinction. Of course, there are ways of making this distinction which most of us would regard as bizarre. To make a distinction between the legitimate and the non-legitimate or between the bizarre and the non-bizarre could be done, but the problem which is in focus here is how it could be shown to those who are placed on the wrong side of the dividing line that it is reasonable to put them there.

I have already given moral questions as an example of a context where a disagreement which could be characterized as a disagreement concerning how the distinction between true and false should be made in a specific context is possible. I want now to give a more concrete example of this. Imagine, therefore, a couple of beliefs which are obviously wrong and which it is important to work against by showing those who believe them that they are wrong – for example, racist beliefs.[22] That such beliefs in most cases are not mistakes due to the racist having misapplied universal criteria is obvious, and rationalistic discussion fails here.[23] Of course, such beliefs can be due to the racist having made a mistake – that is, an error in thinking

---

20 See the section 'The Impossibility of Massive Error' in Chapter 5.

21 Cf. Bouwsma, *Wittgenstein: Conversations 1949–1951*, pp. 5–6.

22 If you do not think that racist beliefs are obviously wrong, you can surely imagine other examples of obviously wrong beliefs.

23 Take all the suggestions for universal criteria which have been mentioned above and apply them to this case. Doing so shows in an obvious way how they all fail. This shows that when coming to practical problems like these, someone who believes in rationalistic discussion faces the same problems as someone who does not. To call racist beliefs irrational – which, of course, both someone who believes in rationalistic discussion and someone who does not can legitimately do – is in many cases in no way a solution to this practical problem.

– anyhow. That depends on how she makes the distinction between true and false
in this context.[24] However, another possibility is that the false beliefs are better not
called mistakes at all. This does not mean that they are not false. What is important
to see is that there are two different ways of being wrong: when this is due to
having made a mistake, and when it is not.[25] What I have argued against in previous
chapters, by showing that you can sometimes rightly say that somebody is wrong
in situations where you are unable to show this to the person in question, is that
every instance of being wrong necessarily is an instance of having made a mistake.
That you cannot show a specific person by means of arguments that she is wrong is
in many cases due to the fact that she has not made a mistake, that is has not made
an error in thinking. A disagreement in the case when the disagreement cannot be
reconciled by means of arguments is then not a disagreement which hides a deeper-
lying agreement (despite the fact that there must be some agreement for the parties
to recognize their disagreement) from which one of them can show argumentatively
that the other is wrong.

Whether somebody who is wrong has made a mistake or not is not determined
by that person herself. That it is difficult to convince somebody that she is wrong
does not necessarily mean that she has not made a mistake – somebody can find
it difficult (or say that she finds it difficult) to see that she has made a mistake for
many different reasons. Such failures in understanding will not be discussed here.[26]
However, when a lack of understanding is recurrent, the person in question does not
make the distinction between true and false in this context in the way you make it.
A disagreement in such cases, when it is not a matter of somebody having made a
mistake, is a disagreement not only about what is true and false here, but also, and
therefore primarily, about how one makes the distinction between true and false in
the field in question.

Since this type of disagreement is possible in many contexts, we cannot exclude
the possibility that we in some context are making the distinction between true and
false in a way which we will replace with another one which we come to see is better,
without this being a matter of argumentatively replacing the first one with another
one. Historically, we have many examples of this.[27] Hence, if we never ceased
making the distinction between true and false in a certain way in a certain context,
progress would in that context only be possible on the level of correcting mistakes
and on the level of doing more, and more thorough, investigations. Therefore, to
cease making the distinction between true and false in a certain way in a certain
context is sometimes good, but it can naturally not be said in advance when this will
be so and when it will not – any break in established ways of making the distinction

---

24 Cf. Wittgenstein, *On Certainty*, p. 11e (§ 74).

25 Cf. ibid., p. 11e (§ 72).

26 However, what I am going to say in the following concerning how it is possible to
show somebody that she is wrong in the case when she has not made a mistake is presumably
also relevant in this case, but that is a question I will not discuss here.

27 Cf. Kuhn, *The Structure of Scientific Revolutions*, pp. 93–5.

between true and false can, after the change, turn out to have made things worse. Such breaks are therefore only based on an experience of dissatisfaction and on the hope that things could get better, as I said in Chapter 4.

How is a specific way of making the distinction between true and false now to be understood? What does it consist of? That making the distinction between true and false is constituted by using certain words and doing certain things is obvious: if it were not, the making could not become visible, and we have seen that it must be possible to make it visible. Making the distinction between true and false in a certain way is also constituted by beliefs. The way one is making the distinction between true and false can, of course, be formulated as general beliefs, but it is above all the case that a specific way of making this distinction must show itself in specific beliefs. Two persons are only in agreement on how the distinction is to be made if this agreement shows itself in specific beliefs.[28]

What constitutes the making of the distinction between true and false (using certain words and doing certain things and holding certain beliefs) hangs together and comes into one's life in the same way – for example, by being born into a society and growing up and being brought up there. Being born into a society and growing up and being brought up there can be expressed as entering a community and living its life – that is, by one interacting with those there before.[29] This is not the only way such beliefs, words and things can come into one's life, however – a community is not needed in all cases for a way to make the distinction between true and false to become established, in the sense that an individual can differ to a large extent from everybody else when it comes to how she makes the distinction between true and false concerning how one should treat other human beings, for example.

That certain beliefs come into one's life in this way – that is, not by means of argumentation – is, of course, the controversial and important point. Here, it must be noticed, however, that these beliefs are so general and self-evident to those who make the distinction between true and false in a specific way that the beliefs are seldom put into words. That it is possible to enter a community and make the distinction between true and false in their way without adopting these beliefs, but by acting as if one believed them, is not a counter-argument here; on the contrary. For an 'acting as if' to be successful, it must imitate how those in the community act as closely as possible, and the acting as if therefore makes all the more obvious how the distinction between true and false is made in different contexts in the community.[30] Furthermore, acting as if is dependent on there being ways of making the distinction between true and false which is not as if: firstly, one's own way of making the

28 Cf. Wittgenstein, *Philosophical Investigations*, p. 75e (§ 242).

29 See Wittgenstein, *Philosophical Investigations*, p. 70e (§ 208); Wittgenstein, *On Certainty*, p. 15e, 19e, 21e, 24e, 38e, 62e–63e (§§ 94, 128, 143, 167, 298, 472, 476).

30 Cf. Phillips, *Introducing Philosophy*, p. 67; Ludwig Wittgenstein, *Letzte Schriften über die Philosophie der Psychologie, Band II: Das Innere und das Äußere: 1949–1951/Last Writings on the Philosophy of Psychology, Volume II: The Inner and the Outer: 1949–1951*, trans. C.G. Luckhardt and Maximilian A.E. Aue (Oxford, 1992), pp. 35e–36e.

distinction between true and false,[31] and secondly, the way of making the distinction between true and false that exists in the community in question.

Furthermore, one way of making the distinction between true and false in a specific context can, when a specific question is discussed, turn out to be indeterminate. For example, a person can be able to distinguish between true and false in a moral context: when it comes to questions about justice, she is able to make this distinction, and when it comes to questions about the value of life, she is able to make this distinction. However, when it comes to the question of whether violence should be used to change a politically unjust situation, she does not know what to say – her way of making the distinction between true and false in the moral context here turns out to be indeterminate, since she is not able to bring together how she deals with questions about the value of life with the way she deals with questions about justice.[32] That a person is unable to make the distinction between true and false when it comes to a specific question is not self-evidently a weakness – it can also be seen as taking the complexities of this question seriously.

The Distinction between True and False in the Context of Religion

Should all disagreements in the context of religion be understood as disagreements within an established way of making the distinction between true and false, or are disagreements about how this distinction is to be made in this context possible? In analytic-theistic philosophy of religion, disagreements about how to make the distinction between true and false in religion have seldom been noticed. Instead it has been implicitly presupposed that the distinction between true and false in this context is to be made in the same way as in the context of empirical questions. The truth or falsity of the belief that God exists has then been determined in the same way as one determines the existence of any other object not immediately visible to the eye, that is by hypothetically concluding from what is visible. This way of philosophically understanding religion could be said to gain strength from how religion is said to be understood commonly nowadays, that is as a theory about reality in its most general sense. Such sayings distort the character of religion, however, as was shown in Chapter 2.[33] This character shows itself in the use of

---

31 For the important distinction between learning language and learning a foreign language, see Wittgenstein, *Philosophical Investigations*, pp. 13e–14e (§ 32).

32 That you cannot answer a certain question is, however, not *necessarily* due to your being unable to make the distinction between true and false in the context in question. Firstly, it can be complicated to argue in the right way, which means that mistakes can be probable. Secondly, some questions cannot be answered until certain investigations have been made. If you are able to make the distinction between true and false in the context in question, you know in principle how these investigations should be conducted, but of course, knowing this is not the same thing as having made them.

33 This is not to say, however, that it is necessarily wrong to make the distinction between true and false in religion in ways foreign to it – that is, to discuss religious questions as if they

words such as 'religion', even by those who express the above understanding. This blindness for disagreements about how to make the distinction between true and false results, in analytic-theistic philosophy of religion, in a defective understanding of why religious disagreements are often so vast and firm, and of why people do not change basic religious beliefs very often. Nor does it give us tools with which to reconcile such disagreements. Here I suggest that why religious disagreements are often so vast and firm can be understood by regarding the disagreements as disagreements about how the distinction between true and false is to be made in the context of religion.

Non-argumentative Ways of Showing

We have now introduced the distinction between two ways of being wrong and stressed the importance of different ways of making the distinction between true and false. It is now time to return to demonstrating that there are other ways to show that somebody is wrong than by means of arguments, and the above example with the racist shows the importance of this. As I have said, argumentation presupposes a common way of making the distinction between true and false.[34] For argumentation to be possible, a common way of making this distinction must therefore be established. The way of showing which is a presupposition to argumentation is thus a matter of establishing a common way of making the distinction between true and false. When it comes to showing somebody, without arguments, that she is wrong, this means that she must begin to make the distinction between true and false in a way which is new for her.[35] In the following, I will point out some different ways of doing this. There are certainly more ways than I will mention here. What I am going to do is only to give some examples, to point out some possibilities – much more than what I am going to say here can be said about how one can make somebody make the distinction between true and false in a way that is new for her. Hence, those ways of making somebody make the distinction between true and false in a way that is new for her which I will mention here must not obscure other ways of doing this.

Before beginning, I will point out something that is important to bear in mind here: just because there *are* ways of making somebody make the distinction between true and false in a way that is new for her, these ways do not have to be used, or do not have to be used on all occasions. This is so for (at least) two reasons. Firstly, a new way of making the distinction between true and false is not necessarily better than the way in which one already makes this distinction. To replace a way of

---

were other types of questions, a subject I will return to.

34 This common way of making the distinction between true and false can be established by one of the interlocutors assuming, for the sake of argument, the way the other makes the distinction between true and false, as I have said before.

35 In some cases, different ways of discussing are mixed: some of the time it may be possible to give fruitful arguments, some of the time other ways of discussing must be tried, ways which will be investigated in the following.

making the distinction between true and false which disregards questions about race when it comes to questions about how to treat other human beings with a racist way which finds questions about race very important would, for example, be a change in existing ways of making the distinction between true and false which is not good.

Secondly, there are risks of violations connected to such ways of making somebody make the distinction between true and false in a way that is new for her. These risks are greater in a context where it is hard to make somebody abandon one way of making the distinction between true and false and take up another, for example in the context of religion. For many believers, religion is a very extensive part of their identity, and paying attention to this fact is important when trying to understand religion; this has been stressed too little in the philosophy of religion. Since for many believers, religion is a very extensive part of their identity, it is natural that it is very hard to make somebody change her religious beliefs radically: it is very dissimilar from making somebody change her beliefs about, for example, the movements of glaciers, which are beliefs in the context of the natural sciences, and it is very dissimilar from making somebody give up one way of making the distinction between true and false concerning questions of etiquette for another.[36]

One aspect of these risks of violations is hence that it is possible to change somebody's very identity. In one's own life, this means that it is possible for somebody to transform one's identity into the identity of somebody one would not like to be. That this is a risk is obvious, but it is also a possibility: it means that it is possible to get out of destructive patterns, to stop living a life one would not like to live, although it might appear as if all hope is gone when one feels stuck in such patterns.

There is therefore a possibility both for destruction and liberation here. Whether or not one should try to make somebody make the distinction between true and false in a way which is new for her must therefore be determined by considering whether this would be a matter of destruction or liberation. This is not the only criterion, however. One must also judge whether the way one is trying to do this is acceptable or not. For most of us, there are certain limits we try not to transgress, limits which it is more important to respect than it is to succeed in showing somebody that she is wrong. It is then more important that the way you treat other people when trying to show them that they are wrong is right than that you succeed in showing them that they are wrong. What should be defended is firstly these limits, and only secondly your own opinions. What these limits are is also up to discussion, however.[37]

---

36 Another possibility, instead of talking about identity, is to describe religious belief as a form of ideology – that is, as a system of ideas which *dominate* the thinking of a person or a group of persons (cf. Althusser, *Lenin and Philosophy and Other Essays*, p. 149). Such a system cannot easily be overthrown by the person or the group in question.

37 One way of arguing for a specific set of limits would be to say that if a person did not respect these limits, people would lose confidence in her, and it would then be more difficult for her to show others that they are wrong. This is probably sometimes true, but it is not relevant here. If these limits were defended by it being said that it is effective to respect them, they would not be so interesting, since then we need not talk about limits, but only about

Furthermore, it is not self-evident that these limits should be defended only within these limits themselves – that is, it is possible that one has to break these limits when defending them against somebody who attacks them. One example of this is that it is sometimes said that a constitution characterized by, among other things, freedom of speech must be defended against those who attack its foundations, by restricting their freedom of speech.

In the following, these risks must hence be borne in mind: what I am going to say *can* be abused and used to manipulate others. This is not a weakness, however: there is always such a risk. If rationalistic discussion were possible, we could avoid this risk, but since rationalistic discussion, in the great majority of cases, is not, the idea of rationalistic discussion is dangerous. It is dangerous because it can make us believe that our starting points in the discussion are self-evident and that we therefore do not have to watch out for manipulation, that we do not have to question what we are doing. Seeing that there is a possibility of abuse can thus make us watchful of this risk.

Interaction

In the following, I am going to discuss three different ways to make somebody make the distinction between true and false in a way which is new for her. The first way is about interaction. The second is about inspiring confidence. The third is about making her see her way of making the distinction in a different light, which can change the character of it. Let us start with the first, a non-discursive way of showing.

Making somebody leave one way of making the distinction between true and false and take up another which takes the place of the former can be done by interacting with her. I have already said that what constitutes the making of the distinction between true and false in a certain way (using certain words and doing certain things and holding certain beliefs) hangs together and comes into one's life in the same way – for example, by one being born into a society, and growing up and being brought up there. Being born into a society, and growing up and being brought up there, can be expressed as entering a community and living its life – by interacting with those there before. This is not only a possibility when it comes to the newborn infant, but is also a possibility in other cases. Intellectual interaction – the only form of interaction which is noticed by those who believe that the only way of showing somebody that she is wrong is by means of arguments – rests, on the contrary, on these other forms of interaction. For intellectual interaction to be fruitful, a way of making the distinction between true and false must already be established, a way which can be established in these other forms of interaction (especially when the interaction takes place over a long period), forms which do not presuppose particular beliefs nor that

---

what is effective. The limits are interesting in just those cases where it would be effective to transgress them, but where we nonetheless respect them, for other reasons than what is effective.

one has already been involved in interaction.[38] Of course, there is no guarantee that such interaction establishes a new way of making the distinction: you can live in a foreign community for a long time and still consider the life there as pointless as you did when you arrived, and this does not have to be regarded as a fault on your side. Close interaction tends to increase the probability for this to happen, however.

There are, of course, many forms of interaction, and I will only give one example here, in order to point to the number of possibilities: when some persons are living near each other and have a common problem, for example a moral or practical problem, which they all want to solve. They might then try to solve the problem together, and might arrive at a solution, which does not have to be a compromise, and which it is possible that none of them would have arrived at on their own. This is not in itself the establishment of a common way of making the distinction between true and false, merely of what one could call a temporary way of making this distinction, the beginning of an establishment of a common way of making this distinction. In this situation, the racist mentioned above, might begin to talk, act and think in a partly new way. Co-operating with people she did not co-operate with before might give rise to a new way of making the distinction between true and false in the context of questions about how to treat other human beings. When making the distinction between true and false in this new way, her racist beliefs are mistakes, and when this is pointed out to her, she will probably give up these beliefs. Another possibility is that nothing happens, or that the development takes another direction. The co-operation might take on an excluding character, and the interaction might therefore give rise to a way of making the distinction between true and false in which anti-racist beliefs are mistakes.

That all of this happens now and then is obvious, and noticing this is sufficient to establish that interaction can bring about new ways of making the distinction between true and false. One context in which this happens now and then is in inter-religious dialogue, where breakthroughs are often caused by interaction in response to a common practical problem rather than by intellectual interaction in response to a theoretical problem. That this way of changing the way in which one makes the distinction between true and false is not something generally blameworthy can be seen by noticing that in many cases, this is how we acquire knowledge.

If the interaction above takes place between many persons, the change in established ways of making the distinction between true and false that this may result in could be called a change to a new society. Interaction is thus in one respect a political process. There are some similarities with the process of integration here, but the similarities must not be exaggerated. 'Integration' is (often) used in situations where the direction of the change is already determined, in situations where a minority group should become a part of the majority. In the situations which are discussed here, no such direction could be determined in advance, since it could

---

38 See James C. Klagge, 'When Are Ideologies Irreconcilable? Case Studies in Diachronic Anthropology', *Philosophical Investigations*, 21 (1998): 270–73.

just as well be the majority that should adopt the ways of speaking and acting of the minority.

When somebody does not want to interact, what I have said above is not of any help. Since interaction can bring about a change in one's identity, a change one may not like, legitimate reasons can be given for not wanting to interact with somebody. If you want to make somebody interact, you can try to make the causes of her unwillingness visible and try to do something about them, however. I will only mention one such possible cause here. An experience of injustice can distort the possibilities of interaction,[39] which means that if the experience of injustice is removed, the possibility that interaction will come about becomes greater.[40] The emphasis on the *experience* of injustice, and not on injustice itself, is important – since we are talking about causes, whether or not there really is an injustice here is not of any importance.[41]

---

39 Another possibility is that the influence goes in the other direction: interaction can sometimes, in itself, make a group of people feel that the relations between them are just.

40 Cf. Emile Durkheim, *The Division of Labor in Society*, trans. George Simpson (New York, 1964), p. 409. Durkheim tends here to see a society without conflicts as a goal in itself, however, and he talks about justice, not, as I do, about the experience of justice.

41 Talking about justice should not be understood here as a substitute for talking about truth or rationality. Moreover, emphasizing justice may lead to the same type of confusion as we saw in Davidson's and Rorty's thinking about truth (which was discussed in Chapter 5). Jacques Derrida mystifies justice in this way when he writes: '... one cannot speak *directly* about justice, thematize or objectivize justice, say "this is just" and even less "I am just," without immediately betraying justice ...'; Jacques Derrida, 'Force of Law: The "Mystical Foundation of Authority"', trans. Mary Quaintance, in Drucilla Cornell, Michel Rosenfeld and David Gray Carlson (eds), *Deconstruction and the Possibility of Justice* (New York, 1992), p. 10.

If somebody says, when it comes to distributive justice, 'That two persons who are alike in nearly all respects (needs, merits, efforts, results) get the same amount of what is to be distributed is just', and Derrida answers, 'To say that is to betray justice', it would be hard to see what his word 'justice' means here and to understand what it is he is actually claiming. To say that we are *always* wrong when we say that something is just, that our experiences concerning what is just and our use of the word 'justice' are *always* illegitimate, is to mystify justice.

However, Derrida has an important point which can be seen in the following:

The structure I am describing here is a structure in which law (*droit*) is essentially deconstructible ... The fact that law is deconstructible is not bad news. We may even see in this a stroke of luck for politics, for all historical progress. ... deconstruction takes place in the interval that separates the undeconstructibility of justice from the deconstructibility of *droit* (authority, legitimacy, and so on). (ibid., pp. 14–15)

In other texts (see, for example, Jacques Derrida, *Specters of Marx: The State of the Debt, the Work of Mourning, and the New International*, trans. Peggy Kamuf (New York, 1994), pp. 28, 59, 64–6), Derrida talks about a certain idea of democracy as that which '... remains irreducible to any deconstruction ...' (ibid., p. 59), '... will never present itself in the form of

Inspiring Confidence

Showing a person by means of arguments that a belief is wrong is done by connecting to beliefs she already has. Another way to change the beliefs of another rather than by means of arguments is to connect to something in the other which is *not* beliefs. That this is a genuine possibility can be seen by noticing how knowledge is often transferred. In some cases, knowledge is transferred in this way: someone who knows something presents all the evidence for a group of beliefs to someone who wants to learn something, and in that way makes it possible for her to evaluate the evidence for herself, and thereby form knowledge. This is not the most common case, however. It is more common that someone who wants to learn something trusts the person who seems to know what she is talking about, trusts the person who inspires confidence. When it comes to learning to *do* something, this is especially evident: here, someone who wants to acquire the ability imitates someone who has this ability.

When it comes to our question, this means that a person who inspires confidence is a person whom people are influenced by,[42] not necessarily against a background of shared beliefs. Hence, it matters here what person you are, not just what beliefs you hold. When it comes to religion, where conflicts in many cases are not only about what to think, but primarily about how to live, the person you are trying to influence could change her mind since she feels attracted to your way of living, since she, in a sense, wants to become like you. Hiding problems in one's own way of thinking, propagating in a disingenuous way, trying to explain away drawbacks of one's own way of thinking and trying to dissimulate are then not only examples of bad argumentation, but are actually things that often count against the point you are trying to make, since they reveal a life which, to many, is not attractive. Therefore, it is hardly a good idea to try to influence somebody by behaving in a favourable way *merely* since this seems to be the easiest way to change her beliefs.

This way of influencing others can, of course, be used in many different cases. However, if it is used merely to make somebody adopt a new belief, without changing how she makes the distinction between true and false, we would have a problem, for this new belief could then stand in conflict with other beliefs she already has, which can result in problems of various kinds. If this way of influencing others is used to make somebody make the distinction between true and false in a new way and adopt beliefs associated with this new way, however, this need not be a problem,

---

full presence ...' (ibid., p. 65). What Derrida is driving at here is how the word 'justice', in the same way as 'true' or 'rational', can serve as a reminder of the fact that what we believe is just has to be questioned in the name of justice itself, and that this questioning can contribute to human progress. This must not result in the belief that what we think is just never is just, however.

42 It is evident that there are considerable risks here: this confidence could, of course, have been earned in a bad way, and there are no guarantees that the one who inspires confidence will not abuse her favourable position.

since then, many beliefs are changed at the same time, and an incoherence need not originate.[43]

Seeing One Way of Making the Distinction in a Different Light

The ways of showing which have just been presented are not parts of philosophy. To make somebody make the distinction between true and false in a specific context in a way which is new for her, can, however, also be to make her see the way she makes the distinction in a different light, by describing it in an alternative way, which can change the character of it.[44] All this is, to use the terminology of this chapter, a matter of describing one way of making the distinction between true and false by applying another way of thinking, with its way of making the distinction between true and false, concerning the subject in question, on it. Many such descriptions are no doubt not philosophical, but it is possible that some of them are – in the next chapter, in the discussion of fideism, we will come back to the issue of the possibility of *philosophical* criticism of religious beliefs. No matter what, this way of showing presupposes a good deal of agreement already, an agreement which interaction, or a person who inspires confidence, might establish.[45]

---

43 For the role and function of confidence in attempts to make somebody change beliefs, cf. Aristotle's account of confidence in Aristotle, *On Rhetoric: A Theory of Civic Discourse*, trans. George A. Kennedy (New York, 1991). According to Aristotle, there are three means of persuasion provided through speech: (1) by means of the speech itself, in so far as it shows or seems to show something (*logos*), (2) by means of the character of the speaker (*ēthos*), and (3) by means of the ability of the speech to lead the hearers to feel emotion (*pathos*); ibid., pp. 37–9 (1356a), cf. ibid., p. 120 (1377b–1378a). When it comes to *ēthos*, Aristotle says that the speaker persuades by means of her character when the speech is spoken in such a way as to make her worthy of confidence; ibid., p. 38 (1356a). A speaker inspires confidence when she seems to be, for example, good or well disposed to us; ibid., p. 77 (1366a).

For our purposes, we can distinguish between *ēthos* and *pathos* by saying that *pathos* makes a belief less menacing and more attractive by *showing* what is attractive about it, as opposed to *saying* what is attractive about it. *Ēthos*, on the other hand, shows what kind of person the one who holds the belief is, and consequently what kind of person one could be if one adopted the belief.

44 Cf. Ludwig Wittgenstein, 'Wittgenstein's Lectures in 1930–33', in James C. Klagge and Alfred Nordmann (eds), *Philosophical Occasions 1912–1951* (Indianapolis, IN, 1993), p. 106; Hodges, 'The Status of Ethical Judgements in the *Philosophical Investigations*': 108.

45 Making somebody see a way of making the distinction between true and false in a specific context in a different light is not only something one subjects other people to. It is, on the contrary, as relevant when one is trying to come to turns with a problem oneself. Moral dilemmas – a case of moral disagreement within oneself, so to speak – cannot be solved just by arguing more carefully. If a moral dilemma is to be solved, a way of making the distinction between true and false must hence be established here. This can be done by looking at the dilemma from a different angle, in the sense explained above.

Criticizing somebody's religious beliefs can thus be a matter of describing how she makes the distinction between true and false in this context in an alternative way. Such a criticism need not be philosophically problematic. It *is* problematic if you believe that the understanding of rationality you are connecting to when criticizing is an understanding which *has* to be prevalent in all contexts of life and in all forms of religious belief. This is not the only possibility, however. If you consciously criticize a form of religious belief from a position foreign to it without believing that this position is privileged *a priori*, and in that way try to change the understanding of rationality the believers themselves have, what you are doing is *not* philosophically problematic.[46] The only problem that may originate in the latter case is that the believers find your criticism irrelevant.

This difference in attitude and in understanding of your own criticism can take expression in different ways. For example, your understanding of your criticism makes a difference to how long you use this form of criticism and when you try another one instead. Furthermore, this understanding makes a difference to how you regard the person you are trying to convince when you fail to do so – as unintelligent, as morally blameworthy, or in some other way.

Criticizing a religious belief for being immoral is therefore, in one sense, better than criticizing it for being irrational, since it is far more difficult to be led into the kind of philosophical confusion I mentioned above when criticizing religious beliefs in this way. The philosophical confusion originates when one is not aware of what one is doing. When criticizing a religious belief for being immoral, this awareness tends to come more easily than when criticizing it for being irrational. This is so for two reasons. Firstly, the awareness of the diversity of moral opinions is greater than the awareness of the diversity of conceptions of rationality and criteria associated therewith. Secondly, the awareness of the difficulty of arriving at a, in the strict sense, neutral position from where to launch the criticism is greater when it comes to morals than when it comes to rationality.

It is hence not necessarily wrong to make the distinction between true and false in religion in ways foreign to it, as we have seen – that is, to describe religious questions as if they were other types of questions. What is wrong is believing that this is the way the distinction *is* made in the context of religion or believing that one's own way of making the distinction is self-evident or necessary. Trying consciously to introduce a new way to make the distinction in the context of religion is not self-evidently wrong, but one must then realize that this is what one is doing. On the contrary, such introductions are sometimes good, since it makes progress not only on the level of correcting mistakes and on the level of doing more, and more thorough, investigations possible, but also on the level of improving the way one makes the distinction between true and false. By making such introductions, the

---

46 It is, of course, not philosophically problematic to say that a certain form of religious belief is, for example, irrational, if this criticism connects to the understanding the believers *themselves* have, explicitly or implicitly, of what rationality amounts to in a religious context – that is, if the criticism is not made from a position foreign to the religious belief in question.

cautionary use of 'true' is brought into focus and ethnocentrism is prevented from becoming a trap,[47] as has been said in a previous chapter. The use of the words 'good' and 'progress' might strike you as problematic here, since it is not possible to show by means of arguments when such introductions are good and when they are not. Two things can be said here, however. Firstly, a consequence of the discussions of rationality and truth in Chapters 4 and 5 is that there is a use of words such as 'good' and 'progress' even in cases where you are not able to show others that you are right. Secondly, this chapter has shown that there are other ways of showing than by means of arguments.

The accusation of fideism levelled against Wittgensteinian philosophy of religion I mentioned in the introduction (according to which this way of doing philosophy of religion results in it being impossible for outsiders to understand and criticize religious beliefs,) is partly answered by means of the above remarks. In the next chapter, we will, among other issues, discuss the issue of the possibility of *philosophical* criticism of religious beliefs, and I will thus continue to answer the accusation of fideism there. In the rest of this chapter, I will continue to answer the accusation of fideism by giving some examples of criticisms of particular religious beliefs; these criticisms may be philosophical or not. These criticisms are not, in contrast to rationalistic criticisms, philosophically problematic, but are a matter of describing religious beliefs in an alternative way, of introducing an alternative way of making the distinction between true and false in this context. In order to make these criticisms philosophically unproblematic, they must sometimes be understood in a way which clashes with the way they were originally understood, but as you will see, it is possible to understand them in another way than originally intended. The examples are furthermore in one obvious sense not new. Making somebody see the way she makes the distinction between true and false in the context of religion in a different light need not be a matter of presenting a way of describing religion she has never heard of before. What makes us justified in talking about a 'different light' is rather that what these descriptions are meant to achieve is her beginning to think about her religious beliefs in a way in which she now does not think about them. It is, moreover, important to remember that different conclusions are possible when discussing beliefs in this way, and that there are more ways of making somebody see the way she makes the distinction between true and false in a specific field in a different light than those I mention here.

Firstly, we have the problem of evil. The problem of evil is often understood as a logical or evidential problem, and it is then neither very interesting nor compelling,[48] as was said in Chapter 1. When the problem is understood as an existential problem, however, the matter is different. What this criticism highlights is the existential inadequateness of certain religious understandings of evil – that is, when the demand

---

47 Cf. Thompson, 'Richard Rorty on Truth, Justification and Justice', pp. 35 and 47.

48 The interest and compulsion the problem of evil has been supposed to have in its logical or evidential forms have, on the contrary, been derived from the existential understanding of the problem. Cf. Phillips, *The Problem of Evil and the Problem of God*, pp. xi–xii.

that a religious belief should enable us to live with the existence of evil is highlighted, such religious beliefs appear inadequate.[49] In that way, an alternative way to make the distinction between true and false in this context might become established, a way in which these questions are important. Sometimes such alternative ways of seeing one's religious belief force themselves in without the help of a description: if life and the world are experienced as permeated by suffering and evil, perhaps as a reaction to events in one's own life, and somebody says that God is good, this saying may appear as void or as an insult. The importance of theological reflection is particularly great when social change brings about new requirements of religion, and with that, new ways of making the distinction between true and false in the context of religion.

Secondly, we have Sigmund Freud's criticism of religious beliefs. His criticism is obviously mostly due to his understanding of religion as something which is to be evaluated in the same way as scientific theories are evaluated,[50] an understanding which is problematic, as we have seen.[51] His criticism contains elements which are not problematic, however. Freud describes religion as a way of dealing with the hardships of human life: the terrors of nature, the cruelty of death, and the sufferings and privations which are necessary for making a social life possible.[52] This description can be understood as a reductive explanation, and is then problematic, but it need not be understood in that way: it can be understood as an alternative to a religious understanding of religion, an alternative which stands on the same level as the religious understanding of religion. That the alternative understanding stands on the same level as the religious understanding of religion means that it does not present the religious understanding as a mistake, as an error in thinking, in the sense I have explained above. If one understands religion in this way, the problem with religion is that it presents the world exactly as one would like it to be, which means that religion appears unbelievable even if one does not evaluate it in the same way as scientific theories are evaluated.[53] What Freud suggests instead is that the hardships of human life should be seen as they are, without adding some optimistic understanding of them. This suggestion would be ill founded, however, if it were not so that religion, even if, in a way, it is *too* adequate (presenting the world exactly as we would like it to be), is also inadequate: it has not succeeded in making us happy and in reconciling us to life in all its aspects.[54] Freud can, of course, not know that an irreligious life would be better for humankind, but we could at least give it a try.[55]

---

49 Cf. Phillips, *Wittgenstein and Religion*, p. 155.

50 See Sigmund Freud, *The Standard Edition of the Complete Psychological Works of Sigmund Freud, Volume XXI: The Future of an Illusion, Civilization and Its Discontents, and Other Works*, trans. James Strachey (London, 1961), pp. 16, 31, 38.

51 See Chapter 2.

52 Ibid., p. 18. See also ibid., pp. 21 and 75.

53 Ibid., pp. 31 and 33.

54 Ibid., pp. 37 and 84–5.

55 Ibid., pp. 48 and 53.

Thirdly, the accusation that religion is a way of legitimizing the social order we can find also in Freud,[56] but it is at the centre of Karl Marx's criticism of religion. Religion is described, as in Freud, as a way of dealing with the hardships of human life, but these hardships, according to Marx, are not necessary, and religion conceals this fact, promising consolation only after death. Religion thus becomes a way of justifying the oppression of the proletariat.[57] By describing religious belief in this way, focusing on its social aspects, Marx can be said to try to make others see it in a different light and make the distinction between true and false in an alternative way here. Many forms of feminist criticism of religious beliefs are a continuation of this type of criticism, by focusing on other forms of oppression.

What must be stressed, however, is that for Marx, criticism of religious beliefs is not very central. This can be seen in Marx's perhaps most well-known saying about religion:

> The struggle against religion is … indirectly a fight against *the world* of which religion is the spiritual *aroma*. *Religious* distress is at the same time the *expression* of real distress and also the *protest* against real distress. Religion is the sigh of the oppressed creature, the heart of a heartless world, just as it is the spirit of spiritless conditions. It is the *opium* of the people. To abolish religion as the *illusory* happiness of the people is to demand their *real* happiness. The demand to give up illusions about the existing state of affairs is the *demand to give up a state of affairs which needs illusions*. The criticism of religion is therefore *in embryo the criticism of the vale of tears*, the *halo* of which is religion.[58]

In the same way as in his 'Theses on Feuerbach', Marx stresses here that criticism of religion could become a starting point for changing the world, as opposed to interpreting it.[59] What Marx criticizes the Young Hegelians for is that their criticism,

---

56 Ibid., pp. 40–41.

57 Karl Marx, 'The Communism of the *Rheinischer Beobachter*', in *Karl Marx Frederick Engels Collected Works, Volume 6: Marx and Engels 1945–48* (London, 1976), p. 231.

58 Karl Marx, 'Contribution to the Critique of Hegel's Philosophy of Law: Introduction', in *Karl Marx Frederick Engels Collected Works, Volume 3: Marx and Engels 1943–44* (London, 1975), pp. 175–6. Translation of Karl Marx, 'Zur Kritik der Hegelschen Rechtsphilosophie: Einleitung', in *Karl Marx Friedrich Engels Gesamtausgabe: Erste Abteilung, Werke Artikel Entwürfe, Band 2, März 1943 bis August 1844: Text* (Berlin, 1982), pp. 170–71: 'Der Kampf gegen die Religion ist … mittelbar der Kampf gegen *jene Welt*, deren geistiges *Aroma* die Religion ist. Das *religiöse* Elend ist in einem der *Ausdruck* des wirklichen Elendes und in einem die *Protestation* gegen das wirkliche Elend. Die Religion ist der Seufzer der bedrängten Kreatur, das Gemüth einer herzlosen Welt, wie sie der Geist geistloser Zustände ist. Sie ist das *Opium* des Volks. Die Aufhebung der Religion als des *illusorischen* Glücks des Volkes ist die Forderung seines *wirklichen* Glücks. Die Forderung, die Illusionen über seinen Zustand aufzugeben, ist die *Forderung, einen Zustand aufzugeben, der der Illisionen bedarf*. Die Kritik der Religion ist also im *Keim* die *Kritik des Jammerthales*, dessen *Heiligenschein* die Religion ist.'

59 Karl Marx, 'Theses on Feuerbach: Edited by Engels', in *Karl Marx Frederick Engels Collected Works, Volume 5: Marx and Engels 1945–47* (London, 1976).

above all of religion, is only theoretical, which means that they put the real relation between human beings' consciousness and their practical activity on its head, when what, on the contrary, can dissolve religion as a social phenomenon is purely a change in the relations of production.[60]

Fourthly, Friedrich Nietzsche establishes new values, and contrasts them to the values he sees in religion (especially in Christianity). The latter values appear, in the light of these new values, as characterized by enmity towards everything which is full of life, and as springing out of hatred, resentment and revenge, a hatred which turns into self-hatred:[61]

> The concept 'God' invented as the antithetical concept to life – everything harmful, noxious, slanderous, the whole mortal enmity against life brought into one terrible unity! The concept 'the Beyond', 'real world' invented so as to deprive of value the *only* world which exists – so as to leave over no goal, no reason, no task for our earthly reality! The concept 'soul', 'spirit', finally even 'immortal soul', invented so as to despise the body, so as to make it sick – 'holy' – so as to bring to all the things in life which deserve

---

60 Karl Marx and Frederick Engels, 'The German Ideology: Critique of Modern German Philosophy According to Its Representatives Feuerbach, B. Bauer and Stirner, and of German Socialism According to Its Various Prophets', in *Karl Marx Frederick Engels Collected Works, Volume 5: Marx and Engels 1945–47* (London, 1976), pp. 23–4, 30, 54; Karl Marx, 'On the Jewish Question', in *Karl Marx Frederick Engels Collected Works, Volume 3: Marx and Engels 1943–44* (London, 1975), p. 151; Marx, 'Contribution to the Critique of Hegel's Philosophy of Law: Introduction', p. 182; Karl Marx, 'A Contribution to the Critique of Political Economy: Part One', in *Karl Marx Frederick Engels Collected Works, Volume 29: Karl Marx 1957–61* (Moscow, 1987), p. 263. See also Frederick Engels, 'Anti-Dühring: Herr Eugen Dühring's Revolution in Science', in *Karl Marx Frederick Engels Collected Works, Volume 25: Frederick Engels Anti-Dühring, Dialectics of Nature* (Moscow, 1987), pp. 300–302:

> All religion … is nothing but the fantastic reflection in men's minds of those external forces which control their daily life … in existing bourgeois society men are dominated by the economic conditions created by themselves, by means of production which they themselves have produced, as if by a alien force. The actual basis of the religious reflective activity therefore continues to exist, and with it the religious reflection itself. … Mere knowledge … is not enough to bring social forces under the domination of society. What is above all necessary for this, is a social *act*. And when this act has been accomplished, when society, by taking possession of all means of production … has freed itself and all its members from the bondage in which they are now held … only then will the last alien force which is still reflected in religion vanish; and with it will also vanish the religious reflection itself, for the simple reason that there will be nothing left to reflect.

61 Friedrich Nietzsche, *Ecce Homo: How One Becomes What One Is*, trans. R.J. Hollingdale (London, 1979), p. 84; Friedrich Nietzsche, *On the Genealogy of Morality*, trans. Carol Diethe (Cambridge, 1994), pp. 18–20, 31–3, 100.

serious attention, the questions of nutriment, residence, cleanliness, weather, a horrifying frivolity![62]

Fifthly, a description meant to make others see religious belief in a different light, a description which Jean-Paul Sartre could have formulated,[63] is that the existence of God would diminish human freedom, by making us into created objects. Sartre writes:

> When we think of God as the creator, we are thinking of him, most of the time, as a supernal artisan. … Thus, the conception of man in the mind of God is comparable to that of the paper-knife in the mind of the artisan: God makes man according to a procedure and a conception, exactly as the artisan manufactures a paper-knife, following a definition and a formula. Thus each individual man is the realization of a certain conception which dwells in the divine understanding.[64]

If there exists a Creator, essence precedes existence, and the choice and responsibility, and the fundamental freedom connected to these, which Sartre emphasizes[65] would not be the centre in an understanding of oneself as a human being.[66] Furthermore,

---

62 Nietzsche, *Ecce Homo*, pp. 103–4. Translation of Friedrich Nietzsche, 'Ecce Homo', in Giorgio Colli and Mazzino Montinari (eds), *Nietzsche Werke: Kritische Gesamtausgabe: Sechste Abteilung: Dritter Band* (Berlin, 1969), pp. 371–2: 'Der Begriff "Gotterfunden" als Gegensatz-Begriff zum Leben, – in ihm alles Schädliche, Vergiftende, Verleumderische, die ganze Todfeindschaft gegen das Leben in eine entsetzliche Einheit gebracht! Der Begriff "Jenseits", "wahre Welt" erfunden, um die *einzige* Welt zu entwerthen, die es giebt, – um kein Ziel, keine Vernunft, keine Aufgabe für unsre Erden-Realität übrig zu behalten! Der Begriff "Seele", "Geist", zuletzt gar noch "unsterbliche Seele", erfunden, um den Leib zu verachten, um ihn krank – "heilig" – zu machen, um allen Dingen, die Ernst im Leben verdienen, den Fragen von Nahrung, Wohnung, geistiger Diät, Krankenbehandlung, Reinlichkeit, Wetter, einen schauerlichen Leichtsinn entgegenzubringen!'.

63 Sartre's atheism is a starting point rather than something he arrives at after a discussion; Sartre, *Existentialism and Humanism*, pp. 27–8 and 56. In some cases, he even seems to think that it is a great problem that God does not exist; ibid., p. 33.

64 Ibid., p. 27. Translation of Sartre, *L'existentialisme est un humanisme*, pp. 19–20: 'Lorsque nous concevons un Dieu créatuer, ce Dieu est assimilé la plupart du temps à un artisan supérieur … Ainsi, le concept d'homme, dans l'esprit de Dieu est assimilable au concept de coupe-papier dans l'esprit de l'industriel: et Dieu produit l'homme suivant des techniques et une conception, exactement comme l'artisan fabrique un coupe-papier suivant une définition et une technique. Ainsi l'homme individuel réalise un certain concept qui est dans l'entendement divin.'

65 Sartre, *Existentialism and Humanism*, p, 29.

66 A more radical form of the same type of criticism is to be found in an anarchist tradition. Max Stirner, for example, dismisses God and all secular equivalents to God for the benefit of the own self:

> To the Christian the world's history is the higher thing, because it is the history of Christ or 'man'; to the egoist only *his* history has value, because he wants to develop only *himself* not the mankind-idea, not God's plan, not the purposes of Providence, not liberty, and the

Sartre appears to think that what good religion promised to deliver was a morality based on absolute foundations.[67] Such a morality is not possible, however, since it is only I myself who can decide what I should do,[68] so when it comes to questions about morality, it does not matter whether God exists or not,[69] and religion then has no positive function and can be rejected.

Sixthly, making somebody see the way she makes the distinction between true and false in a specific field, for example in the context of religion, in a different light can also be done by focusing on some aspect in the person's past. Since our identities are often complex, it is often possible to find a critical vantage point somewhere in the person's identity.[70] Your identity is not something you determine completely on your own. What influences your identity is, among other things, those people with whom you have something in common (or are regarded as having something in common with). A change in identity can then be effected by being given an alternative picture of which people you have something in common with, people you may not like and therefore try not to be like, or people you like and therefore want to be like. One way of facilitating such a change is by showing the person you are in discussion with that the position you propose contains what made the criticized belief nevertheless attractive – that is, by showing that what makes somebody stick to this position is not lost when giving it up. Another way is by appealing to unconscious desires and fears.[71]

---

like. He does not look upon himself as a tool of the idea or a vessel of God, he recognizes no calling, he does not fancy that he exists for the further development of mankind and that he must contribute his mite to it, but he lives himself out, careless of how well or ill humanity may fare thereby. (Max Stirner, *The Ego and Its Own*, trans. Steven Tracy Byington (Cambridge, 1995), p. 323; see also ibid., pp. 153 and 183)

Michael Bakunin, for example, exalts thought and rebellion as the central things (Michael Bakunin, *God and the State*, trans. Benjamin Tucker (New York, 1970), pp. 9 and 12), and sums up this type of criticism in a good way (ibid., pp. 27–8):

... if God is, he is necessarily the eternal, supreme, absolute master, and, if such a master exists, man is slave ... if God existed, only in one way could he serve human liberty – by ceasing to exist. ... *if God really existed, it would be necessary to abolish him.*

Thus Bakunin proves that God does not exist by the following deduction: 'If God is, man is a slave; now, man can and must be free; then, God does not exist'; ibid., p. 25.

67 Sartre, *Existentialism and Humanism*, p. 33.

68 Ibid., pp. 31 and 38.

69 Ibid., p. 56

70 Cf. Richard Rorty, *Achieving Our Country: Leftist Thought in Twentieth-century America* (Cambridge, 1998), pp. 3–4.

71 The appeal to unconscious desires and fears in particular contains great risks: there is a genuine possibility here of vast violations, violations which in many cases pass unseen for the person who is exposed to them.

The strength in these possibly fruitful criticisms is that they attack *particular* religious beliefs or forms of religious belief. This certainly means that they do not manage to criticize *every* religious belief or *every* form of religious belief, if that was the intention. However, for this reason, the criticism is more fruitful when it is relevant.

Furthermore, none of these criticisms is decisive, since the conclusion that there is no God is not imperative. That this is so does not frustrate their function as criticism, however – that would be so only if the only real criticism was a matter of inference, was a matter of logical compulsion. We have thus not arrived at a level where differences between people are no longer possible, a level which then could be a secure starting point. Discussing and developing possibilities for discussion is, on the contrary, a permanent task. By highlighting another way of dealing with the problem, I have hopefully contributed something, but not, of course, the one and only solution, for every enumeration of strategies for action has to be open-ended. Criticism of religious beliefs then becomes something different from what it has traditionally been in analytic-theistic philosophy of religion.[72]

Conclusion

In this chapter, I have answered the question 'How is fruitful discussion of religious beliefs possible?' by showing, firstly, that there is no guarantee that it always is possible. Furthermore, I have given an account of how the difference between the case in which it is possible and the case in which it is not can be understood. Starting from that account, I have presented some examples of possibly fruitful criticism of particular religious beliefs and forms of belief.

This question had to be asked because of certain observations we made by relating to Wittgenstein and Wittgensteinian philosophy of religion – the picture of religious beliefs according to which they are beliefs of a scientific type, based on hypothetical, scientific reasoning, overlooks certain characteristics of religious belief; the belief that the distinction between true and false, between rational and irrational, is made in the same way in all areas of human life overlooks how these distinctions are rooted in the diverse ways we deal with the world around us. The answer I have given in this chapter to the question 'How is fruitful discussion of religious beliefs possible?' could thus also be seen as a way of answering the criticism of Wittgensteinian philosophy of religion for being fideist, a criticism I mentioned in the introduction. In the next chapter, I will discuss the problem of fideism, and show how what I have said here is a way of answering the criticism of Wittgensteinian philosophy of religion for being fideist. Above all, I will try to get to the bottom of the problem by discussing in what

---

72 For a somewhat different account of how it is possible to effect changes of beliefs in the context of vast disagreements, see Hugo Strandberg, 'Att ändra sig och andra: En diskussion kring relationen mellan en skeptisk inställning och en konservativ hållning', in Erica Appelros, Stefan Eriksson and Catharina Stenqvist (eds), *Makt och religion i könsskilda världar: Religionsfilosofiska perspektiv* (Lund, 2003), pp. 169–75.

sense, if any, Wittgenstein's philosophy could be said to be a critical philosophy. That will lead us to the question of whether there could be a *philosophical* criticism of religious beliefs – a question we have left open in this chapter.

Chapter 7

Wittgenstein, Conservatism and Fideism

In Chapter 2, I showed, by relating to Wittgenstein's philosophy, that our beliefs about the world in the most general sense are not based on theoretical, hypothetical thinking. We saw that this idea overlooks how our ways of speaking are conceptually connected to our ways of acting and living in the world generally. Since our ways of making the distinction between true and false are not based on hypothetical reasoning, but are rooted in the diverse ways we deal with the world around us, it is possible that this distinction is not made in the same way in all contexts and by all persons. Therefore, it is not *necessary* to see religious beliefs as the same sort of beliefs as scientific beliefs. If we furthermore observe the differences between how we actually act when it comes to religion and when it comes to science, we realize that perceiving religious beliefs to be a form of scientific beliefs distorts the specific character of religious beliefs.

The problem was, however, that the above observations mean that a specific kind of disagreement is possible: disagreements which are not disagreements concerning whether a mistake has been made within a shared way of making the distinction between true and false, but which are disagreements about how the distinction between true and false should be made in a certain context, as I showed in Chapter 6. In such situations, there does not have to be a way to make the distinction between true and false which we can step back to, to reconcile the disagreement. If there does not have to be such a way, there does not have to be a position we can step back to, and from there criticize particular religious beliefs in a self-evident way. For this reason, Wittgenstein's philosophy has been said to have fideist consequences. However, in the last chapter, I showed that there are forms of criticism which do not presuppose a self-evident starting point. That is not enough, however, since it is possible that the problem has deeper roots. 'Wittgensteinian fideism' is, for example, said to be a consequence of Wittgensteinian sayings such as 'It [philosophy] leaves everything as it is',[1] and concepts such as language-game and form of life, designating something said to be given and in some sense self-contained. Therefore, in the following, we must discuss the problem of fideism, in relation to Wittgenstein's philosophy, more directly, to see if there is anything that deserves to be called *philosophical* criticism of religious beliefs. This will be done in a rather unusual way. I will start by discussing a question which is closely related to the question of fideism, but which is too seldom *de facto* related to it, namely the question of conservatism: is a

---

1   Wittgenstein, *Philosophical Investigations*, p. 42e (§ 124): 'Sie [die Philosophie] läßt alles wie es ist.'

critical attitude towards the status quo compatible with Wittgenstein's philosophy? Paying attention to the discussions of this question could deepen the discussions of the question of fideism by letting us approach it from a different direction.

Those who have answered the question of conservatism in the negative have often done this against a background of a discussion of Wittgenstein's own political views. I will therefore begin the discussion of the question of conservatism by discussing Wittgenstein's own political views, and thereafter discuss the relation between his philosophy and conservatism. I want to point out right at the beginning that I do not give any verdict on the question about strong and direct connections between Wittgenstein's political views and his philosophy. All I am doing is to point out that seeing Wittgenstein as politically conservative is a gross simplification. This is simply directed against those who are dependent on seeing him as politically conservative, those who actually see a connection between his political views and his philosophy, and criticize his philosophy for what they see when it comes to his political views. However, investigating Wittgenstein's political views does not only have such an indirect purpose. Such an investigation can also make it clear that a Wittgensteinian philosophy could be combined with different political views and positions, and thus make possibilities visible which we otherwise could have missed.

After the discussion of the question of conservatism, I address the main question in this chapter, the question of 'Wittgensteinian fideism'. The answer to the question of conservatism is used here to shed light upon this second question.

Wittgenstein and Conservatism

In the following discussion of Wittgenstein's own political views, I want to make and argue for four claims. The first claim is that Wittgenstein's political views have both radical and conservative traits. The second is that according to Wittgenstein, philosophy ought to have political implications, in the sense that it should make you more careful about how you use certain words. The third is that Wittgenstein is to some extent a cultural pessimist, which does not mean, however, that progress is bad (whatever that would mean), only that the question of whether or not something is progress is more complicated than is often thought, among other things due to the fact that progress is connected to questions about aims. The fourth and last claim is that according to Wittgenstein, it is possible to try to influence the future, and that we in some sense must also try to influence the future, since progress will not come by itself. Of course, this depends on how you understand the word 'progress', a question that will be discussed below.

Conservative or Radical?

No doubt examples can be given of situations where Wittgenstein expresses a conservative opinion or expresses himself in a way which indicates a conservative view.[2] Wittgenstein writes, for example: 'Where there is bad management in the state, I believe, bad management is fostered in the families too. A worker who is ready for a strike at any time will not bring up his children to respect order either.'[3] However, when one focuses too intensely on such examples, one misses the fact that other examples can be given at the same time, examples of situations where Wittgenstein expresses a radical opinion or expresses himself in a way which indicates a radical view,[4] or where he expresses a wavering or a mixed opinion.[5] This can be interpreted as a matter of Wittgenstein changing his views, or as a matter of his views being paradoxical and contradictory.[6] These interpretations are not unreasonable, but in the following I will describe the matter in another way (a description not necessarily in conflict with these interpretations). I will describe Wittgenstein's political views as basically ambiguous, an ambiguity which stems from the fact that Wittgenstein's political views often have a distinctive ethical/existential ground. By giving a couple of examples where this ground shows itself and leads to ambiguous political views, I show in this section that labelling Wittgenstein as *either* a conservative or a radical is not very meaningful. Such a labelling overlooks the fact that Wittgenstein's political views are often political views only secondarily, since they grow out of other views.

---

2   See, for example, Maurice O'Connor Drury, 'Conversations with Wittgenstein', in F.A. Flowers III (ed.), *Portraits of Wittgenstein, Volume 3* (Bristol, 1999), p. 201; Paul Engelmann, 'A Memoir', trans. L. Furtmüller, in F.A. Flowers III (ed.), *Portraits of Wittgenstein, Volume 2* (Bristol, 1999), p. 45; Ray Monk, *Ludwig Wittgenstein: The Duty of Genius* (London, 1990), pp. 72, 188–9, 192, 195–6; Fania Pascal, 'Wittgenstein: A Personal Memoir', in F.A. Flowers III (ed.), *Portraits of Wittgenstein, Volume 2* (Bristol, 1999), p. 225; Wittgenstein, *Culture and Value*, p. 64e; Ludwig Wittgenstein, 'Movements of Thought: Diaries 130–1 932, 1 936–1 937', in James C. Klagge and Alfred Nordmann (eds), *Public and Private Occasions* (Lanham, MD, 2003), p. 67.

3   Wittgenstein, *Culture and Value*, p. 72e: 'Wo schlechte Wirtschaft im Staat ist wird, glaube ich, auch schlechte Wirtschaft in den Familien begünstigt. Der jederzeit zum Streike bereite Arbeiter wird auch seine Kinder nicht zur Ordnung erziehen.'

4   See, for example, Monk, *Ludwig Wittgenstein: The Duty of Genius*, pp. 189, 194–5, 343, 353–4, 480, 486; Pascal, 'Wittgenstein: A Personal Memoir', p. 228; George Thomson, 'Wittgenstein: Some Personal Recollections', in F.A. Flowers III (ed.), *Portraits of Wittgenstein, Volume 2* (Bristol, 1999), p. 220.

5   See, for example, Rush Rhees, 'Postscript', in F.A. Flowers III (ed.), *Portraits of Wittgenstein, Volume 3* (Bristol, 1999), pp. 275–6; Lodwig Wittgenstein, 'Ludwig Hänsel– Ludwig Wittgenstein: A Friendship, 1929–1940', in James C. Klagge and Alfred Nordmann (eds), *Public and Private Occasions* (Lanham, MD, 2003), pp. 269–71.

6   Cf. Georg Henrik von Wright, 'Wittgenstein and the Twentieth Century', in Leila Haaparanta, Martin Kusch and Ilka Niiniluoto (eds), *Acta Philosophica Fennica 49: Language, Knowledge, and Intentionality. Perspectives on the Philosophy pf Jaakko Hintikka* (1990), p. 53.

Throughout his life, Wittgenstein was more concerned with ethical and existential issues than with political ones, a focus which can take apolitical expressions.[7] This ethical/existential view had obvious political implications, as we will see. For example, during the 1930's Wittgenstein thought about moving to the Soviet Union. These thoughts had little to do with politics in the first place, however, but more with the life he thought one lived there, a life characterized by hardship, primitivity, manual labour and spirituality.[8] Fania Pascal, who taught Russian to Wittgenstein in the 1930s, writes: 'To my mind, his feeling for Russia would have had at all times more to do with Tolstoy's moral teachings, with Dostoevsky's spiritual insights, than with any political or social matters. He would view the latter, which certainly were not indifferent to him, in terms of the former.'[9]

In 1935, Wittgenstein travelled to the Soviet Union, and after the journey he hinted that he did not like what he saw. At the same time, however, he expressed his sympathy for the Soviet regime, and he spoke admiringly of the educational system there.[10] To Rush Rhees, a student and close friend of Wittgenstein, he said that: '... 'the important thing is that people have *work*'.[11] Rhees again:

> He thought the new regime in Russia did provide work for the mass of the people. If you spoke of regimentation of Russian workers, of workers not being free to leave or change their jobs, or perhaps of labour camps, Wittgenstein was not impressed. It would be terrible if the mass of the people there – or in any society – had no regular work. He also thought it would be terrible if the society were ridden by 'class distinctions', although he said less about this.[12] 'On the other hand, *tyranny* ...?' – with a questioning gesture, shrugging his shoulders – 'doesn't make me feel indignant.'[13]

To Maurice O'Connor Drury, a student and close friend of Wittgenstein, Wittgenstein said:

> People have accused Stalin of having betrayed the Russian Revolution. But they have no idea of the problems that Stalin had to deal with; and the dangers he saw threatening

---

7   See, for example, Ludwig Wittgenstein, *Notebooks 1914–1916*, trans. G.E.M. Anscombe (Chicago, IL, 1979), p. 73e; Wittgenstein, *Culture and Value*, pp. 51e and 60e; Engelmann, 'A Memoir', pp. 17–18; Monk, *Ludwig Wittgenstein: The Duty of Genius*, pp. 17–18 and 213; Pascal, 'Wittgenstein: A Personal Memoir', p. 229.

8   Monk, *Ludwig Wittgenstein: The Duty of Genius*, p. 343.

9   Pascal, 'Wittgenstein: A Personal Memoir', p. 245.

10   Monk, *Ludwig Wittgenstein: The Duty of Genius*, p. 353.

11   Rhees, 'Postscript', p. 278.

12   In a note, Rhees says the following: 'When I said that the "rule of bureaucracy" in Russia was bringing in class distinctions there, he told me: "If anything could destroy my sympathy with the Russian regime, it would be the growth of class distinctions"'; Rhees, 'Postscript', p. 278.

13   Ibid.

Russia. I was looking at a picture of the British Cabinet and I thought to myself, 'a lot of wealthy old men'.[14]

No matter what exactly Wittgenstein meant here, he apparently stressed, as a good side of the Soviet regime, that it provided people with work, but he did not care about its tyrannical and anti-democratic sides. This could have made Wittgenstein express sympathy for the Nazi regime as well. However, Wittgenstein did not do that at all.[15] One of the main differences between Communism and Nazism, according to Wittgenstein, was, presumably, the latter's racist, patriot and chauvinist side.[16] Wittgenstein reacted strongly against the patriotism and chauvinism he saw in England in the 1930s[17], so the far more excessive patriotism and chauvinism of Nazi Germany was probably even more distasteful to him.

What we can see from these few examples is that Wittgenstein's political views, which should be seen as implications of his more fundamental ethical/existential view, are to some extent radical, but are at the same time mixed with conservative, even reactionary and totalitarian, elements, and this makes it hard to characterize Wittgenstein's general political view as either conservative or radical – these labels are not appropriate. They are inappropriate due, firstly, to the fact that Wittgenstein's political view consists of elements which point in different directions, as we saw already at the beginning of this section. Secondly, they are inappropriate because different things could be intended by the words 'conservative' and 'radical', which means that in order to be usable in this context, these words need to be clarified. We can therefore conclude that labelling Wittgenstein as *either* a conservative or a radical is not very meaningful.

Political Implications of Philosophy

One interesting and important episode in the life of Wittgenstein occurred in the autumn of 1939, as reported by Norman Malcolm,[18] a student and close friend of Wittgenstein. Malcolm and Wittgenstein were walking and saw a news-vendor's sign which announced that the German government accused the British government of instigating a recent attempt to assassinate Hitler with a bomb. Whereas Wittgenstein believed that this accusation could be true, Malcolm said that he could not believe that the top people in the British government would do such a thing, and motivated his disbelief by talking of the British national character being decency and civilized

---

14 Drury, 'Conversations with Wittgenstein', p. 228.

15 See ibid., p. 223; Rhees, 'Postscript', p. 277.

16 It is important here to remember that Wittgenstein, and of course also his brother and sisters living in Austria, were Jews according to the definition in the Nuremberg laws. See David Stern, 'Was Wittgenstein a Jew?', in James C. Klagge (ed.), *Wittgenstein: Biography and Philosophy* (New York, 2001), p. 239.

17 Monk, *Ludwig Wittgenstein: The Duty of Genius*, pp. 423–4.

18 See Norman Malcolm, *Ludwig Wittgenstein: A Memoir* (Oxford, 1984), pp. 30 and 35.

behaviour. Wittgenstein then became very angry, and commented on the event later in a letter to Malcolm, saying that studying philosophy is not of much use if all it does is to enable you to talk and think about logic, certainty, probability, perception and the like, and does not '... improve your thinking about the important questions of everyday life ...'[19]. The affective character of Wittgenstein's letter shows that this was something he regarded as extremely important. Thus we have here an example of how Wittgenstein connects philosophical and political thinking in a way which is unusual for him. According to Wittgenstein, philosophy ought to have political implications in the sense that it should make you more careful in how you use terms such as 'national character'.[20]

Cultural Pessimism

When it is said that Wittgenstein was conservative, what is often referred to is his 'cultural pessimism'.[21] Roughly, this means a view of the modern age as a period of decay, an age characterized by the rise of science, technology, industry and business, and by the decline of art and music, a period where there is no room for originality. This is so for the cultural pessimist not only concerning the present, but also concerning the future: things are getting, and will be in some sense worse. This development is inevitable, and all we can do is to accept it, see what it is possible to do in our time and do that, and grieve that we are not living in a time of cultural prosperity. A prime example here is Oswald Spengler, who writes:

> ... we have to reckon with the hard cold facts of a *late* life ... Of great painting or great music there can no longer be, for Western people, any question. Their architectural possibilities have been exhausted these hundred years. Only *extensive* possibilities are left to them. ... The lesson, I think, would be of benefit to the coming generations, as showing

---

19 Ibid., p. 35.

20 See also what Rhees writes concerning Wittgenstein and the political implications of philosophy:

> ... he [Wittgenstein] did think it was important to teach students to *think* – or to try to *make* them think – even though they be students with no talent for philosophy. (When I was commenting on the indifferent lot in one of my classes, Wittgenstein replied: 'Teach them to *think*. Work against the government.') Work against the corruption which it is almost impossible for ordinary people to withstand. (Rush Rhees, 'On Wittgenstein', *Philosophical Investigations*, 24 (2001): 161–2)

If Rhees (or Wittgenstein) here thinks that those who are not ordinary (that is, philosophers?) can withstand this corruption without working against it, that must, of course, be questioned.

21 See, for example, David Bloor, *Wittgenstein: A Social Theory of Knowledge* (London, 1983), pp. 162–4; Rudolf Haller, *Questions on Wittgenstein* (London, 1988), p. 75; Janos Cristoph Nyíri, 'Wittgenstein's New Traditionalism', in Jaakko Hintikka (ed.), *Acta Philosophica Fennica 28: Essays on Wittgenstein in Honour of G.H. von Wright* (1976), pp. 503–5.

them what is possible – and therefore necessary – and what is excluded from the inward potentialities of their time. Hitherto an incredible total of intellect and power has been squandered in false directions. ... And I can only hope that men of the new generation may be moved by this book to devote themselves to technics instead of lyrics, the sea instead of the paint-brush, and politics instead of epistemology. Better they could not do.[22]

Wittgenstein's cultural pessimism is often explicated by means of those he is said to have been influenced by in this respect: thinkers such as Otto Weininger and, above all, Spengler.[23] What is important, however, is to see Wittgenstein's cultural pessimism as it is, and thus be open to similarities and differences between Wittgenstein and thinkers such as Spengler.[24] I will therefore begin by giving some examples of sayings by Wittgenstein where he seems to give expression to a cultural pessimism.

Wittgenstein seems to agree with Spengler that in our time, culture is no longer possible, and that we ought to direct our powers in other directions: '... in these times genuine & strong characters simply turn away from the field of the arts & towards other things ...'[25]. When it comes to architecture for example, Wittgenstein says that the house building of today better be non-architectonic: 'Architecture immortalizes

---

22 Oswald Spengler, *The Decline of the West, Volume I: Form and Actuality*, trans. Charles Francis Atkinson (New York, 1926), pp. 40–41. Translation of Oswald Spengler, *Der Untergang des Abendlandes: Umrisse einer Morphologie der Weltgeschichte: Erster Band: Gestalt und Wirklichkeit* (München, 1920), pp. 56–7: '... wir haben mit den harten und kalten Tatsachen eines *späten* Lebens zu rechnen ... Von einer großen Malerei und Musik wird für den westeuropäischen Menschen nicht mehr die Rede sein. Seine architektonischen Möglichkeiten sind seit hundert Jahren erschöpft. Ihm sind nur extensive Möglichkeiten geblieben. ... Ich betrachte diese Lehre als eine Wohltat für die kommende Generation, weil sie ihr zeigt, was möglich und also notwendig ist und was nicht zu den innern Möglichkeiten der Zeit gehört. Es ist bisher eine Unsumme von Geist und Kraft auf falschen Wegen verschwendet worden. ... Wenn unter dem Eindruck dieses Buches sich Menschen der neuen Generation der Technik statt der Lyrik, der Marine statt der Malerei, der Politik statt der Erkenntniskritik zuwenden, so tun sie, was ich wünsche, und man kann ihnen nichts Besseres wünschen.'

23 Monk, *Ludwig Wittgenstein: The Duty of Genius*, pp. 20 and 299. See also Wittgenstein, *Culture and Value*, p. 16e.

24 There are some examples of situations where Wittgenstein explicitly says that he is influenced by Spengler (see, for example, Wittgenstein, 'Movements of Thought', pp. 25, 27, 55). Many who emphasize this influence exaggerate its importance enormously in a speculative fashion, however (see, for example, Bloor, *Wittgenstein: A Social Theory of Knowledge*, p. 162; Clack, *Wittgenstein, Frazer and Religion*, pp. 163–76; Brian R. Clack, *An Introduction to Wittgenstein's Philosophy of Religion* (Edinburgh, 1999), pp. 128–9; Janos Cristoph Nyíri, 'Wittgenstein's Later Work in Relation to Conservatism', in Brian McGuinness (ed.), *Wittgenstein and His Times* (Oxford, 1982), p. 51). These reports are exaggerated since they do not mention that Wittgenstein on some occasions explicitly repudiates those sides of Spengler which could be used to motivate a cultural pessimisim (see, for example, Wittgenstein, *Culture and Value*, pp. 21e and 30e–31e). More examples will be given below.

25 Wittgenstein, *Culture and Value*, p. 8e: '... echte & starke Naturen wenden sich eben in dieser Zeit von dem Gebiet der Künste ab & anderen Dingen zu ...'.

& glorifies something. Hence there can be no architecture where there is nothing to glorify.'[26]

When it comes to philosophy, it is also evident that the view of our time as a time of decay also affects how philosophy is done. In a lecture in 1930, Wittgenstein said:

> The nimbus of philosophy has been lost. For we now have a method of doing philosophy, and can speak of *skilful* philosophers. ... But once a method has been found the opportunities for the expression of personality are correspondingly restricted. The tendency of our age is to restrict such opportunities; this is characteristic of an age of declining culture or without culture. A great man need be no less great in such periods, but philosophy is now being reduced to a matter of skill and the philosopher's nimbus is disappearing.[27]

Although it is not clear whether or not Wittgenstein is talking about his own philosophy here,[28] those who want to read him as a cultural pessimist must see that Wittgenstein in that case is ambivalent towards the discovery of his method. On the one hand, this method makes it possible to get something done.[29] On the other hand, it is a part of an age and a cultural decline which Wittgenstein does not admire. So if the above quote is read as a saying about Wittgenstein's own philosophy, Wittgenstein is saying that when there are no opportunities for other kinds of philosophy any more, this decline should be accepted, in the same way as the field of the arts should be turned away from, and architecture should not be a means of expression.

However, to what extent is this conservatism? Pessimism can be described as consisting of two components: (1) that something is bad, and (2) that we cannot do anything about it. In this section, I will discuss the first component, to see whether and to what extent Wittgenstein is conservative in this respect, leaving the second one to the next section.

The question, then, is whether we are justified in calling him conservative in the light of what he considers to be bad. Without doubt, Wittgenstein's cultural taste was predominantly conservative, especially when it comes to music.[30] However, this does not necessarily mean that he is also conservative politically.[31] If we want to call

---

26 Ibid., p. 74e: 'Architektur verewigt & verherrlicht etwas. Darum kann es Architektur nicht geben, wo nichts zu verherrlichen ist.'

27 Wittgenstein, *Wittgenstein's Lectures: Cambridge, 1930–1932*, p. 21.

28 For examples of interpretations (which are not wholly convincing, however) according to which Wittgenstein is talking here about his own philosophy, see Monk, *Ludwig Wittgenstein: The Duty of Genius*, pp. 263–4; Jacques Bouveresse, '"The Darkness of This Time": Wittgenstein and the Modern World', in A. Phillips Griffiths (ed.), *Wittgenstein Centenary Essays* (Cambridge, 1991), pp. 12–14; Clack, *Wittgenstein, Frazer and Religion*, p. 174.

29 See Drury, 'Conversations with Wittgenstein', p. 199.

30 See, for example, ibid., pp. 201, 213, 245.

31 See Hans-Johann Glock, 'Wittgenstein and Reason', in James C. Klagge (ed.), *Wittgenstein: Biography and Philosophy* (New York, 2001), p. 204; Joachim Schulte, 'Wittgenstein and Conservatism', *Ratio*, 25 (1983): 73.

him conservative in the light of what he considers bad, we have to find something more directly connected to politics. In this context, we can cite what is most often referred to[32] as an example of Wittgenstein's cultural pessimism, the foreword to the book later called *Philosophical Remarks*, a foreword written during the autumn of 1930. There, he did try to describe the spirit in which he was writing,[33] and thus gave an expression of his personality:

> This book is written for those who are in sympathy with the spirit in which it is written. This spirit is, I believe, different from that of the prevailing European and American civilization. The spirit of <u>this civilization</u> the expression of which is the industry, architecture, music of present day fascism & socialism, is a <u>spirit that is alien & uncongenial to the author</u>. … in these times genuine & strong characters simply turn away from the field of the arts & towards other things … Even if it is clear to me then that the disappearance of a culture does not signify the disappearance of human value but simply of certain means of expressing this value, still the fact remains that I contemplate the current of European civilization without sympathy, without understanding its aims if any. … It is all one to me whether the typical western scientist understands or appreciates my work since in any case he does not understand the spirit in which I write. Our civilization is characterized by the word progress. Progress is its form, it is not one of its properties that it makes progress. <u>Typically</u> it constructs. Its <u>activity</u> is to construct a more and more complicated structure. And even clarity is only a means to this end & not an end in itself.[34]

---

32 See, for example, Bloor, *Wittgenstein: A Social Theory of Knowledge*, p. 164; Bouveresse, '"The Darkness of This Time": Wittgenstein and the Modern World', pp. 11 and 27–8; Haller, *Questions on Wittgenstein*, pp. 75–6; Nyíri, 'Wittgenstein's New Traditionalism', p. 503; Nyíri, 'Wittgenstein's Later Work in Relation to Conservatism', p. 57; Janos Cristoph Nyíri, 'Wittgenstein 1929–31: The Turning Back', in Stuart Shanker (ed.), *Ludwig Wittgenstein: Critical Assessments, Volume Four: From Theology to Sociology: Wittgenstein's Impact on Contemporary Thought* (London, 1986), p. 47; Georg Henrik von Wright, 'Wittgenstein in Relation to His Time', in Brian McGuinness (ed.), *Wittgenstein and His Times* (Oxford, 1982), pp. 114 & 117; Wright, 'Wittgenstein and the Twentieth Century', pp. 51–2.

33 Even if he was in doubt whether or not the foreword ought to be written. See Wittgenstein, *Culture and Value*, pp. 10e–11e.

34 Ibid., pp. 8e–9e: 'Dieses Buch ist für diejenigen geschrieben, die dem Geist, in dem es geschrieben ist freundlich gegenüberstehn. Dieser Geist ist, glaube ich, ein anderer als <u>der der</u> großen europäischen & amerikanischen Zivilisation. Der Geist <u>dieser Zivilisation</u> dessen Ausdruck die Industrie, Architektur, Musik der Faschismus & Socialismus der Jetztzeit ist, ist ein dem Verfasser <u>fremder & unsympathischer Geist</u>. … echte & starke Naturen wenden sich eben in dieser Zeit von dem Gebiet der Künste ab & anderen Dingen zu … Ist es mir so klar daß das Verschwinden einer Kultur nicht das Verschwinden menschlichen Wertes bedeutet sondern bloß gewisser Ausdrucksmittel dieses Werts so bleibt dennoch die Tatsache bestehen daß ich dem Strom der Europäischen Zivilisation ohne Sympathie zusehe, ohne Verständnis für die Ziele wenn sie welche hat. … Ob ich von dem typischen westlichen Wissenschaftler verstanden oder geschätzt werde ist mir gleichgültig weil er den Geist in dem ich schreibe doch nicht versteht. Unsere Zivilisation ist durch das Wort Fortschritt charakterisiert. Der Fortschritt ist ihre Form nicht eine ihrer Eigenschaften daß sie fortschreitet. Sie ist <u>typisch</u> aufbauend.

This foreword could be used as an argument for Wittgenstein being politically conservative, by saying that Wittgenstein is against progress, above all against technical development. Such a reading overlooks some interesting sayings in the foreword, however.[35] Firstly, Wittgenstein intimates that our civilization has no aims (at least he is unable to notice these aims), that in our civilization, nothing is an end in itself. Without any aims, talk about progress is empty. Secondly, progress is therefore only a form of our civilization, but making progress is not one of its properties. Wittgenstein thus questions whether the progress of our time really is progress, by highlighting that this progress is either a movement without any aims at all, or at best is only a matter of working for the attainment of aims which it is unclear about, aims laid down in advance. There is another understanding of progress, however, according to which it has to do with considering the aims in themselves, with also trying to make progress at the level of aims. If this was really done, making progress could be a property of our civilization.[36]

Wittgenstein himself does not say much about what his aims are. He mentions 'clarity' in the foreword, but this is not much of a political aim, and cannot be said to be either radical or conservative. What his distinction between form and property shows, however, is that his view is not, as now and then is claimed, a '... rejection of belief in progress ...'[37] on the whole, but only a rejection of a certain view of what such a belief in progress means. What Wittgenstein is calling for is a more balanced

---

Ihre <u>Tätigkeit</u> ist es ein immer komplizierteres Gebilde zu konstruieren. Und auch die Klarheit dient doch nur wieder diesem Zweck & ist nicht Selbstzweck.' For other versions of the foreword, see Ludwig Wittgenstein, *Philosophical Remarks*, trans. Raymond Hargreaves and Roger White (Oxford, 1975), p. 7, and Michael Nedo, 'Aus Ludwig Wittgensteins ‚Taschen-Notizbuch' von 1931', *Deutsche Zeitschrift für Philosophie*, 45 (1997).

35   Furthermore, such a reading overlooks the context in which it is written. To understand the foreword properly, it must be read against the background of what Wittgenstein probably dissociates himself from here: Rudolf Carnap's foreword to his *The Logical Structure of the World: Pseudoproblems in Philosophy*, trans. Rolf A. George (Berkeley, CA, 1967), pp. xv–xviii, and the manifesto of the Vienna Circle: Otto Neurath, 'The Scientific Conception of the World', *Empiricism and Sociology* (Dordrecht, 1973), pp. 299–318. See S. Stephen Hilmy, *The Later Wittgenstein: The Emergence of a New Philosophical Method* (Oxford, 1987), pp. 213, 307–8, 314–5, for more about the relations between these two documents and Wittgenstein's foreword.

36   In this context, compare what Wittgenstein is saying elsewhere: '... the proposition, "Such-and-such means progress," must never occur in a sociologist's description.' It is hence possible that one of the things Wittgenstein in the foreword objects to is the putative descriptive use of the word 'progress', a use which consequently overlooks its normative character. If that is so, the foreword is about, among other things, the ethical: 'What is ethical cannot be taught. ... Here there is nothing to be stated any more; all I can do is to step forth as an individual and speak in the first person'; Ludwig Wittgenstein, *Wittgenstein and the Vienna Circle*, trans. Joachim Schulte and Brian McGuinness (Oxford, 1979), pp. 116–17. See also ibid., pp. 68–9 and 92–3; Wittgenstein, *Tractatus*, pp. 145 and 147 (§§ 6.42–6.421); Wittgenstein, 'A Lecture on Ethics', pp. 39–40.

37   Haller, *Questions on Wittgenstein*, p. 75.

discussion of progress, where we see that progress and decline are connected. Rhees reports Wittgenstein to have said: '... we may call it progress because it opens up new opportunities. But in the course of this change, opportunities which were there before may be lost. In one way it was progress, in another it was decline.'[38] Before we compare the present with the past in order to see whether or not we are making progress, and if so, in what way, we must question and discuss the way the comparison is made, in order to avoid just presupposing what we find valuable right now. In that respect, progress is intimately connected to a critical discussion of aims.

Formerly, it was perhaps easier to call somebody conservative who did not regard technical development *in itself* as something positive. In the course of time, however, we have become more aware of, for example, ecological problems connected with technical development. Wittgenstein's emphasis on the question of aims and his distinction between form and property are, in this context, rather promising politically. Wittgenstein is thus to some extent a cultural pessimist, but that does not mean that he regards progress as bad (whatever that would mean), only that the question of whether or not something is progress is more complicated than is often thought, among other things due to the fact that progress is connected to questions about aims.

The Possibility of Progress

However, Wittgenstein's cultural pessimism could justify our calling him conservative if he thinks that we cannot do anything about the bad aspects of our civilization. One of the results of our discussion above was that whether or not something is progress must be determined by evaluating the aims. This means that progress is not a historical necessity, since it is possible that a development we now see and regard as progressive will in the future be seen as decline. If we understood progress as a form, on the other hand, and presupposed that human beings solve the tasks they set themselves, we would be sure that we will make progress.

If making progress is understood as a possible property, the matter is then different. When we have made clear what our aims are, we can answer the question of whether or not progress is possible by determining whether a better state of affairs than the present one is possible or impossible, and if progress is possible, we must determine whether or not we can do anything to bring it about. However, Wittgenstein writes: 'Who knows the laws according to which society unfolds? I am sure even the cleverest has no idea. If you fight, you fight. If you hope, you hope. You can fight, hope & even believe, without believing *scientifically*.'[39] We have seen that Wittgenstein rejects the belief that it is a necessity that the future will bring progress.

---

38 Rhees, 'Postscript', p. 275.

39 Wittgenstein, *Culture and Value*, p. 69e: 'Wer kennt die Gesetze, nach denen die Gesellschaft sich entwickelt? Ich bin überzeugt, daß auch der Gescheiteste keine Ahnung hat. Kämpfst Du, so kämpfst Du. Hoffst Du, so hoffst Du. Man kann kämpfen, hoffen & auch glauben, ohne *wissenschaftlich* zu glauben.'

Now we see, in addition, that he also rejects every comprehensive view of the future which claims to be based on science.[40] Wittgenstein is not as close to Spengler as has sometimes been said, then, since Spengler's is a prime example of an attempt to find laws for the development of society. According to Wittgenstein, we can fight, hope and believe. To resign, as Spengler suggests we do, is then not necessary.

Although Wittgenstein says that we can fight, hope and believe, it is of course possible that Wittgenstein himself was unable to hope, and therefore thought that nothing could be done about the bad aspects of our civilization. However, Wittgenstein's philosophy can be seen as a struggle against one aspect of our civilization that he considered bad, namely the destructive influence of the scientific world-view.[41] Wittgenstein hinted now and then that this was the case. One example is how, in *The Blue Book*, he discusses why it is difficult to do philosophy in the way he proposes. The reason he gives is '... our craving for generality'[42] and '... contemptuous attitude towards the particular case'[43], a craving which '... is the resultant of a number of tendencies connected with particular philosophical confusions'.[44] Wittgenstein mentions four such tendencies and confusions. The last one of them he expresses in this way:

> Our craving for generality has another main source: our preoccupation with the method of science. I mean the method of reducing the explanation of natural phenomena to the smallest possible number of primitive natural laws; and, in mathematics, of unifying the treatment of different topics by using a generalization. Philosophers constantly see the method of science before their eyes, and are irresistibly tempted to ask and answer questions in the way science does. This tendency is the real source of metaphysics, and leads the philosopher into complete darkness.[45]

Wittgenstein is certainly not attacking this tendency directly, but by giving examples of its failures, he tries to make us aware of the limitations of this kind of thinking. Wittgenstein's struggle against the destructive influence he thought the scientific world-view had can hence be seen as one example of how he tries to influence the future by means of his philosophy, even if he had only small hopes when it comes to the prospects of its success.[46] Hence, we can conclude that according to Wittgenstein, it is possible to try to influence the future, and that we in some sense must try to influence the future, since progress will not come by itself.[47]

---

40 Cf. Wittgenstein, *Last Writings on the Philosophy of Psychology II*, pp. 81e–82e.

41 Cf. Hilmy, *The Later Wittgenstein*, p. 190; Wright, 'Wittgenstein and the Twentieth Century', pp. 52–3 and 60.

42 Wittgenstein, *The Blue and Brown Books*, p. 17.

43 Ibid., p. 18.

44 Ibid., p. 17.

45 bid., p. 18.

46 Wittgenstein, *Philosophical Investigations*, p. xe.

47 Cf. here also Bouwsma, *Wittgenstein: Conversations 1949–1951*, p. 35.

Although Wittgenstein is to some extent a cultural pessimist, this does not justify us in calling him conservative.[48] When we now go over to the question about the relation between Wittgenstein's philosophy and conservatism, it could be helpful to bear in mind the four claims I have argued for here. Firstly, Wittgenstein's political views have both radical and conservative traits. Secondly, according to Wittgenstein philosophy ought to have political implications in the sense that it should make you more careful about how you use certain words. Thirdly, Wittgenstein is to some extent a cultural pessimist, which does not mean that progress is bad (whatever that would mean), however, only that the question of whether or not something is progress is more complicated than is often thought, among other things due to the fact that progress is connected to questions about aims. Fourthly, according to Wittgenstein, it is possible to try to influence the future. These claims can remind us of the complexity of the issue, and thereby prevent us from delivering simplistic answers to the question.

The Relation between Wittgenstein's Philosophy and Conservatism

The chief criticism of Wittgenstein's philosophy as being a conservative one is that it regards the actual use of language as the only decisive standard, and thereby makes criticisms of practices and traditions impossible.[49] In the following, I will begin by presenting Herbert Marcuse's criticism of Wittgenstein's philosophy, as formulated in his *One Dimensional Man,* since his criticism is rather extensive and directly connected to political issues. After this, I will present another way of relating Wittgenstein's philosophy and conservatism, and lastly, I will evaluate them. By doing this, we begin to see an answer to the question about the possibility of philosophical criticism of religious beliefs.

Marcuse's starting point is that our society appears to be rational, but is irrational, which means, among other things, that: 'Its productivity is destructive of the free development of human needs and faculties, its peace maintained by the constant threat

---

48 One example of a political view which is both pessimistic, although in a different sense than Wittgenstein's, and without doubt seen as radical is Herbert Marcuse's. In the last pages of his *One Dimensional Man*, the hopes for change seems to be very limited, and he ends the book by writing:

The critical theory of society ... holding no promise and showing no success, it remains negative. Thus it wants to remain loyal to those who, without hope, have given and give their life to the Great Refusal. At the beginning of the fascist era, Walter Benjamin wrote: *Nur um der Hoffnungslosen willen ist uns die Hoffnung gegeben.* It is only for the sake of those without hope that hope is given to us. (Herbert Marcuse, *One Dimensional Man: Studies in the Ideology of Advanced Industrial Society* (London, 1964), p. 257)

49 See, for example, Maurice Cornforth, *Marxism and the Linguistic Philosophy* (London, 1965), p. 163; Ernest Gellner, *Relativism and the Social Sciences* (Cambridge, 1985), pp. 172–3; Nyíri, 'Wittgenstein 1929–31: The Turning Back', pp. 38–9.

of war, its growth dependent on the repression of the real possibilities for pacifying the struggle for existence …'.[50] This society is capable of preventing, in different ways, all forms of social change:[51] the productive apparatus determines individual needs and aspirations through manipulation of needs,[52] technology establishes more effective and pleasant forms of social control,[53] and seemingly rational barriers of thought are created through ideological means.[54] This indoctrination is, according to Marcuse, not planned. Instead, it has a seemingly rational character, to such a degree and in such a sense that the distinction between 'real' needs and needs imposed by society becomes purely theoretical.[55]

Due to this seemingly rational character of society, what is needed, according to Marcuse, is an analysis that shows the irrationality, in the sense mentioned above, of society – that is, a questioning of the presuppositions of today's technology, natural and social sciences, and philosophy. One example of such a questioning is Marcuse's criticism of the attempts to eliminate all concepts which cannot be defined in the way operationalism, behaviourism and radical empiricism respectively demand.[56] One of Marcuse's examples is that 'democracy' in the social sciences is defined to mean the political system we have, which means that studies about the extent to which an election is an expression of a democratic process are settled in advance.[57]

In philosophy, Marcuse launches his criticism against certain kinds of linguistic philosophy. The problem here is the same as with operationalism: this kind of philosophy claims to cure thought and speech of confusing notions, but by doing that, it rejects those notions which stand in opposition to prevailing discourse and behaviour, and could be a means of changing it.[58] Wittgenstein's philosophy is severely criticized here: '… Wittgenstein's assurance that philosophy "leaves everything as it is" … provides an intellectual justification for that which society has long since accomplished – namely, the defamation of alternative modes of thought which contradict the established universe of discourse.'[59]

The basic problem with Wittgenstein's philosophy is then, according to Marcuse, that its therapeutic character merely makes it possible for the patient to function normally in a sick world, without helping her to understand the world in terms of what it is and what it could be. For Marcuse, philosophy is therefore the opposite to that which leaves everything as it is:[60] '… what is at stake is the chance of preserving and protecting the right, the *need* to think and speak in terms other than those of

---

50 Marcuse, *One Dimensional Man*, p. ix.
51 Ibid., p. xii.
52 Ibid., pp. xv and 3.
53 bid., p. xv.
54 Ibid., p. 14.
55 Ibid., pp. 8–9.
56 Ibid., pp. 12–13.
57 Ibid., pp. 114–16.
58 Ibid., pp. 170–71.
59 Ibid., p. 173.
60 Ibid., p. 183.

common usage – terms which are meaningful, rational, and valid precisely because they are other terms'.[61]

The second way of relating Wittgenstein's philosophy to conservatism I want to mention here is formulated by David Bloor and J.C. Nyíri. Bloor says that Wittgenstein was a 'conservative thinker', in giving '... priority to the Concrete over the Abstract, Life over Reason, ... Practice over Norms ... Being ... over Thought'.[62] J.C. Nyíri reasons in about the same way by saying that Wittgenstein is a conservative philosopher since he claimed 'That one must "recognize certain authorities in order to make judgements at all", or that one cannot even err – that is, that one loses altogether the capacity for rational thought – if one does not *judge in conformity* with some group or other ...'.[63] Nyíri claims, furthermore, that Wittgenstein's thought contains the elements of a conservative anthropology:

> His later writings ... imply an image of man which stands in glaring contradiction to the liberal, classically bourgeois image of man. The concept of the internally or mentally autonomous, rational individual, of the human subject acting in accordance with the light of his reason, sovereign within his own mental world, reveals itself as absurd ...[64]

It is now time to evaluate these ways of relating Wittgenstein's philosophy to conservatism. We start with Bloor and Nyíri. That their picture of the relation between Wittgenstein's philosophy and conservatism is erroneous is easy to see. Firstly, it is a bit peculiar to say that somebody who gives priority to the concrete over the abstract, life over reason, practice over norms, being over thought and criticizes a liberal anthropology for that reason alone should be counted as a conservative thinker. If that were so, Karl Marx could be said to be a conservative thinker, in emphasizing how social change has its basis in the social reality that human beings find themselves in, and not in philosophical thought.[65] Secondly, an important distinctive feature of conservatism is its image of society, according to which there are no real social antagonisms, an image according to which illusory antagonisms are mediated by society and the individuals in it being seen as an organic whole where everybody has their different role and function, a whole which we ought to subordinate ourselves to. Such an image of society Wittgenstein does not express.[66] Thirdly, and most

---

61 Ibid., p. 178.

62 Bloor, *Wittgenstein: A Social Theory of Knowledge*, p. 161. See also ibid., p. 162.

63 Nyíri, 'Wittgenstein's Later Work in Relation to Conservatism', p. 50. Nyíri refers to Wittgenstein, *On Certainty*, pp. 65e and 23e (§§ 493 and 156).

64 Nyíri, 'Wittgenstein 1929–31: The Turning Back', p. 39. See also Anthony O'Hear, 'Wittgenstein and the Transmission of Traditions', in A. Phillips Griffiths (ed.), *Wittgenstein Centenary Essays* (Cambridge, 1991), p. 43.

65 See, for example, 'Theses on Feuerbach'; Karl Marx, 'The Eighteenth Brumaire of Louis Bonaparte', in *Karl Marx Frederick Engels Collected Works, Volume 11: Marx and Engels 1951–53* (London, 1979), p. 103; Marx, 'A Contribution to the Critique of Political Economy', pp. 263–4; Marx and Engels, 'The German Ideology', pp. 23–4.

66 Perhaps the above-mentioned foreword (Wittgenstein, *Culture and Value*, pp. 8e–9e; Wittgenstein, *Philosophical Remarks*, p. 7) can be referred to as an expression of such an

importantly, Wittgenstein certainly said things akin to what Bloor and Nyíri claim he said (that one must recognize certain authorities in order to make judgements at all, for example), but this justifies calling him a conservative thinker or philosopher only if these remarks are interpreted in a specific way, a way which is neither argued for nor self-evident. It is, on the contrary, evident that the point of these remarks is not what Bloor and Nyíri claim it is. Wittgenstein was a conservative philosopher, in Bloor's and Nyíri's sense, only if he would say to someone who tried not to follow a certain political or religious authority, or tried to argue against a certain traditional political or religious idea by means of seemingly rational arguments, that this is not possible. Such an interpretation of Wittgenstein relies on an interpretation of his philosophical activity as being a matter of stating how things *must* be, instead of pointing out the range of possibilities. Wittgenstein's remarks can therefore be read, in contrast to Bloor's and Nyíri's reading, as a reminder of the fact not that some specific things cannot be questioned, but that there always are *some* things which are taken for granted and not questioned.[67] These things show themselves in what we, in fact, are not questioning, and are not laid down in advance.[68] They are not opinions, but rather ways of acting and thinking.[69] This means, furthermore, that these things which are not questioned just now can come to be questioned in the future, but then other things will serve as what makes judgement and argument what it then is.[70] Since political and religious authorities *are* actually questioned, since we are *not* in agreement on political and religious matters, these remarks of Wittgenstein cannot be used to support cither side in the political or religious debate.[71]

Bloor's and Nyíri's way of relating Wittgenstein's philosophy to conservatism is therefore not successful. To what extent is Marcuse's criticism correct, then, and to what extent is it incorrect? To begin with, it is important to see that there are similarities, which Marcuse does not see, between his and Wittgenstein's philosophy. Marcuse wants to retain such notions which stand in opposition to prevailing discourse and behaviour, notions which could be a means of changing it. In one sense, Wittgenstein is doing precisely the same thing when he, by means of the notion of family resemblance,[72] shows that concepts do not, in general, need strict definitions – for example, general operationalist definitions – and when he shows the variety of linguistic expressions. Therefore, when Wittgenstein says that philosophy leaves everything as it is, it also leaves the kind of linguistic use which Marcuse

---

image of society, but in that case, it is only a single example, and doubtful as well. Examples which points in other directions can be given, as we have seen.

67 See, for example, Wittgenstein, *On Certainty*, pp. 16e, 22e, 44e (§§ 105, 150, 342–3).

68 See, for example, ibid., pp. 17e, 22e, 28e, 62e–63e (§§ 110, 148, 152, 204, 476).

69 See Wittgenstein, *Philosophical Investigations*, p. 75e (§ 241).

70 See, for example, Wittgenstein, *On Certainty*, p. 15e (§§ 96–9).

71 Cf. Derrida, *Specters of Marx*, p. 54.

72 Wittgenstein, *Philosophical Investigations*, pp. 27e–29e (§ 66–71).

stresses as it is, as opposed to the attempt to make language fit into some ideological form.[73]

To leave everything as it is is thus both undogmatic and critical – critical of dogmatic ways of doing philosophy. When you are obsessed with a philosophical problem, the aim of Wittgenstein is to make you aware of the fact that you do not need to hold fast to a certain idea.[74] This means there is a change in how you see what lies before you.[75] Wittgenstein therefore writes: '"But it must be like this!" is not a philosophical proposition. Philosophy only states what everyone admits.'[76]

Here, two examples of how these undogmatic and critical sides intermingle in Wittgenstein's philosophy will be given. Firstly, when Wittgenstein, in his lectures on religious beliefs, criticizes Father O'Hara for making questions in religion questions of science,[77] he says that O'Hara behaves in a way which he would not do if he really believed that religious questions were scientific questions. Of course, one possibility for O'Hara would be to start behaving in accordance with the conception of religious questions as being a kind of scientific questions. Since a descriptive philosophy could do no more than point out how what somebody says contradicts what she does, if O'Hara did this, Wittgenstein could then do no more. In this sense, Wittgenstein's philosophy is undogmatic as well as critical.

---

73 See ibid., pp. 40e, 43e (§§ 109, 128, 131). Cf. Tommi P. Uschanov, 'Ernest Gellner's Criticisms of Wittgenstein and Ordinary Language Philosophy', in Gavin Kitching and Nigel Pleasants (eds), *Marx and Wittgenstein: Knowledge, Morality and Politics* (London/New York, 2002), pp. 34–5 and 39; Rupert Read, 'Marx and Wittgenstein on Vampires and Parasites: A Critique of Capital and Metaphysics', in Gavin Kitching and Nigel Pleasants (eds), *Marx and Wittgenstein: Knowledge, Morality and Politics* (London/New York, 2002), p. 274. Nigel Pleasants ('Towards a Critical Use of Marx and Wittgenstein', in Gavin Kitching and Nigel Pleasants (eds), *Marx and Wittgenstein: Knowledge, Morality and Politics* (London/New York, 2002), p. 169) even claims that what Wittgenstein is saying when he says that philosophy leaves everything as it is is about the same as what Marx is saying in his eleventh thesis on Feuerbach (Marx, 'Theses on Feuerbach', p. 8): according to Pleasants, both Wittgenstein and Marx meant that if one really wants to change things, doing philosophy is not the way to go about it.

74 Malcolm, *Ludwig Wittgenstein: A Memoir*, p. 43.

75 See Wittgenstein, *Philosophical Investigations*, pp. 31e–32e, 40e (§§ 79, 109); Wittgenstein, 'Philosophy', p. 161; Wittgenstein, 'Discussions between Wittgenstein, Waddington, and Thouless', p. 382.

76 Wittgenstein, *Philosophical Investigations*, p. 132e (§ 599): '"Es muß sich doch so verhalten!" ist kein Satz der Philosophie. Sie stellt nur fest, was Jeder ihr zugibt.' See also Wittgenstein, *Wittgenstein's Lectures: Cambridge, 1932–1935*, p. 97; Wittgenstein, *Lectures on the Foundations of Mathematics*, p. 103; Wittgenstein, *Wittgenstein and the Vienna Circle*, p. 183.

77 Wittgenstein, *Lectures and Conversations on Aesthetics, Psychology and Religious Belief*, pp. 57–9.

Secondly, the same goes for Wittgenstein's discussion with Alan Turing about mathematics.[78] When they discuss questions such as whether there are discoveries and experiments in mathematics, Wittgenstein disagrees sharply in one sense with Turing, and tries by means of examples to make him change his mind, but in another sense they agree, claims Wittgenstein:

> Turing doesn't object to anything I say. He agrees with every word. He objects to the idea he thinks underlies it. He thinks we're undermining mathematics, introducing Bolshevism into mathematics. But not at all.[79]

> Turing thinks that he and I are using the word "experiment" in two different ways. But I want to show that this is wrong. That is to say, I think that if I could make myself quite clear, then Turing would give up saying that in mathematics we make experiments. If I could arrange in their proper order certain well-known facts, then it would become clear that Turing and I are not using the word "experiment" differently.[80]

In this case, too, Wittgenstein could be said to be undogmatic (Turing and Wittgenstein are not in disagreement, they are not holding different dogmas to be true) as well as against certain ideas (saying that we do experiments in mathematics is problematic, according to Wittgenstein). Thus Wittgenstein leaves everything as it is at the same time as he changes how we see things.[81] In this context, he changes how we understand mathematics, by pointing out that saying that we do experiments in mathematics is misleading, that saying so overlooks certain aspects of mathematics, and so on.

Since Wittgenstein's philosophy has an undogmatic character, Wittgenstein justifies neither society as it is nor a certain opinion about how society should be, when it comes to political questions. In this way, too, philosophy leaves everything (among other things, *both* sides in the political debate) as it is. Marcuse is thus wrong in saying that Wittgenstein's philosophy supports society as it is, since we can change society without our view of how society should be being *philosophically* more justified than the way in which society now is. Marcuse has a point, however, in that there are questions which are difficult to discuss substantially when trying to live up to Wittgenstein's methodological ideals. What Wittgenstein tries to do is to show that there are more possibilities than we think there are, and thereby making it possible for us to get out of the grip of certain puzzlements and stop being troubled by them. When it comes to questions about one's life and society, this way of doing philosophy can be helpful in making the number of possible answers visible, but when it then comes to settling for a more or less reasonable answer, Wittgenstein does not have much to contribute, and it would be negative if we stopped being

---

78 See Wittgenstein, *Lectures on the Foundations of Mathematics*, esp. pp. 45–7, 62–8, 92–102, 228–9, 261–5.

79 Ibid., p. 67.

80 Ibid., p. 102.

81 Cf. Wittgenstein, *Philosophical Investigations*, p. 49e (§ 144); Gordon P. Baker, *Wittgenstein's Method: Neglected Aspects* (Oxford, 2004), pp. 82 and 91.

troubled by these questions. Wittgenstein's philosophy is hence not conservative in itself, but if it becomes the only way of thinking and thereby silences the thorough discussion about one's life and society, it becomes conservative.

One way of countering this criticism of Wittgenstein's philosophy would be to say that there certainly are questions where his way of thinking does not have much to contribute, but such questions are not philosophical. Such a proposed definition of what questions are philosophical is not in accordance with the history of the subject, however, and the main reason for regarding questions about one's life and society as non-philosophical – namely, that they cannot be discussed in a thorough way – is one of the things which, with the help of Wittgenstein's philosophy, I have been trying to argue against in this study, by pointing out that discussion is not just a matter of argumentation.

Wittgenstein's philosophy can, moreover, be used to argue *against* such a restriction of philosophy, by highlighting other possibilities, when one is inclined to say that there is only one possible form of philosophy, that philosophy *must* be this and that. Michael P. Hodges writes:

> ... does it [the fact that philosophy must leave everything as it is] imply that there is no sort of reflective criticism that can be brought against our practices? There will, of course, be no neutral perspective from which to launch such a critique, but the supposition that only such a value-free critique would do is itself a prejudice of traditional philosophy in just the sense that Wittgenstein's methods are meant to displace. Any such assessment would itself be rooted in values. What we cannot do is to find a transcendental perch from which to examine our practices in their totality ... Perhaps Wittgenstein would not engage in this sort of criticism, but at least he leads us to the door behind which the possibility lies.[82]

If we are emphasizing questions about one's life and society as philosophical questions, have we then not stepped out of what could be called Wittgensteinian philosophy? In a way, this is an uninteresting question, since it does not matter much whether we answer yes or no. However, it is important to see that we are not necessarily compelled to understand Wittgensteinian philosophy, or any other kind of philosophy, in a monolithic way. In line with the way Wittgenstein discusses other concepts, we can talk about a diversity of aims within philosophy. Clarity[83] is then not the only aim, but formulating new ideas and describing things in new ways are other aims.[84] Clarity is no less presuppositionless or less political than these aims – the political presuppositions behind these different aims merely show themselves in different ways.

---

82 Hodges, 'The Status of Ethical Judgements in the *Philosophical Investigations*': 112. See also Michael P. Hodges, 'Faith: Themes from Wittgenstein, Kierkegaard and Nietzsche', in Robert L. Arrington and Mark Addis (eds), *Wittgenstein and Philosophy of Religion* (London, 2001), p. 76.

83 See, for example, Wittgenstein, *Philosophical Investigations*, p. 44e (§ 133); Wittgenstein, *Wittgenstein and the Vienna Circle*, p. 183; Wittgenstein, 'Philosophy', p. 181.

84 See Chapter 6.

Fideism

It is now time to go on to the main question of 'Wittgensteinian fideism'. The term 'Wittgensteinian fideism' was coined by Kai Nielsen in an article with the same title.[85] In that article, Nielsen is not discussing and criticizing Wittgenstein's philosophy in itself, merely philosophers inspired by Wittgenstein, but in later writings, this criticism is aimed at Wittgenstein too.[86] In his article of 1967, Nielsen does not define 'fideism', but the question is whether an outsider can understand and criticize religion. Since religion being criticizable by outsiders implies that religion can be understood by outsiders, the possibility of criticism is the more fundamental question. There are, of course, different forms of understanding, and it can be claimed that there are forms of understanding which are impossible for an outsider to attain. Such forms of understanding would then be internally related to being religious. If religious beliefs are criticizable by outsiders, however, there are at least some forms of understanding which they can attain – forms which make criticism possible.

The question of Wittgensteinian fideism has been answered implicitly in the above discussion of conservatism. As we have seen, Wittgenstein does not preclude the possibility of criticism, and hence not criticism of religion. Whether *philosophy* can criticize religion is more doubtful, but as was argued above, the reasons for excluding such criticism from philosophy presuppose such philosophical prejudices as Wittgenstein tried to uncover. The philosophical value of a criticism can then be that it makes it possible for us to see a religious belief in a *new* way. The criticisms of religious beliefs mentioned in the last part of the last chapter therefore had a philosophical value when Freud, Marx and the others formulated them. In order to make this value visible, we sometimes had to understand them in a way which clashes with the way they were understood by those who formulated them, however. These criticisms may furthermore have a value in a person's own philosophical thinking, in so far as they are new for her. When it comes to philosophy in general, however, there is no element of newness to these criticisms when they are simply reiterated, so if these criticisms have a general philosophical value today, this value must be due to some other factor. Moreover, if they have no philosophical value, this does not mean that they have no value.

Hence, we have seen that philosophical criticism of religious beliefs is possible. Therefore, what we are going to do in the rest of this chapter is simply to discuss some specific questions which arise in this context, primarily whether there is anything which the words 'criticism of religion' might stand for which satisfies Nielsen.

In Chapter 6, it was shown that there is no guarantee that criticism is always possible. In those cases where it turns out not to be possible to make another person give up a specific belief by appealing to other beliefs she has, you can try to make her give up that belief by making her make the distinction between true and false in

---

85 Nielsen, 'Wittgensteinian Fideism'.

86 See, for example, Kai Nielsen, *Naturalism and Religion* (Amherst, MA, 2001), pp. 335–42.

a way that is new for her. This can be done by, for example, making her see the way she makes the distinction in a different light, by describing it in an alternative way. The latter form of criticism does not start from principles claimed to be self-evident or given *a priori*, but from a position which is as possible to question as the position it criticizes. Nielsen's requirements for what criticism must be are then not satisfied in any of these cases, requirements which can be seen in the following:

> To argue, as I do ... that the very first-order discourse of this form of life [religion] is incoherent or irrational can be nothing but a confusion [according to the Wittgensteinian fideist] ... Philosophy cannot relevantly criticise religion [according to the Wittgensteinian fideist] ... But I do *not* agree that the first-order discourse of religion is in order as it is, and I do not agree that philosophy cannot relevantly criticise religions or forms of life.[87]

Nielsen presupposes here that religion is something homogeneous which can be criticized in its entirety,[88] since he assumes that there is *one* first-order discourse of religion, and he consequently overlooks the diversity in what we call religion.[89] The reason why he thinks that the first-order discourse of religion is not in order as it is is that religious claims are not publicly testable.[90] Hence, he presupposes that public testability is necessarily a relevant criterion. Public testability is of course sometimes a relevant criterion, but we cannot presuppose that it is necessarily relevant, or that it always is relevant. As we saw in Chapter 2, we have to notice the diversity of the ways we deal with the world around us. Therefore, we must not presuppose that religion is necessarily to be judged in the same way as we judge other human activities, for example science. The philosophical discussion can then not take for granted that its aim is to fix a *general* meaning to concepts such as 'rationality' and thereafter to use the concept to settle every controversy.

That it is problematic to think that there are criteria which are always relevant and whose meaning is evident can be seen from Nielsen's own examples of what he takes to be obviously meaningful criticisms: '"Foot-binding was for a long time an established institution but it was really cruel and irrational" may be false but it is not nonsense.'[91] That foot-binding is cruel is obvious, and even if it is not obvious, we understand what a person who says so claims. What does it mean, however, to say that foot-binding is irrational? Obviously, it could not just mean that it is cruel. To understand what somebody who is saying that foot-binding is irrational is claiming, we need to know more about how she understands rationality and irrationality, or more about the context of the institution of foot-binding. We need to know, for

---

87 Nielsen, 'Wittgensteinian Fideism': 193.

88 Cf. Stephen Mulhall, 'Wittgenstein and the Philosophy of Religion', in D.Z. Phillips and Timothy Tessin (eds), *Philosophy of Religion in the 21st Century* (Basingstoke, 2001), pp. 107–8.

89 Cf. Bouwsma, *Wittgenstein: Conversations 1949–1951*, p. 55.

90 Nielsen, 'Wittgensteinian Fideism': 203. See also Nielsen, *Naturalism and Religion*, p. 351.

91 Nielsen, 'Wittgensteinian Fideism': 206.

example, whether this practice is supposed to achieve anything, and in that case, what. When we know this, we can go on to discuss whether the means is a suitable way of achieving the end, whether this end is desirable, and so on, and in that way we can begin to see what 'rational' and 'irrational' might mean in this context.

The same goes for another of Nielsen's examples: '... gambling is illogical'.[92] If gambling is understood here as a means of earning money, we understand what a person who is saying this is claiming, although it is, of course, possible to disagree. If gambling is seen as a form of entertainment, however, as a way of getting some excitement, what could it then possibly mean to say that it is *illogical*?

Thus Nielsen can be said to give a confused account of what we are actually doing when we criticize religious beliefs, and is thus not, as he thinks he is, saving criticism of religious beliefs from those who attack its possibility. D.Z. Phillips says in this context:

> ... it may be said ... [that Wittgenstein] does not leave all criticism where it is. Even if this were true, it would not be because it is *criticism*, but because it is bad philosophy ... But the charge is not even true, since it cannot be said that Wittgenstein rules out *any* genuine form of criticism. What he does not allow is something which purports to be criticism, but which is itself a species of philosophical confusion.[93]

Phillips is claiming that it could be right – that is, not confused – to say that a certain form of religious belief is irrational, if this criticism is thought to connect to the understanding the believers themselves have, explicitly or implicitly, of what rationality amounts to in a religious context. It is not obvious, however, whether Phillips recognizes that criticizing a certain form of religious belief for being irrational by connecting to an understanding of rationality which is not the understanding of the believers need not be a form of philosophical confusion. In Chapter 6, I showed that such a criticism need not be a form of philosophical confusion, by pointing out the difference between two cases. Firstly, we have the case where you believe that the understanding of rationality you are connecting to is an understanding which has to be prevalent in all contexts of life. Secondly, we have the case where you consciously criticize a form of religious belief from a position foreign to it, without believing that this position is privileged *a priori*. The latter form of criticism runs the risk of the believers finding it irrelevant, but it is not, as the first form is, a matter of philosophical confusion.

What we have to be clear about, therefore, is what we do when we criticize in a certain way, what our philosophical pretensions are when we criticize. Religion stands in a relation to all other human activities, and *may* be influenced by all of them, but is not *necessarily* influenced by any of them if they are taken separately. It is possible, however, to claim that religion ought to be influenced by some and ought not be influenced by others. The same goes for the influence of religious beliefs on other human activities. Thus all human activities are related to each other, some

---

92 Ibid.
93 Phillips, *Wittgenstein and Religion*, p. 97.

more closely and some more distantly, and we can change the character of a specific activity by relating it more closely to another activity, or by separating it more from another activity. Stressing that human activities are related must not, however, lead us to believe that all different activities really are of the same kind, that the distinction between true and false is made in the same way in all areas of human life.[94]

Conclusion

In this chapter, I have argued that Wittgenstein's relation to conservatism is rather complicated. On the one hand, Wittgenstein's political views have both radical and conservative traits; on the other hand, this distinction is sometimes problematic in itself when it comes to Wittgenstein. Furthermore, I have argued that a critical attitude towards the status quo is compatible with Wittgenstein's way of doing philosophy. However, there are certainly questions (for example, when it comes to settling for a more or less reasonable answer to questions about one's life and society) which are difficult to discuss substantially when trying to live up to Wittgenstein's methodological ideals, so if such questions are to be seen as part of philosophy, we have to give room for different ways of dealing with philosophical problems. I have also argued that the accusation of fideism directed at Wittgensteinian philosophy of religion relies on a defective understanding of what criticism amounts to in this context, an understanding which presupposes that all human activities should be judged in the same way. Since, both in this chapter, especially in the discussion of fideism, and in the previous one, we have dwelled upon how discussion and criticism of religious beliefs can be understood, by way of conclusion we ought to say some things about what this means for the philosophy of religion as a critical enterprise.

---

94 Cf. ibid., pp. 67, 69, 71–2, 87.

Chapter 8

Philosophy of Religion and Enlightenment Thinking

One of the conclusions so far is that the question 'Is religious belief rational?' is not very meaningful unless we specify what is meant by 'rational' here and show why this conception of rationality is to be preferred. That this needs to be done in order to make the question meaningful removes some of the interest of the question – the fact that the question did not need to be specified was what made it interesting, since if we did not need to show why our particular way of specifying the question is to be preferred, the question would provide us with a way of criticizing religious beliefs from a neutral basis.

Often, this question has been filled with content by it being presupposed as self-evident that religious beliefs are some sort of scientific or empirical beliefs. However, another conclusion so far is that such a conception of religious beliefs is misguided. By reminding ourselves of aspects of religious belief which are easily forgotten when theorizing about religion, we have come to see that religious beliefs have a different character to scientific beliefs: for the religious believer, her religious belief is not tentative or some form of hypothesis in need of evidence for its probability.[1]

However, the question 'Is religious belief rational?' is important, since it points at a wish to discuss religious beliefs critically, a wish that is important to entertain, for two main reasons. Firstly, all of us dislike and want to work against *some* religious beliefs (unless we define 'religious' in some peculiar way), and it is better to discuss than to simply fight. Of course, there is not *always* a need for criticism. All I am saying is that there *sometimes* is such a need, that there are cases where simply understanding is not enough, even if understanding is a presupposition for a fruitful critical discussion.[2] Secondly, since not everything is as we want it to be, there is a need for improvement and change of one's mind.

Since the question 'Is religious belief rational?' needs to be specified, and thus is not a question which can always be answered without discussing questions about values and aims, the question does not stand out from or above questions like 'Is religious belief moral?' or 'Is religious belief existentially adequate?' On the contrary, by focusing on the latter questions, the question about the rationality of religious beliefs can be filled with content. There are, of course, many different ways of filling such a question with content, but the advantage of stressing moral, political and

---

1   See, for example, Phillips, *Recovering Religious Concepts*, pp. 3–6.
2   Cf. Winch, *Trying to Make Sense*, pp. 192–3.

existential issues is that it is far more difficult to be led into philosophical confusion when criticizing religious beliefs by focusing on such issues rather than in terms of rationality. The reason why it is more difficult to be led into philosophical confusion here is, firstly, that the awareness of the diversity of, for example, moral opinions is greater than the awareness of the diversity of conceptions of rationality and criteria associated therewith. The second reason is that the awareness of the difficulty of arriving at a, in the strict sense, neutral position from where to launch the criticism is greater when it comes to morals than when it comes to rationality. Stressing moral, political and existential issues must not, however, lead us to believe that religion is identical to a moral, political or existential issue.

The first-mentioned objection here – to critically discussing religious belief by focusing on moral, political and existential issues by saying that it is not a neutral and presuppositionless form of criticism – is thus not a feasible objection. The obvious counter-argument to such an objection is that the idea of neutrality is problematic, that it often conceals questionable presuppositions. The importance of the idea of neutrality is that it expresses ideals such as willingness to change one's mind and listen to others, being open to improvements, and now and then discussing one's own presuppositions critically, but all these ideals can be taken care of without the idea of neutrality. Showing the problems with the idea of a presuppositionless way of doing philosophy thus opens the way for a critical form of philosophy of religion.

A second possible objection to critically discussing religious beliefs by focusing on moral, political and existential issues is that there is no immediate connection between the nature of reality and our existential and moral aspirations.[3] The objection is thus that it is one thing to discuss whether a religious belief is true or not, and another to discuss whether or not we ought to wish that it is true, and that the only responsibility one needs to take to one's religious beliefs is therefore *epistemic* responsibility. However, it is important to notice a difference between believing that some fact is true, even though we wish it were not true, and the belief in God. To believe in God is *not* to believe that some powerful creature exists, which is to be believed and obeyed no matter what evil things it commands, which is to be obeyed since if we do not, this creature will punish us. To believe in God is, on the contrary, to *assent to* a way of living and an attitude towards the world (in the most general meaning of the word). Hence, beliefs which are called religious have the character of being closely related to behaviour – that is, a belief which is unrelated to behaviour is not called religious, even if words such as 'God' occur in the expression of the belief. Since religious beliefs are closely related to behaviour, they must also be discussed in relation to moral, political and existential issues, but perhaps not exclusively in relation to such issues.[4]

A third possible way of objecting to this way of critically discussing religious beliefs is to compare religious beliefs with poetry: it could then be said that in the

---

3   See Mikael Stenmark, 'Theological Pragmatism: A Critical Evaluation', *Heythrop Journal*, 41 (2000): 190.

4   This also seems to be Stenmark's conclusion. See ibid.: 193 and 197.

same way as a poem should only be evaluated by focusing on aesthetic aspects and not on its liberating or oppressive potential, religious beliefs should not be evaluated due to their liberating or oppressive potentials. The problem with this objection is, however, that there is a difference between religious beliefs and poetry, in that one can read poetry for many different reasons without believing in what the poem in question expresses (if it does express something). Religion, on the other hand, almost always demands of us that it should have a significance for our life in general. If a poem is read for the view of life it expresses, however, it must be judged like any other view of life.

That neglecting to discuss religious beliefs in relation to moral, political and existential issues is a problem has been shown above all by feminist philosophers of religion and feminist theologians. Pamela Sue Anderson, for example, has proposed that the question 'For whom has a particular religious belief been constructed?' is to be answered before the question of the justification of the belief is raised.[5] Although this is a good question,[6] this is not the only question to be asked, for it is possible that a certain belief cannot be said to be constructed for any particular person or group of persons, but that the belief nevertheless ought to be questioned. Another important question is therefore: 'Which behaviour and attitude does the belief in question promote?'[7] When answering such a question, the context of the belief must be examined – a belief can promote different behaviours and attitudes in different contexts.

The problem Anderson stresses is especially obvious in Alvin Plantinga's reformed epistemology. Plantinga claims that the religious believer should not start from a position where God's existence is not affirmed, and from such a position argue for the justification of her religious belief. Instead, she should take her religious belief for granted, and show that it is justified by showing that it is properly basic – that is, comparable with saying 'I see a tree' when standing in front of a tree.[8] Plantinga's way of criticizing what he calls the evidentialist objection to theistic

5   Pamela Sue Anderson, *A Feminist Philosophy of Religion: The Rationality and Myths of Religious Beliefs* (Oxford/Malden, 1998), p. 36.

6   Anderson's formulation is a little misleading, however. The formulation can make us believe that when we have answered the question 'For whom has a particular religious belief been constructed?', we can go on justifying beliefs in the way it is usually done in the philosophy of religion. In this book, I have approached the question of justification – a word I have shunned since it can lead us astray – from a different direction. The question which is important here is how we can show somebody that a particular religious belief is wrong or right, and that can seldom by done by means of a general philosophical justification.

7   This is not to say that a belief can be understood isolated from all forms of behaviour, only that a distinction between beliefs and some forms of behaviour can be made, forms to which such behaviour which is promoted by the belief might belong.

8   See, for example, Alvin Plantinga, 'The Reformed Objection to Natural Theology', in John B. Brough, Daniel O. Dahlstrom and Henry B. Veatch (eds), *Proceedings of the American Catholic Philosophical Association, Volume LIV: Philosophical Knowledge* (1980), pp. 50–51; Alvin Plantinga, 'Is Belief in God Properly Basic?', *Noûs*, 15 (1981): 44–8.

belief[9] by regarding religious beliefs as beliefs akin to perceptual beliefs is then problematic. It is problematic since it shuts out religious beliefs from the sphere where moral, political and existential criticism is relevant, and he tries in that way artificially to hinder new ways of making the distinction between true and false in the context of religion. That Plantinga, in his 'Advice to Christian Philosophers',[10] mentions as important tasks for the Christian philosopher systematizing, deepening, exploring and articulating her perspective,[11] but not discussing her religious beliefs critically, is then not surprising. What being a Christian means and takes seems to be fixed for Plantinga, and the military vocabulary he uses ('on the move', 'march', 'unity', 'being all of one piece', 'courage', 'boldness', 'strength', 'armor')[12] reveals that for him, such a critical discussion would perhaps be seen as a weakness, or even treachery.

Critical Thinking and the Enlightenment Tradition

As I said above, it is important to entertain the wish to discuss religious belief critically. In Chapter 5, I showed, by discussing the concept of truth, that the distinction between believing that something is true and this being true can be upheld without presupposing that it is possible to take up a position from where what we believe can be compared with what is true and in that manner change our beliefs in the right direction. In Chapter 6, I showed in a more concrete way that the wish to discuss religious beliefs critically can be entertained, and how this can be done. As we have seen, Plantinga does not entertain this wish. However, the kind of philosophy which his is a reaction to does not entertain this wish either, as we will see. Rejecting the rationalistic way of critically discussing religious beliefs thus opens the way for a form of philosophy of religion which, in one important sense, is a more proper extension of the Enlightenment tradition, and this I will show in the following. Analytic-theistic philosophy of religion, by having laid down a fixed way of critically discussing religious beliefs, prides itself on being the legitimate heir of the bench-mark of critical thought, namely the Enlightenment tradition, but in so far as the Enlightenment tradition is such a bench-mark, this can be questioned.

In analytic-theistic philosophy of religion, the question of the justification of religious belief is central. The kind of philosophy of religion which Plantinga's is a reaction to discusses this question by means of arguments supposed to show the existence or the non-existence of God, arguments supposed to show the coherence or the incoherence of the concept of God, and arguments supposed to show the consistency or the inconsistency of certain properties of the concept of God with facts about the world. Both the defenders and the opponents of religious belief agree that if all these arguments were to point in a certain direction, that would point to the

---

9   Ibid., p. 41.
10   Alvin Plantinga, 'Advice to Christian Philosophers', *Faith and Philosophy*, 1 (1984).
11   Ibid.: 268 and 271.
12   See ibid.: 253–4.

justification of religious belief. What makes this way of doing philosophy of religion problematic, however, is that it discusses the justification of religious belief without discussing its liberating or oppressing potential – in short, that responsibility for the beliefs under discussion is not taken.[13] Anderson writes that '… these theistic arguments … assume the status quo of patriarchal beliefs. … my contention is that the popular empiricist … methods of defending or attacking theistic beliefs confirm the status quo of patriarchy in the history of western philosophy'.[14] The problem with this tradition of philosophy of religion is that it takes a certain conception of religious belief for granted, without arguing for it. The intellectual aspect and the behavioural aspect of religious belief is here sharply distinguished, and it is the first aspect which is seen as the primary locus of rationality, and thereby the primary subject of philosophical criticism. In that respect, such philosophy of religion is uncritical.

Enlightenment philosophy has often been understood as insisting on one universal norm of rationality based on science, and it is then uncritical in the same respect as analytic-theistic philosophy of religion, and consequently not a benchmark of critical thought. However, what enlightenment is can be understood in another way. What I now want to do, in dialogue with a central text of the Enlightenment, Immanuel Kant's 'An Answer to the Question: What Is Enlightenment?',[15] is therefore to show that it is possible to give another account of the critical aspect of enlightenment thinking. Enlightenment thinking is then seen as an insistence on the importance of improving oneself and others.[16]

Kant begins that text by writing *'Enlightenment is the human being's emergence from his self-incurred minority [Unmündigkeit]. Minority* is inability to make use of

---

13 The objection that the only responsibility which one need to take in this context is epistemic responsibility was discussed earlier in this chapter.

14 Anderson, *A Feminist Philosophy of Religion*, p. 16.

15 Kant, *Practical Philosophy*, pp. 17–22.

16 Kant also discusses what enlightenment is also in other places. He writes, for example:

Thinking for oneself means seeking the supreme touchstone of truth in oneself (i.e. in one's own reason); and the maxim of always thinking for oneself is **enlightenment**. Now there is less to this than people imagine when they place enlightenment in the acquistion of *information*; for it is rather a negative principle in the use of one's faculty of cognition, and often he who is richest in information is the least enlightened in the use he makes of it. … Thus it is quite easy to ground enlightenment in *individual subjects* through their education; one must only begin early to accustom young minds to this reflection. But to enlighten an *age* is very slow and arduous; for there are external obstacles which in part forbid this manner of education and in part make it more difficult. (Immanuel Kant, *Religion and Rational Theology*, trans. Allen W. Wood (Cambridge, 1996), 18)

The reflection Kant talks about here is to be done in a specific way, but Kant is nevertheless far from insisting on one universal norm of rationality based on science – on the contrary.

one's own understanding without direction of another.'[17] This saying should not be accepted without discussion.[18] Namely, Kant seems to be exaggerating: being able to use one's own understanding requires learning – that is, direction[19] – and being aware of one's dependence on others is therefore important. Furthermore, to believe that people in the past did not think for themselves, and that we now do, is unfair to the past and naïve regarding the present. What is important in Kant's saying, however, is the insistence on taking care of possibilities, when they arise, to break with old and obsolete authorities. These possibilities are of different sizes at different times, and arise as a result of, among other things, political processes. However, possibilities must be taken care of, so although we are no isolated subjects who can think completely for ourselves, the phrase 'to think for oneself' has an obvious use in concrete situations, and is then an important ideal.

Kant specifically relates his answer to religious issues, by saying that enlightenment requires freedom to make a public use of your understanding, a freedom which is restricted by certain persons, among others clergymen, who do not want people to think for themselves.[20] Moreover, Kant regards it as impossible to bind a society to something said to be eternal and beyond possible change and improvement.[21] The reason why this is impossible is, according to Kant, that this '… would be a crime against human nature, whose original vocation lies … in … progress',[22] that this would be '… to violate the sacred right of humanity and trample it underfoot'.[23]

---

17 Kant, *Practical Philosophy*, p. 17. Translation of Immanuel Kant, *Was ist Aufklärung?: Ausgewählte kleine Schriften* (Hamburg, 1999), p. 20: '*Aufklärung ist der Ausgang des Menschen aus seiner selbstverschuldeten Unmündigkeit. Unmündigkeit* ist das Unvermögen, sich seines Verstandes ohne Leitung eines anderen zu bedienen.'

18 Apart from the problem mentioned, there are some problems of translation. *Verstand* is above translated as 'understanding', but this is not fully satisfying. 'Understanding' is primarily what comes to existence when one understands something, whereas *Verstand*, as used by Kant, is the faculty for thinking of objects of sensible intuition, the faculty by which we bring intuitions under concepts and thereby make them understandable; Kant, *Critique of Pure Reason*, pp. 193–4 (A51/B75). Furthermore, the noun *Verstand* has the adjective *verständig*, which in English is 'intelligent' or the like. One possible alternative translation of *Verstand* is therefore 'intelligence' or 'intellect'. In the following, however, I stick to 'understanding' (and the problem of translation should then be borne in mind), and sometimes speak more loosely about 'thinking for oneself'. The other problem concerns the translation of *Leitung* as 'direction'. *Leitung* may have a stronger sense here, more in the direction of 'command', but we do not have to settle for a definite translation here, since there is another and more serious set of problems.

19 Kant is aware of this. See Kant, *Religion and Rational Theology*, p. 18.

20 Kant, *Practical Philosophy*, p. 18.

21 Ibid., pp. 19–20.

22 Ibid., p. 20. Translation of Kant, *Was ist Aufklärung?*, p. 24: '… wäre ein Verbrechen wider die menschliche Natur, deren ursprüngliche Bestimmung … in … Fortschreiten besteht …'.

23 Kant, *Practical Philosophy*, p. 20. Translation of Kant, *Was ist Aufklärung?*, p. 25: '… die heiligen Rechte der Menschheit zu verletzen und mit Füßen treten'.

To talk about human nature and sacred rights is of course problematic, but it is not needed: it suffices to say that to bind society to something beyond possible change and improvement would be to prevent others from thinking for themselves.

For the philosophy of religion, this means that the critical discussion of religious beliefs must be kept open: the critical discussion of a specific religious belief may not be cancelled from the philosophical agenda in order to hinder possible improvements. The Enlightenment tradition is not something unique which we must remain loyal to, however, but is a part of a developing history, where criticism, and especially self-criticism, is central.[24] This means – and this is the important point – that rejecting the rationalistic way of critically discussing religious belief is not to reject enlightenment thinking. On the contrary, discussing religious beliefs in relation to moral, political and existential issues is, in one sense, a more proper extension of the Enlightenment tradition. Analytic-theistic philosophy of religion has been preoccupied with the question of the justification of religious belief, understood mainly in terms of proofs for and against the existence of God. Philosophers in that tradition differ, of course, when it comes to the question of whether such a proof or disproof will ever be conclusive or not, but the final aim of their discussion is conclusive proofs – that is, to close the question definitively. The critical discussion in relation to moral, political and existential issues is open to different persons' different ways of seeing things, however, and lets us then, in discussion with others, make use of our own understanding – and, to echo Kant, this is what enlightenment is.

---

24 Cf. Derrida, *Specters of Marx*, p. 88; Ricoeur, *From Text to Action*, pp. 306–7; Theodor W. Adorno and Max Horkheimer, *Dialectic of Enlightenment*, trans. John Cumming (London, 1997), pp. xiii–xvi.

Bibliography

Adorno, Theodor W., *Negative Dialectics*, trans. E.B. Ashton (New York: Continuum, 1973).

Adorno, Theodor W. and Horkheimer, Max, *Dialectic of Enlightenment*, trans. John Cumming (London: Verso, 1997).

Allen, Amy, 'MacIntyre's Traditionalism', *The Journal of Value Inquiry*, 31 (1997): 511–25.

Althusser, Louis, *Lenin and Philosophy and Other Essays*, trans. Ben Brewster (London: NLB, 1971).

Anderson, Pamela Sue, *A Feminist Philosophy of Religion: The Rationality and Myths of Religious Beliefs* (Oxford/Malden: Blackwell, 1998).

Apel, Karl-Otto, *Towards a Transformation of Philosophy*, trans. Glyn Adey and David Frisby (London: Routledge & Kegan Paul, 1980).

Appelros, Erica, *God in the Act of Reference: Debating Religious Realism and Non-realism* (Aldershot: Ashgate, 2002).

Arendt, Hannah, *Between Past and Future: Eight Exercises in Political Thought* (New York: The Viking Press, 1968).

Aristotle, *The Nicomachean Ethics*, trans. Hippocrates G. Apostle (Dordrecht/ Boston, MA: D. Reidel, 1975).

——, *On Rhetoric: A Theory of Civic Discourse*, trans. George A. Kennedy (New York: Oxford University Press, 1991).

——, *Metaphysics: Books Γ, Δ and E*, trans. Christopher Kirwan, 2nd edn (Oxford: Clarendon Press, 1993).

Ayer, Alfred Jules, *Language, Truth and Logic*, 2nd edn (London: Victor Gollancz, 1946).

Baghramian, Maria, *Relativism* (London: Routledge, 2004).

Baker, Gordon P., *Wittgenstein's Method: Neglected Aspects*, ed. Katherine Morris (Oxford: Blackwell Publishing, 2004).

Baker, Gordon P. and Hacker, Peter M.S., *Scepticism, Rules and Language* (Oxford: Basil Blackwell, 1984).

——, *An Analytical Commentary on the* Philosophical Investigations, *Volume 2: Wittgenstein: Rules, Grammar and Necessity* (Oxford: Basil Blackwell, 1985).

Bakunin, Michael, *God and the State*, trans. Benjamin Tucker (New York: Dover Publications, 1970).

Bell, Catherine M., '"The Chinese Believe in Spirits": Belief and Believing in the Study of Religion', in Nancy K. Frankenberry (ed.), *Radical Interpretation in Religion* (Cambridge: Cambridge University Press, 2002), pp. 100–116.

Bell, Richard H., 'Religion and Wittgenstein's Legacy: Beyond Fideism and Language Games', in Timothy Tessin and Mario von der Ruhr (eds), *Philosophy and the Grammar of Religious Belief* (New York: St. Martin's Press, 1995), pp. 215–47.

Benhabib, Seyla, *Situating the Self: Gender, Community and Postmodernism in Contemporary Ethics* (Cambridge: Polity Press, 1992).

Berman, Marshall, *All That Is Solid Melts Into Air: The Experience of Modernity* (New York: Simon and Schuster, 1982).

Bernstein, Richard J., *Beyond Objectivism and Relativism: Science, Hermeneutics, and Praxis* (Oxford: Basil Blackwell, 1983).

Bilgrami, Akeel, 'Norms and Meaning', in Ralf Stoecker (ed.), *Reflecting Davidson: Donald Davidson Responding to an International Forum of Philosophers* (Berlin: Walter de Gruyter, 1993), pp. 121–44.

Bloor, David, *Wittgenstein: A Social Theory of Knowledge* (London: Macmillan, 1983).

Bouveresse, Jacques, '"The Darkness of This Time": Wittgenstein and the Modern World', in A. Phillips Griffiths (ed.), *Wittgenstein Centenary Essays* (Cambridge: Cambridge University Press, 1991), pp. 11–39.

Bouwsma, Oets Kolk, *Wittgenstein: Conversations 1949–1951*, ed. J.L. Craft and Ronald E. Hustwit (Indianapolis, IN: Hackett, 1986).

Brandom, Robert, 'Perception and Rational Constraint', *Philosophy and Phenomenological Research*, 58 (1998): 369–74.

Cahn, Steven M., 'The Irrelevance to Religion of Philosophic Proofs for the Existence of God', *American Philosophical Quarterly*, 6 (1969): 170–72.

Carnap, Rudolf, *The Logical Structure of the World: Pseudoproblems in Philosophy*, trans. Rolf A. George (Berkeley, CA: University of California Press, 1967).

Churchill, John, 'The Squirrel Does Not Infer by Induction: Wittgenstein and the Natural History of Religion', in Timothy Tessin and Mario von der Ruhr (eds), *Philosophy and the Grammar of Religious Belief* (New York: St. Martin's Press, 1995), pp. 48–78.

Clack, Brian R., *Wittgenstein, Frazer and Religion* (New York: St. Martin's Press, 1999).

——, *An Introduction to Wittgenstein's Philosophy of Religion* (Edinburgh: Edinburgh University Press, 1999).

Copleston, Frederick, *A History of Philosophy, Volume I: Greece and Rome*, rev. edn (London: Burns and Oates, 1947).

Cornford, Francis MacDonald, *From Religion to Philosophy: A Study in the Origins of Western Speculation* (London: Edward Arnold, 1912).

Cornforth, Maurice, *Marxism and the Linguistic Philosophy* (London: Lawrence & Wishart, 1965).

Craig, Edward, 'Davidson and the Sceptic: The Thumbnail Version', *Analysis*, 50 (1990): 213–14.

Crary, Alice, 'Wittgenstein's Philosophy in Relation to Political Thought', in Alice Crary and Rupert Read (eds), *The New Wittgenstein* (London: Routledge, 2000), pp. 118–45.

Dalferth, Ingolf U., *Die Wirklichkeit des Möglichen: Hermeneutische*

Religionsphilosophie (Tübingen: Mohr Siebeck, 2003).

Davidson, Donald, 'Reply to Jerry Fodor and Ernest Lepore', in Ralf Stoecker (ed.), *Reflecting Davidson: Donald Davidson Responding to an International Forum of Philosophers* (Berlin: Walter de Gruyter, 1993), pp. 77–84.

——, 'Reply to Andreas Kemmerling', in Ralf Stoecker (ed.), *Reflecting Davidson: Donald Davidson Responding to an International Forum of Philosophers* (Berlin: Walter de Gruyter, 1993), pp. 117–19.

——, 'Reply to A.C. Genova', in Lewis Edwin Hahn (ed.), *The Philosophy of Donald Davidson* (Chicago, IL: Open Court, 1999), pp. 192–4.

——, 'Reply to Barry Stroud', in Lewis Edwin Hahn (ed.), *The Philosophy of Donald Davidson* (Chicago, IL: Open Court, 1999), pp. 162–6.

——, 'Reply to Peter Pagin', in Urszula M. Żegleń (ed.), *Donald Davidson: Truth, Meaning and Knowledge* (London: Routledge, 1999), pp. 72–4.

——, 'Reply to Roger F. Gibson', in Urszula M. Żegleń (ed.), *Donald Davidson: Truth, Meaning and Knowledge* (London: Routledge, 1999), pp. 134–5.

——, *Inquiries into Truth and Interpretation*, 2nd edn (Oxford: Oxford University Press, 2001).

——, *Subjective, Intersubjective, Objective* (Oxford: Oxford University Press, 2001).

——, 'Externalisms', in Petr Kotatko, Peter Pagin and Gabriel Segal (eds), *Interpreting Davidson* (Stanford, CT: CSLI Publications, 2001), pp. 1–16.

——, *Problems of Rationality* (Oxford: Oxford University Press, 2004).

——, *Truth, Language, and History* (Oxford: Oxford University Press, 2005).

——, *Truth and Predication* (Cambridge/London: The Belknap Press of Harvard University Press, 2005).

D'Costa, Gavin, 'Whose Objectivity? Which Neutrality? The Doomed Quest for a Neutral Vantage Point from Which to Judge Religions', *Religious Studies*, 29 (1993): 79–95.

Derrida, Jacques, 'Force of Law: The "Mystical Foundation of Authority"', trans. Mary Quaintance, in Drucilla Cornell, Michel Rosenfeld and David Gray Carlson (eds), *Deconstruction and the Possibility of Justice* (New York: Routledge, 1992), pp. 3–67.

——, *Specters of Marx: The State of the Debt, the Work of Mourning, and the New International*, trans. Peggy Kamuf (New York: Routledge, 1994).

——, *Of Grammatology*, corr. edn, trans. Gayatri Chakravorty Spivak (Baltimore, MD: The John Hopkins University Press, 1997).

Descartes, René, *The Philosophical Writings of Descartes, Volume II*, trans. John Cottingham, Robert Stoothoff and Dugald Murdoch (Cambridge: Cambridge University Press, 1984).

Diamond, Cora, 'Rules: Looking in the Right Place', in D.Z. Phillips and Peter Winch (eds), *Wittgenstein: Attention to Particulars: Essays in Honour of Rush Rhees (1909–89)* (London: Macmillan, 1989), pp. 12–34.

Diogenes Laertius, *Lives of Eminent Philosophers: In Two Volumes: I*, trans. R.D.

Hicks (London: William Heinemann, 1925).

Drury, Maurice O'Connor, 'Conversations with Wittgenstein', in F.A. Flowers III (ed.), *Portraits of Wittgenstein, Volume 3* (Bristol: Thoemmes Press, 1999), pp. 188–252.

Durkheim, Emile, *The Division of Labor in Society*, trans. George Simpson (New York: The Free Press, 1964).

Edwards, Steve, 'Formulating a Plausible Relativism', *Philosophia*, 22 (1993): 63–74.

Engelmann, Paul, 'A Memoir', trans. L. Furtmüller, in F.A. Flowers III (ed.), *Portraits of Wittgenstein, Volume 2* (Bristol: Thoemmes Press, 1999), pp. 5–62.

Engels, Frederick, 'Anti-Dühring: Herr Eugen Dühring's Revolution in Science', in *Karl Marx Frederick Engels Collected Works, Volume 25: Frederick Engels Anti-Dühring, Dialectics of Nature* (Moscow, Progress Publishers, 1987), pp. 1–309.

Eriksson, Stefan, *Ett mönster i livets väv: Tro och religion i ljuset av Wittgensteins filosofi* (Nora: Nya Doxa, 1998).

———, 'The Resurrection and the Incarnation – Myths, Facts or What?', *Studia Theologica*, 55 (2001): 129–44.

Flax, Jane, 'Postmodernism and Gender Relations in Feminist Theory', in Linda J. Nicholson (ed.), *Feminism/Postmodernism* (New York: Routledge, 1990), pp. 39–62.

Flew, Antony, *God and Philosophy* (London: Hutchinson, 1966).

Foley, Richard and Fumerton, Richard, 'Davidson's Theism?', *Philosophical Studies*, 48 (1985): 83–9.

Frankenberry, Nancy K., 'Pragmatism, Truth, and the Disenchantment of Subjectivity', in Nancy K. Frankenberry and Hans H. Penner (eds), *Language, Truth, and Religious Belief: Studies in Twentieth-century Theory and Method in Religion* (Atlanta, GA: Scholars Press, 1999), pp. 507–32.

Frankenberry, Nancy K. and Penner, Hans H., 'From Functionalism to Relativism: Introduction', in Nancy K. Frankenberry and Hans H. Penner (eds), *Language, Truth, and Religious Belief: Studies in Twentieth-Century Theory and Method in Religion* (Atlanta, GA: Scholars Press, 1999), pp. 275–9.

Fraser, Nancy and Nicholson, Linda J., 'Social Criticism without Philosophy: An Encounter between Feminism and Postmodernism', in Linda J. Nicholson (ed.), *Feminism/Postmodernism* (New York: Routledge, 1990), pp. 19–38.

Frege, Gottlob, 'Logic', in Michael Beaney (ed.), *The Frege Reader* (Oxford: Blackwell, 1997), pp. 227–50.

Freud, Sigmund, *The Standard Edition of the Complete Psychological Works of Sigmund Freud, Volume XXI: The Future of an Illusion, Civilization and Its Discontents, and Other Works*, trans. James Strachey (London: The Hogarth Press, 1961).

Gadamer, Hans-Georg, *Kleine Schriften I: Philosophie Hermeneutik* (Tübingen: J.C.B. Mohr (Paul Siebeck), 1967).

———, *Philosophical Hermeneutics*, trans. and ed. David E. Linge (Berkeley, CA:

University of California Press, 1976).

——, *Gesammelte Werke: Band 1: Hermeneutik I: Wahrheit und Methode: Grundzüge einer philosophischen Hermeneutik*, 5th edn (Tübingen: J.C.B. Mohr (Paul Siebeck), 1986).

——, *Truth and Method*, 2nd edn, trans. Joel Weinsheimer and Donald G. Marshall (New York: Continuum, 1989).

Gellman, Jerome, 'Religious Diversity and the Epistemic Justification of Religious Belief', *Faith and Philosophy*, 10 (1993): 345–64.

Gellner, Ernest, *Relativism and the Social Sciences* (Cambridge: Cambridge University Press, 1985).

Genova, A.C., 'The Very Idea of Massive Truth', in Lewis Edwin Hahn (ed.), *The Philosophy of Donald Davidson* (Chicago, IL: Open Court, 1999), pp. 167–91.

Glock, Hans-Johann, 'Wittgenstein and Reason', in James C. Klagge (ed.), *Wittgenstein: Biography and Philosophy* (New York: Cambridge University Press, 2001), pp. 195–220.

Godlove, Terry F., *Religion, Interpretation, and Diversity of Belief: The Framework Model from Kant to Durkheim to Davidson* (Cambridge: Cambridge University Press, 1989).

Goethe, Johann Wolfgang von, *Faust: Parts One and Two*, trans. George Madison Priest (Chicago, IL: Encyclopædia Britannica, 1952).

Gustafsson, Martin, 'Systematic Meaning and Linguistic Diversity: The Place of Meaning-theories in Davidson's Later Philosophy', *Inquiry,* 41 (1998): 435–53.

——, The Rule-follower and his Community: Remarks on an Apparent Tension in Wittgenstein's Discussions of Rule-following', *Language Sciences*, 26 (2004): 125–45.

Haack, Susan, *Manifesto of a Passionate Moderate: Unfashionable Essays* (Chicago, IL: The University of Chicago Press, 1998).

Habermas, Jürgen, *The Philosophical Discourse of Modernity: Twelve Lectures*, trans. Frederick Lawrence (Cambridge, MA: The MIT Press, 1987).

——, 'Rortys pragmatische Wende', *Deutsche Zeitschrift für Philosophie*, 44 (1996): 715–41.

——, *Truth and Justification*, ed. and trans. Barbara Fultner (Cambridge: Polity Press, 2003).

Haller, Rudolf, *Questions on Wittgenstein* (London: Routledge, 1988).

Harding, Sandra, 'Feminism, Science, and the Anti-Enlightenment Critiques', in Linda J. Nicholson (ed.), *Feminism/Postmodernism* (New York: Routledge, 1990), pp. 83–106.

Hegel, Georg Wilhelm Friedrich, *Hegel's Philosophy of Right*, trans. T.M. Knox (Oxford: Oxford University Press, 1952).

——, *Natural Law: The Scientific Ways of Treating Natural Law, Its Place in Moral Philosophy, and Its Relation to the Positive Sciences of Law*, trans. T.M. Knox (Philadelphia, PA: University of Pennsylvania Press, 1975).

Heidegger, Martin, *Being and Time*, trans. John Macquarrie and Edward Robinson

(Oxford: Blackwell, 1962).

——, *Identity and Difference*, trans. Joan Stambaugh (Chicago, IL: The University of Chicago Press, 1969).

——, *Poetry, Language, Thought*, trans. Albert Hofstadter (New York: Harper & Row, 1971).

——, *Sein und Zeit*, 18th edn (Tübingen: Max Niemeyer Verlag, 2001).

Herrmann, Eberhard, *Religion, Reality, and a Good Life: A Philosophical Approach to Religion* (Tübingen: Mohr Siebeck, 2004).

Hiley, David R., *Philosophy in Question: Essays on a Pyrrhonian Theme* (Chicago, IL: The University of Chicago Press, 1988).

Hilmy, S. Stephen, *The Later Wittgenstein: The Emergence of a New Philosophical Method* (Oxford: Basil Blackwell, 1987).

Hodges, Michael P., 'The Status of Ethical Judgements in the *Philosophical Investigations*', *Philosophical Investigations*, 18 (1995): 99–112.

——, 'Faith: Themes from Wittgenstein, Kierkegaard and Nietzsche', in Robert L. Arrington and Mark Addis (eds), *Wittgenstein and Philosophy of Religion* (London: Routledge, 2001), pp. 66–84.

Hollis, Martin and Lukes, Steven, 'Introduction', in Martin Hollis and Steven Lukes (eds), *Rationality and Relativism* (Oxford: Basil Blackwell, 1982), pp. 1–20.

Hume, David, *Dialogues Concerning Natural Religion* (London: Routledge, 1991).

——, *An Enquiry Concerning Human Understanding* (Oxford: Oxford University Press, 1999).

Hyman, John, 'Wittgensteinianism', in Philip L. Quinn and Charles Taliaferro (eds), *A Companion to Philosophy of Religion* (Cambridge: Blackwell publishers, 1997), pp. 150–57.

Jantzen, Grace M., 'What's the Difference? Knowledge and Gender in (Post)Modern Philosophy of Religion', *Religious Studies,* 32 (1996): 431–48.

Kant, Immanuel, *Practical Philosophy*, trans. and ed. Mary J. Gregor (Cambridge: Cambridge University Press, 1996).

——, *Religion and Rational Theology*, trans. and ed. Allen W. Wood (Cambridge: Cambridge University Press, 1996).

——, *Critique of Pure Reason*, trans. and ed. Paul Guyer and Allen W. Wood (Cambridge: Cambridge University Press, 1998).

——, *Was ist Aufklärung?: Ausgewählte kleine Schriften* (Hamburg: Felix Meiner Verlag, 1999).

Kirk, Robert, *Relativism and Reality: A Contemporary Introduction* (London: Routledge, 1999).

Klagge, James C., 'When Are Ideologies Irreconcilable? Case Studies in Diachronic Anthropology', *Philosophical Investigations*, 21 (1998): 268–79.

Knorpp, William Max, 'What Relativism Isn't', *Philosophy*, 73 (1998): 277–300.

Kompridis, Nikolas, 'So We Need Something Else for Reason to Mean', *International Journal of Philosophical Studies*, 8 (2000): 271–95.

Kuhn, Thomas S., *The Structure of Scientific Revolutions*, 2nd edn (Chicago, IL: The

University of Chicago Press, 1970).

Kusch, Martin, *Knowledge by Agreement: The Programme of Communitarian Epistemology* (Oxford/New York: Oxford University Press, 2002).

Kölbel, Max, 'Indexical Relativism versus Genuine Relativism', *International Journal of Philosophical Studies*, 12 (2004): 297–313.

Lynch, Michael P., *Truth in Context: An Essay on Pluralism and Objectivity* (Cambridge, MA/London: The MIT Press, 1998).

McDowell, John, *Mind and World* (Cambridge, MA: Harvard University Press, 1994).

——, *Mind, Value, and Reality* (Cambridge – London: Harvard University Press, 1998).

——, 'Towards Rehabilitating Objectivity', in Robert B. Brandom (ed.), *Rorty and His Critics* (Malden: Blackwell, 2000), pp. 109–23.

MacIntyre, Alasdair, *Whose Justice? Which Rationality?* (London: Duckworth, 1988).

Malcolm, Norman, *Ludwig Wittgenstein: A Memoir*, 2nd edn (Oxford: Oxford University Press, 1984).

——, *Nothing Is Hidden: Wittgenstein's Criticism of His Early Thought* (Oxford: Basil Blackwell, 1986).

Marcuse, Herbert, *One Dimensional Man: Studies in the Ideology of Advanced Industrial Society* (London: Routledge & Kegan Paul, 1964).

Marx, Karl, 'On the Jewish Question', in *Karl Marx Frederick Engels Collected Works, Volume 3: Marx and Engels 1843–44* (London: Lawrence & Wishart, 1975), pp. 146–74.

——, 'Contribution to the Critique of Hegel's Philosophy of Law: Introduction', in *Karl Marx Frederick Engels Collected Works, Volume 3: Marx and Engels 1843–44* (London: Lawrence & Wishart, 1975), pp. 175–87.

——, 'Theses on Feuerbach: Edited by Engels', in *Karl Marx Frederick Engels Collected Works, Volume 5: Marx and Engels 1845–47* (London: Lawrence & Wishart, 1976), pp. 6–8.

——, 'The Communism of the *Rheinischer Beobachter*', in *Karl Marx Frederick Engels Collected Works, Volume 6: Marx and Engels 1845–48* (London: Lawrence & Wishart, 1976), pp. 220–34.

——, 'The Eighteenth Brumaire of Louis Bonaparte', in *Karl Marx Frederick Engels Collected Works, Volume 11: Marx and Engels 1851–53* (London: Lawrence & Wishart, 1979), pp. 99–197.

——, 'Zur Kritik der Hegelschen Rechtsphilosophie: Einleitung', in *Karl Marx Friedrich Engels Gesamtausgabe, Erste Abteilung, Werke Artikel Entwürfe: Band 2, März 1843 bis August 1844: Text* (Berlin: Dietz Verlag, 1982), pp. 170–83.

——, 'A Contribution to the Critique of Political Economy: Part One', in *Karl Marx Frederick Engels Collected Works, Volume 29: Karl Marx 1857–61* (Moscow: Progress Publishers, 1987), pp. 257–418.

Marx, Karl and Engels, Frederick, 'The German Ideology: Critique of Modern German Philosophy According to Its Representatives Feuerbach, B. Bauer and

Stirner, and of German Socialism According to Its Various Prophets', in *Karl Marx Frederick Engels Collected Works, Volume 5: Marx and Engels 1845–47* (London: Lawrence & Wishart, 1976), pp. 19–539.

Merleau-Ponty, Maurice, *Phenomenology of Perception*, trans. Colin Smith (London: Routledge, 1962).

——, 'Un inédit de Maurice Merleau-Ponty', *Revue de Métaphysique et de Morale*, 67 (1962): 401–9.

——, 'An Unpublished Text by Maurice Merleau-Ponty: A Prospectus of His Work', trans. Arleen B. Dallery, in James M. Edie (ed.), *The Primacy of Perception and Other Essays on Phenomenological Psychology, the Philosophy of Art, History and Politics* (Evanston, IL: Northwestern University Press, 1964), pp. 3–11.

Monk, Ray, *Ludwig Wittgenstein: The Duty of Genius* (London: Jonathan Cape, 1990).

Montaigne, Michel Eyquem de, *The Essays of Michel Eyquem de Montaigne*, trans. Charles Cotton, ed. W. Carew Hazlitt (Chicago, IL: Encyclopædia Brittanica, 1952).

Moser, Paul K., *Philosophy after Objectivity: Making Sense in Perspective* (New York: Oxford University Press, 1993).

Mulhall, Stephen, 'Wittgenstein and the Philosophy of Religion', in D.Z. Phillips and Timothy Tessin (eds), *Philosophy of Religion in the 21st Century* (Basingstoke: Palgrave, 2001), pp. 95–118.

Nedo, Michael, 'Aus Ludwig Wittgensteins ‚Taschen-Notizbuch' von 1931', *Deutsche Zeitschrift für Philosophie*, 45 (1997): 429–33.

Neurath, Otto, *Empiricism and Sociology,* ed. Marie Neurath and Robert S. Cohen (Dordrecht: D. Reidel, 1973).

Nielsen, Kai, 'Wittgensteinian Fideism', *Philosophy,* 42 (1967): 191–209.

——, *Naturalism and Religion* (Amherst, MA: Prometheus Books, 2001).

Nietzsche, Friedrich, 'Ecce homo', in Giorgio Colli and Mazzino Montinari (eds), *Nietzsche Werke: Kritische Gesamtausgabe, Sechste Abteilung: Dritter Band* (Berlin: Walter de Gruyter, 1969), pp. 253–372.

——, *Ecce Homo: How One Becomes What One Is*, trans. R.J. Hollingdale (London: Penguin Books, 1979).

——, *On the Genealogy of Morality*, ed. Keith Ansell-Pearson, trans. Carol Diethe (Cambridge: Cambridge University Press, 1994).

Nyíri, Janos Cristoph, 'Wittgenstein's New Traditionalism', in Jaakko Hintikka (ed.), *Acta Philosophica Fennica 28: Essays on Wittgenstein in Honour of G.H. von Wright* (1976), pp. 503–12.

——, 'Wittgenstein's Later Work in Relation to Conservatism', in Brian McGuinness (ed.), *Wittgenstein and His Times* (Oxford: Basil Blackwell, 1982), pp. 44–68.

——, 'Wittgenstein 1929–31: The Turning Back', in Stuart Shanker (ed.), *Ludwig Wittgenstein: Critical Assessments, Volume Four: From Theology to Sociology: Wittgenstein's Impact on Contemporary Thought* (London: Croom Helm, 1986), pp. 29–59.

O'Grady, Paul, *Relativism* (Teddington: Acumen, 2002).

——, 'Wittgenstein and Relativism', *International Journal of Philosophical Studies*, 12 (2004): 315–37.

O'Hear, Anthony, 'Wittgenstein and the Transmission of Traditions', in A. Phillips Griffiths (ed.), *Wittgenstein Centenary Essays* (Cambridge: Cambridge University Press, 1991), pp. 41–60.

O'Neill, Martin, 'Explaining "The Hardness of the Logical Must": Wittgenstein on Grammar, Arbitrariness and Logical Necessity', *Philosophical Investigations*, 24 (2001): 1–29.

Pascal, Fania, 'Wittgenstein: A Personal Memoir', in F.A. Flowers III (ed.), *Portraits of Wittgenstein, Volume 2* (Bristol: Thoemmes Press, 1999), pp. 222–48.

Peano, Giuseppe, 'The Principles of Arithmetic, Presented by a New Method', trans. Jean van Heijenoort, in Jean van Heijenoort (ed.), *From Frege to Gödel: A Source Book in Mathematical Logic, 1879–1931* (Cambridge, MA: Harvard University Press, 1967), pp. 85–97.

Penner, Hans H., 'Why Does Semantics Matter?', in Nancy K. Frankenberry and Hans H. Penner (eds), *Language, Truth, and Religious Belief: Studies in Twentieth-Century Theory and Method in Religion* (Atlanta, GA: Scholars Press, 1999), pp. 473–506.

Perelman, Chaïm, *The Realm of Rhetoric*, trans. William Kluback (Notre Dame, IN: University of Notre Dame Press, 1982).

Peterson, Michael, Hasker, William, Reichenbach, Bruce and Basinger, David, *Reason and Religious Belief: An Introduction to the Philosophy of Religion*, 2nd edn (New York/Oxford: Oxford University Press, 1998).

Phillips, Dewi Zephaniah, *Faith and Philosophical Enquiry* (London: Routledge & Kegan Paul, 1970).

——, *Belief, Change and Forms of Life* (London: Macmillan, 1986).

——, *Wittgenstein and Religion* (New York: St. Martin's Press, 1993).

——, *Introducing Philosophy: The Challenge of Scepticism* (Oxford: Blackwell, 1996).

——, *Philosophy's Cool Place* (Ithaca, NY: Cornell University Press, 1999).

——, *Recovering Religious Concepts: Closing Epistemic Divides* (Basingstoke: Macmillan, 2000).

——, *Religion and Friendly Fire: Examining Assumptions in Contemporary Philosophy of Religion* (Aldershot/Burlington, VT: Ashgate, 2004).

——, *The Problem of Evil and the Problem of God* (London: SCM Press, 2004).

Plantinga, Alvin, *God and Other Minds: A Study in the Rational Justification of Belief in God* (Ithaca, NY: Cornell University Press, 1967).

——, 'The Reformed Objection to Natural Theology', in John B. Brough, Daniel O. Dahlstrom and Henry B. Veatch (eds), *Proceedings of the American Catholic Philosophical Association, Volume LIV: Philosophical Knowledge* (1980), pp.

49–62.

——, 'Is Belief in God Properly Basic?', *Noûs*, 15 (1981): 41–51.

——, 'Advice to Christian Philosophers', *Faith and Philosophy*, 1 (1984): 253–71.

Plato, *The Dialogues of Plato, Volume I: Euthyphro, Apology, Crito, Meno, Gorgias, Menexenus*, trans. R.E. Allen (New Haven, CT/London: Yale University Press, 1984).

——, *The Theaetetus of Plato*, trans. M.J. Levett and Myles Burnyeat (Indianapolis, IN: Hackett, 1990).

——, *The Dialogues of Plato, Volume 3: Ion, Hippias Minor, Laches, Protagoras*, trans. R.E. Allen (New Haven, CT/London: Yale University Press, 1996).

——, *Complete Works*, ed. John M. Cooper (Indianapolis, IN: Hackett, 1997).

Pleasants, Nigel, 'Towards a Critical Use of Marx and Wittgenstein', in Gavin Kitching and Nigel Pleasants (eds), *Marx and Wittgenstein: Knowledge, Morality and Politics* (London/New York: Routledge, 2002), pp. 160–81.

Pojman, Louis P., 'Fideism: Faith without/against Reason', in Louis P. Pojman (ed.), *Philosophy of Religion: An Anthology*, 2nd edn (Belmont, TN: Wadsworth, 1994), pp. 436–8.

Popkin, Richard H., 'Origins of Western Philosophic Thinking: Introduction', in Richard H. Popkin (ed.), *The Columbia History of Western Philosophy* (New York: Columbia University Press, 1999), pp. 1–5.

Popper, Karl, 'Normal Science and Its Dangers', in Imre Lakatos and Alan Musgrave (eds), *Criticism and the Growth of Knowledge: Proceedings of the International Colloquium in the Philosophy of Science, London, 1965, Volume 4* (Cambridge: Cambridge University Press, 1970), pp. 51–8.

Preston, John, 'On Some Objections to Relativism', *Ratio*, 5 (1992): 57–73.

Putnam, Hilary, *Meaning and the Moral Sciences* (London: Routledge & Kegan Paul, 1978).

——, *Reason, Truth and History* (Cambridge: Cambridge University Press, 1981).

——, *Realism and Reason: Philosophical Papers, Volume 3* (Cambridge: Cambridge University Press, 1983).

——, *Realism with a Human Face*, ed. James Conant (Cambridge, MA: Harvard University Press, 1990).

——, *Renewing Philosophy* (Cambridge, MA: Harvard University Press, 1992).

Rappaport, Steven, 'Must a Metaphysical Relativist Be a Truth Relativist?', *Philosophia*, 22 (1993): 75–85.

Read, Rupert, 'Marx and Wittgenstein on Vampires and Parasites: A Critique of Capital and Metaphysics', in Gavin Kitching and Nigel Pleasants (eds), *Marx and Wittgenstein: Knowledge, Morality and Politics* (London/New York: Routledge, 2002), pp. 254–81.

Rhees, Rush, *Rush Rhees on Religion and Philosophy*, ed. D.Z. Phillips (Cambridge: Cambridge University Press, 1997).

——, 'Postscript', in F.A. Flowers III (ed.), *Portraits of Wittgenstein, Volume 3* (Bristol: Thoemmes Press, 1999), pp. 253–81.

——, 'On Wittgenstein', ed. D.Z. Phillips, *Philosophical Investigations*, 24 (2001):

153–62.

Richter, Duncan, *Wittgenstein at His Word* (London/New York: Continuum, 2004).

Ricoeur, Paul, *From Text to Action: Essays in Hermeneutics, II*, trans. Kathleen Blamey and John B. Thompson (London: The Athlone Press, 1991).

Rorty, Richard, *Objectivity, Relativism, and Truth: Philosophical Papers Volume 1* (Cambridge: Cambridge University Press, 1991).

——, *Truth and Progress: Philosophical Papers, Volume 3* (Cambridge: Cambridge University Press, 1998).

——, *Achieving Our Country: Leftist Thought in Twentieth-Century America* (Cambridge, MA: Harvard University Press, 1998).

——, *Philosophy and Social Hope* (London: Penguin Books, 1999).

——, 'Universality and Truth', in Robert B. Brandom (ed.), *Rorty and His Critics* (Malden: Blackwell, 2000), pp. 1–30.

——, 'Response to Jürgen Habermas', in Robert B. Brandom (ed.), *Rorty and His Critics* (Malden: Blackwell, 2000), pp. 56–64.

——, 'Response to Donald Davidson', in Robert B. Brandom (ed.), *Rorty and His Critics* (Malden: Blackwell, 2000), pp. 74–80.

——, 'Response to John McDowell', in Robert B. Brandom (ed.), *Rorty and His Critics* (Malden: Blackwell, 2000), pp. 123–8.

——, 'Response to Akeel Bilgrami', in Robert B. Brandom (ed.), *Rorty and His Critics* (Malden: Blackwell, 2000), pp. 262–7.

——, 'Response to Bjørn Ramberg', in Robert B. Brandom (ed.), *Rorty and His Critics* (Malden: Blackwell, 2000), pp. 370–77.

——, 'Response to Molly Cochran', in Matthew Festenstein and Simon Thompson (eds), *Richard Rorty: Critical Dialogues* (Cambridge: Polity Press, 2002), pp. 200–202.

Rosen, Michael, 'The Role of Rules', *International Journal of Philosophical Studies*, 9 (2001): 369–84.

Russell, Bertrand, *The Collected Papers of Bertrand Russell, Volume 10: A Fresh Look at Empiricism, 1927–42*, ed. John G. Slater with the assistance of Peter Köllner (London: Routledge, 1996).

Sartre, Jean-Paul, *L'existentialisme est un humanisme* (Paris: Nagel, 1946).

——, *Existentialism and Humanism*, trans. Philip Mairet (Brooklyn, NY: Haskell House, 1948).

Schroeder, Severin, 'The Demand for Synoptic Representations and the Private Language Discussion: PI 243–315', in Erich Ammereller and Eugen Fischer (eds), *Wittgenstein at Work: Method in the* Philosophical Investigations (London: Routledge, 2004), pp. 147–69.

Schulte, Joachim, 'Wittgenstein and Conservatism', *Ratio,* 25 (1983): 69–80.

Segerdahl, Pär, *Språkteorier och språkspel: Fem moderna språkteorier ur en Wittgensteininspirerad synvinkel* (Lund: Studentlitteratur, 1998).

Sextus Empiricus, *Outlines of Scepticism*, trans. Julia Annas and Jonathan Barnes (Cambridge: Cambridge University Press, 1994).

Siegel, Harvey, *Relativism Refuted: A Critique of Contemporary Epistemological*

Relativism (Dordrecht: D. Reidel, 1987).

Slob, Wouter H., *Dialogical Rhetoric: An Essay on Truth and Normativity after Postmodernism* (Dordrecht: Kluwer Academic Publishers, 2002).

Spengler, Oswald, *Der Untergang des Abendlandes: Umrisse einer Morphologie der Weltgeschichte: Erster Band: Gestalt und Wirklichkeit*, 22nd edn (Munich: C.H. Beck'sche Verlagsbuchhandlung Oskar Beck, 1920).

——, *The Decline of the West, Volume I: Form and Actuality*, trans. Charles Francis Atkinson (New York: Alfred A. Knopf, 1926).

Stenmark, Mikael, 'The End of the Theism–atheism Debate? A Response to Vincent Brümmer', *Religious Studies*, 34 (1998): 261–80.

——, 'Theological Pragmatism: A Critical Evaluation', *Heythrop Journal*, 41 (2000): 187–98.

Stern, David, 'Was Wittgenstein a Jew?', in James C. Klagge, *Wittgenstein: Biography and Philosophy* (New York: Cambridge University Press, 2001), pp. 237–72.

Stirner, Max, *The Ego and Its Own*, ed. David Leopold, trans. Steven Tracy Byington (Cambridge: Cambridge University Press, 1995).

Stout, Jeffrey, *Democracy and Tradition* (Princeton, NJ: Princeton University Press, 2004).

Strandberg, Hugo, 'Att ändra sig och andra: En diskussion kring relationen mellan en skeptisk inställning och en konservativ hållning', in Erica Appelros, Stefan Eriksson and Catharina Stenqvist (eds), *Makt och religion i könsskilda världar: Religionsfilosofiska perspektiv* (Lund: Religio, 2003), pp. 161–75.

Strawson, Peter F., 'Truth', *Analysis*, 9 (1949): 83–97.

Swinburne, Richard, *An Introduction to Confirmation Theory* (London: Methuen, 1973).

——, *The Coherence of Theism* (Oxford: Clarendon Press, 1977).

——, *Faith and Reason* (Oxford: Oxford University Press, 1981).

——, *The Existence of God*, rev. edn (Oxford: Clarendon Press, 1991).

——, *Is There a God?* (Oxford: Oxford University Press, 1996).

——, *Epistemic Justification* (Oxford: Clarendon Press, 2001).

Tarski, Alfred, 'The Semantic Conception of Truth and the Foundations of Semantics', *Philosophy and Phenomenological Research,* 4 (1944): 341–75.

Taylor, Charles, *Philosophical Arguments* (Cambridge, MA/London: Harvard University Press, 1995).

Taylor, Christopher C.W., 'Introduction', in C.C.W. Taylor (ed.), *Routledge History of Philosophy, Volume I: From the Beginning to Plato* (London: Routledge, 1997), pp. 1–18.

Thomas Aquinas, *Summa Theologica: Complete English Edition in Five Volumes, Volume One* (London: Sheed & Ward, 1981).

Thompson, Simon, 'Richard Rorty on Truth, Justification and Justice', in Matthew Festenstein and Simon Thompson (eds), *Richard Rorty: Critical Dialogues* (Cambridge: Polity Press, 2001), pp. 33–50.

Thomson, George, 'Wittgenstein: Some Personal Recollections', in F.A. Flowers III (ed.), *Portraits of Wittgenstein, Volume 2* (Bristol: Thoemmes Press, 1999), pp. 219–21.

Uschanov, Tommi P., 'Ernest Gellner's Criticisms of Wittgenstein and Ordinary Language Philosophy', in Gavin Kitching and Nigel Pleasants (eds), *Marx and Wittgenstein: Knowledge, Morality and Politics* (London/New York: Routledge, 2002), pp. 23–46.

Vattimo, Gianni, 'The Trace of the Trace', trans. David Webb, in Jacques Derrida and Gianni Vattimo (eds), *Religion* (Cambridge: Polity Press, 1998), pp. 79–94.

Wainwright, William J., 'Objections to Traditional Theism', in William L. Rowe and William J. Wainwright (eds), *Philosophy of Religion: Selected Readings*, 2nd edn (San Diego, CA: Harcourt Brace Jovanovich, 1989), pp. 262–5.

Walzer, Michael, *Thick and Thin: Moral Arguments at Home and Abroad* (Notre Dame, IN: University of Notre Dame Press, 1994).

Weil, Simone, *Lettre à un religieux* (Paris: Gallimard, 1951).

——, *Letter to a Priest*, trans. A.F. Willis (London: Routledge, 2002).

Williams, Michael, 'Scepticism without Theory', *Review of Metaphysics*, 41 (1988): 547–88.

Winch, Peter, *Trying to Make Sense* (Oxford: Basil Blackwell, 1987).

——, 'On Wittgenstein', *Philosophical Investigations*, 24 (2001): 180–84.

Wittgenstein, Ludwig, *Tractatus Logico-Philosophicus/Logisch-Philosophische Abhandlung*, 2nd impr., trans. D.F. Pears and B.F. McGuinness (London: Routledge & Kegan Paul, 1963).

——, *Lectures and Conversations on Aesthetics, Psychology and Religious Belief*, compiled from notes taken by Yorick Smythies, Rush Rhees and James Taylor, ed. Cyril Barrett (Oxford: Basil Blackwell, 1966).

——, *Zettel*, ed. G.E.M. Anscombe and G.H. von Wright, trans. G.E.M. Anscombe (Berkeley, CA/Los Angeles, CA: University of California Press, 1967).

——, *The Blue and Brown Books*, 2nd edn (Oxford: Basil Blackwell, 1969).

——, *Bemerkungen über die Grundlagen der Mathematik*, rev. and enl. edn, ed. G.E.M. Anscombe, Rush Rhees and G.H. von Wright (Frankfurt am Main: Suhrkamp Verlag, 1974).

——, *Philosophical Grammar*, ed. Rush Rhees, trans. Anthony Kenny (Berkeley, CA: University of California Press, 1974).

——, *Über Gewissheit/On Certainty*, repr. with corr., ed. G.E.M. Anscombe and G.H. von Wright, trans. Denis Paul and G.E.M. Anscombe (Oxford: Blackwell, 1974).

——, *Philosophical Remarks*, ed. Rush Rhees, trans. Raymond Hargreaves and Roger White (Oxford: Basil Blackwell, 1975).

——, *Wittgenstein's Lectures on the Foundations of Mathematics, Cambridge, 1939*, from the notes of R.G. Bosanquet, Norman Malcolm, Rush Rhees and Yorick Smythies, ed. Cora Diamond (Chicago, IL: The University of Chicago Press, 1976).

——, *Remarks on the Foundations of Mathematics*, rev. ed., ed. G.H. von Wright, R. Rhees and G.E.M. Anscombe, trans. G.E.M. Anscombe (Cambridge, MA: The

MIT Press, 1978).

——, *Wittgenstein and the Vienna Circle*, conversations recorded by Friedrich Waismann, ed. Brian McGuinness, trans. Joachim Schulte and Brian McGuinness (Oxford: Basil Blackwell, 1979).

——, *Wittgenstein's Lectures: Cambridge, 1932–1935*, from the notes of Alice Ambrose and Margaret Macdonald, ed. Alice Ambrose (New York: Prometheus Books, 1979).

——, *Notebooks 1914–1916*, 2nd edn, ed. G.H. von Wright and G.E.M. Anscombe, trans. G.E.M. Anscombe (Chicago, IL: The University of Chicago Press, 1979).

——, *Wittgenstein's Lectures: Cambridge, 1930–1932*, from the notes of John King and Desmond Lee, ed. Desmond Lee (Oxford: Basil Blackwell, 1980).

——, *Bemerkungen über die Philosophie der Psychologie, Band I/Remarks on the Philosophy of Psychology, Volume I*, ed. G.E.M. Anscombe and G.H. von Wright, trans. G.E.M. Anscombe (Chicago, IL: The University of Chicago Press, 1980).

——, *Bemerkungen über die Philosophie der Psychologie: Band II/Remarks on the Philosophy of Psychology, Volume II*, ed. G.H. von Wright and Heikki Nyman, trans. C.G. Luckhardt and M.A.E. Aue (Chicago, IL: The University of Chicago Press, 1980).

——, *Letzte Schriften über die Philosophie der Psychologie, Band II: Das Innere und das Äußere: 1949–1951/Last Writings on the Philosophy of Psychology, Volume II: The Inner and the Outer: 1949–1951*, ed. G.H. von Wright and Heikki Nyman, trans. C.G. Luckhardt and Maximilian A.E. Aue (Oxford: Blackwell, 1992).

——, 'A Lecture on Ethics', in James C. Klagge and Alfred Nordmann (eds), *Philosophical Occasions 1912–1951* (Indianapolis, IN: Hackett, 1993), pp. 37–44.

——, 'Wittgenstein's Lectures in 1930–33', notes taken by G.E. Moore, in James C. Klagge and Alfred Nordmann (eds), *Philosophical Occasions 1912–1951* (Indianapolis, IN: Hackett, 1993), pp. 46–114.

——, 'Bemerkungen über Frazers *Golden Bough*'/'Remarks on Frazer's *Golden Bough*', trans. John Beversluis, in James C. Klagge and Alfred Nordmann (eds), *Philosophical Occasions 1912–1951* (Indianapolis, IN: Hackett, 1993), pp. 118–55.

——, 'Philosophie/Philosophy', ed. Heikki Nyman, trans. C.G. Luckhardt and M.A.E. Aue, in James C. Klagge and Alfred Nordmann (eds), *Philosophical Occasions 1912–1951* (Indianapolis, IN: Hackett, 1993), pp. 160–99.

——, 'Notes for Lectures on "Private Experience" and "Sense Data"', some trans. Rush Rhees and David G. Stern, in James C. Klagge and Alfred Nordmann (eds), *Philosophical Occasions 1912–1951* (Indianapolis, IN: Hackett, 1993), pp. 202–88.

——, 'The Language of Sense Data and Private Experience', notes taken by Rush Rhees, in James C. Klagge and Alfred Nordmann (eds), *Philosophical Occasions 1912–1951* (Indianapolis, IN: Hackett, 1993), pp. 290–367.

——, 'Ursache und Wirkung: Intuitives Erfassen/Cause and Effect: Intuitive Awareness', trans. Peter Winch, in James C. Klagge and Alfred Nordmann (eds),

Philosophical Occasions 1912–1951 (Indianapolis, IN: Hackett, 1993), pp. 370–426.

——, 'Notes for the "Philosophical Lecture"', in James C. Klagge and Alfred Nordmann (eds), *Philosophical Occasions 1912–1951* (Indianapolis, IN: Hackett, 1993), pp. 447–58.

——, *Vermischte Bemerkungen: Eine Auswahl aus dem Nachlaß/Culture and Value: A Selection from the Posthumous Remains*, ed. G.H. von Wright in collaboration with Heikki Nyman, rev. edn of the text by Alois Pichler, trans. Peter Winch (Oxford: Blackwell, 1998).

——, *Philosophische Untersuchungen/Philosophical Investigations*, 3rd edn, ed. G.E.M. Anscombe and R. Rhees, trans. G.E.M. Anscombe (Oxford: Blackwell Publishers, 2001).

——, 'Movements of Thought: Diaries 1930–1932, 1936–1937', in James C. Klagge and Alfred Nordmann (eds), *Public and Private Occasions* (Lanham, MD: Rowman & Littlefield, 2003), pp. 3–255.

——, 'Ludwig Hänsel–Ludwig Wittgenstein: A Friendship, 1929–1940', in James C. Klagge and Alfred Nordmann (eds), *Public and Private Occasions* (Lanham, MD: Rowman & Littlefield, 2003), pp. 257–327.

——, 'Discussions between Wittgenstein, Waddington, and Thouless: Summer 1941', in James C. Klagge and Alfred Nordmann (eds), *Public and Private Occasions* (Lanham, MD: Rowman & Littlefield, 2003), pp. 381–96.

Wright, Georg Henrik von, 'Wittgenstein in Relation to His Times', in Brian McGuinness (ed.), *Wittgenstein and His Times* (Oxford: Basil Blackwell, 1982): pp. 108–20.

——, 'Dante between Ulysses and Faust', in Monika Asztalos, John E. Murdoch and Ilkka Niiniluoto (eds), *Acta Philosophica Fennica 48: Knowledge and the Sciences in Medieval Philosophy. Proceedings of the Eighth International Congress of Medieval Philosophy, Vol. I* (1990), pp. 1–9.

——, 'Wittgenstein and the Twentieth Century', in Leila Haaparanta, Martin Kusch and Ilka Niiniluoto (eds), *Acta Philosophica Fennica 49. Language, Knowledge, and Intentionality: Perspectives on the Philosophy of Jaakko Hintikka* (1990), pp. 47–67.

Xenophanes of Colophon, *Fragments: A Text and Translation with a Commentary by J. H. Lester* (Toronto: University of Toronto Press, 1992).

Yeatman, Anna, 'A Feminist Theory of Social Differentiation', in Linda J. Nicholson (ed.), *Feminism/Postmodernism* (New York: Routledge, 1990), pp. 281–99.

Index

Althusser, Louis 111, 134
analytic-theistic philosophy of religion
      132–3, 147, 176–7, 179
anarchism 145–6
Anderson, Pamela Sue 175, 177
Apel, Karl-Otto 123–4
argumentation 2, 41, 54, 71, 78–80, 123–8,
      130, 132–33, 138, 164
arguments for the existence of God, *see* God
Aristotle v, 87, 115, 139

Bakunin, Michael 146
Bayes's theorem 20–21
belief 6, 78, 98–9, 117
Benhabib, Seyla 124
Bernstein, Richard J. 41, 72
Bloor, David 163–4
body 68–71

cause and effect 36-8
certainty 110–12
change 6, 54, 60, 67–8, 71, 75, 77, 81–6,
      89, 91, 107, 111–3, 120, 125, 130–1,
      134, 136, 138, 140–41, 154, 161–3,
      165–6, 173–4, 176–9; *see also*
      progress; self-criticism
charity, principle of 97–100
colour 32–3, 38–9, 109
conceptual investigation 30, 32, 39, 41,
      51–2, 100, 111–2, 129
conceptual priority 28, 30, 35–6, 40, 53
confusion 12, 140
conservatism 74–5, 149–51, 153–4, 156–9,
      161, 163–4, 167
criterial notion of reasoning 53–4, 86–8
criticism 5, 10, 85, 107, 126, 147, 159, 161,
      165, 167–74, 176–7, 179; *see also*
      religious beliefs; self-criticism
cultural pessimism 154-9, 161

Davidson, Donald 51–2, 73–4, 88, 91–107,
      110, 112–3, 115–20, 123

demand for universality, *see* universality
democracy 126, 137–8, 162
Derrida, Jacques 45, 137–8
Descartes, René 70
discussion 4–6, 124–5, 147, 167; *see also*
      rationalistic discussion
dissatisfaction 84–5

embodiment, *see* body
enlightenment 176–9
ethnocentrism 75–9, 84, 141
evil, *see* problem of evil
existence of God, *see* God

Faust 85
feminist philosophy 5, 56, 143, 175
fideism 4–5, 141, 149–50, 168–70
Frege, Gottlob 115–6
Freud, Sigmund 142–3, 168
fruitful 4–6

Gadamer, Hans-Georg 66–8, 87
God 17–24, 27–9, 40, 69, 98, 132, 142,
      144–6, 174–6, 179

Habermas, Jürgen 79, 81, 124
Hegel, G.W.F. 122–3
Heidegger, Martin 27, 60–65, 67–8, 115
history 12–13, 65–7, 72, 79, 159, 167
hypothetical reasoning 19–23, 29, 31–41,
      132

identity 134, 137, 146
ideology 111, 134
induction 36–7, 100
interpretation 31–2, 71, 88, 93–4, 104, 123,
      143; *see also* radical interpretation
inter-religious dialogue 5, 136

justice 137–8
justification 33, 54, 56, 76–7, 79, 109–10,
      114–5, 117–9, 175–7, 179

Kant, Immanuel 59, 62, 87, 122–3, 177–9
Kompridis, Nikolas 86
Kuhn, Thomas S. 5, 48, 52, 55, 77

liberalism 77–8, 163

McDowell, John 88, 117–9
MacIntyre, Alasdair 80–81
making the distinction between true and
        false 33–4, 41–3, 45, 47, 49–53,
        55–7, 60, 106, 128–36, 138–43,
        146–7, 149, 168–9, 171, 176; *see
        also* truth
Marcuse, Herbert 161–2, 164, 166
Marx, Karl 143–4, 163, 165, 168
massive error 102–5, 107–10
mathematics 33–4, 81, 107–9, 128, 166
meaning, linguistic 31–4, 38–40, 51, 71–4,
        91–104, 106, 108–9, 111, 115, 161,
        165, 169
Merleau-Ponty, Maurice 69–70
metaphysics 27, 29–30, 51, 160
mistake 11–12, 30, 32, 35, 41, 48, 73–4,
        89, 99–100, 102, 105, 107–10, 125,
        128–30, 132, 136, 140, 142, 149

Nielsen, Kai 4, 55–6, 168–70
Nietzsche, Friedrich 144–5
Nyíri, J.C. 163–4

objectivity 90, 105–7, 110, 112, 117

pain 30, 35–6, 39–40, 69–70
Penner, Hans H. 98
pessimism; *see* cultural pessimism
Phillips, D.Z. 4, 170
philosophy v, 2–3, 5, 7–13, 29, 54, 65, 127,
        139, 153–4, 156, 160, 162–9, 171,
        174, 179
Plantinga, Alvin 175–6
Plato 9, 44–5, 47–8
Popper, Karl 55
primitive reactions, *see* reaction
principle of charity, *see* charity
private language 39, 72–3
problem of evil 20, 25–6, 141–2
progress 150, 157–61; *see also* change
Putnam, Hilary 47–8, 54, 56, 106–7,
        110–11, 113–14, 118

Pyrrhonism, *see* Sextus Empiricus

radical interpretation 51–2, 73, 91–104
rationalistic discussion 17–8, 20, 22–6, 43,
        121–4, 126, 129, 135, 141, 176, 179
rationality 2–3, 5–6, 17, 27, 41, 54–6,
        59–60, 65–7, 71–2, 74–5, 78–82,
        84–9, 107, 117–8, 120, 123, 129,
        137–8, 140, 147, 162–3, 169–70,
        173–4, 177
reactions 28–9, 31, 33–7, 39–41, 111, 142
reason 2, 70, 72, 79, 81, 86, 163, 177; *see
        also* argumentation; discussion;
        rationality
relativism 42–60, 88, 113
religious beliefs 2–3, 6, 18–19, 23–30,
        39–41, 83, 98, 106, 132–4, 138, 149,
        165, 169–70, 173–5, 177
    criticism of 3–5, 24–7, 40, 42, 98,
        139–42, 148–9, 161, 168–74, 176,
        179
        philosophical 139, 141, 148–9, 161,
            168–9, 179
religious experience 23–4; *see also* reactions
representation 76–7, 117–9
revelation, *see* religious experience
Rorty, Richard 56, 75–9, 94, 107, 110–14,
        116, 119, 137
rule following 31–2, 53, 71, 87–90, 93–4,
        108–9

Sartre, Jean-Paul 24, 145–6
science 5, 8–12, 25–9, 47–8, 60, 127–8,
        134, 142, 149, 154, 157–60, 165,
        169, 173, 177
self-criticism 6, 10, 122, 179; *see also*
        change; criticism
self-reference 7, 10, 44–7, 116
Sextus Empiricus 45–7
Siegel, Harvey 26, 55–6
simplicity 21–3, 25
situatedness 60, 65–7, 71–2, 74–5, 79, 81,
        83, 85, 88
Socrates 3–4, 9
Spengler, Oswald 154–5, 160
Stirner, Max 145–6
Swinburne, Richard 19–24, 28

Tarski, Alfred 94, 96, 116, 118

Taylor, Charles 60, 68–70, 86, 125
teleological argument, *see* God
theism 19–23, 175–7
Trier, Lars von 1
Thomas Aquinas 19
tradition 56, 60, 65–6, 72, 80–81, 114–5,
 161, 164, 176, 179
triangulation 73, 105–6, 117–8
truth 34, 49, 55, 57, 60, 65–7, 71–2, 74–5,
 88–91, 94, 96–107, 109–21, 127–8,
 137–8, 141, 174, 176; *see also* making the distinction between true and
 false; relativism

cautionary use of 107, 110–13, 120,
 140–41
coherence theory of 115, 118–20
correspondence theory of 115–20

universality 7, 10, 17, 27, 42, 48, 53–4,
 56–61, 65, 74–6, 81, 83, 88–91,
 120–6, 129, 177

Wittgenstein, Ludwig 4, 5, 8–12, 29, 31–2,
 35–7, 39, 42, 71–3, 87, 93–4, 107–9,
 112, 115, 132, 147–68, 170–71
Wittgensteinian fideism, *see* fideism